Collins easy learning

Italian
Grammar

Era pieno
di gente.

*Hanno quasi
finito.*

Published by Collins
An imprint of HarperCollins Publishers
Westerhill Road
Bishopbriggs
Glasgow G64 2QT

Third edition 2016

ISBN 978-0-00-814202-5

10 9 8 7 6 5 4

© HarperCollins Publishers 2006, 2016

www.collinsdictionary.com
www.collins.co.uk/languagesupport

Typeset by Davidson Publishing Solutions,
Glasgow

Printed in Italy by GRAFICA VENETA S.p.A.

A catalogue record for this book is available
from the British Library.

If you would like to comment on any aspect
of this book, please contact us at the given
address or online.
E-mail: dictionaries@harpercollins.co.uk
🄵 www.facebook.com/collinsdictionary
🐦 @collinsdict

Acknowledgements
We would like to thank those authors
and publishers who kindly gave permission
for copyright material to be used in the
Collins Corpus. We would also like to
thank Times Newspapers Ltd for providing
valuable data.

MANAGING EDITOR
Maree Airlie

CONTRIBUTORS
Francesca Logi
Janice McNeillie

FOR THE PUBLISHER
Gerry Breslin
Craig Balfour
Chloe Osborne

CONTENTS

Note on trademarks

Entered words which we have reason to believe constitute trademarks have been designated as such. However, neither the presence nor the absence of such designation should be regarded as affecting the legal status of any trademark.

Foreword for language teachers

The *Easy Learning Italian Grammar* is designed to be used with both young and adult learners, as a group reference book to complement your course book during classes, or as a recommended text for self-study and homework/coursework.

The text specifically targets learners from beginners to intermediate or GCSE level, and therefore its structural content and vocabulary have been matched to the relevant specifications up to and including Higher GCSE.

The approach aims to develop knowledge and understanding of grammar and to improve the ability of learners to apply it by:

- defining parts of speech at the start of each major section, with examples in English to clarify concepts
- minimizing the use of grammar terminology and providing clear explanations of terms both within the text and in the **Glossary**
- illustrating all points with examples (and their translations) based on topics and contexts which are relevant to beginner and intermediate course content

The text helps you develop positive attitudes to grammar learning in your classes by:

- giving clear, easy-to-follow explanations
- prioritizing content according to relevant specifications for the levels
- sequencing points to reflect course content, e.g. verb tenses
- highlighting useful **Tips** to deal with common difficulties
- summarizing **Key points** at the end of sections to consolidate learning

In addition to fostering success and building a thorough foundation in Italian grammar, the optional **Grammar Extra** sections will encourage and challenge your learners to further their studies to higher and advanced levels.

Introduction for students

Whether you are starting to learn Italian for the very first time, brushing up on topics you have studied in class, or revising for your GCSE exams, the *Easy Learning Italian Grammar* is here to help. This easy-to-use guide takes you through all the basics you will need to speak and understand modern everyday Italian.

Learners sometimes struggle with the technical terms they come across when they start to explore the grammar of a new language. The *Easy Learning Italian Grammar* explains how to get to grips with all the parts of speech you will need to know, using simple language and cutting out jargon.

The text is divided into sections, each dealing with a particular area of grammar. Each section can be studied individually, as numerous cross-references in the text point you to relevant points in other sections of the book for further information.

Every major section begins with an explanation of the area of grammar covered on the following pages. For quick reference, these definitions are also collected together on pages viii–xii in a glossary of essential grammatical terms.

What is a verb?
A **verb** is a word which describes what somebody or something does, what they are, or what happens to them, for example, *play, be, disappear*.

Each grammar point in the text is followed by simple examples of real Italian, with English translations, to help you understand the rules. Underlining has been used in examples throughout the text to highlight the grammatical point being explained.

➤ To say *the one* in Italian use **quello** to refer to masculine nouns or **quella** to refer to feminine nouns. The relative pronoun is **che**.

    È <u>quello</u> che non funziona.   That's the one which isn't working.

This book marks which vowel is stressed in some Italian words by putting those vowels into italic.

        il m*a*nager   the manager

⇨ *For more information on **Stress**, see page 196.*

Tips and **Information** notes throughout the text are useful reminders of the things that often trip learners up when learning Italian.

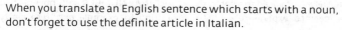

Tip

When you translate an English sentence which starts with a noun, don't forget to use the definite article in Italian.

Le macchine costano caro.	Cars cost a lot.
La frutta fa bene.	Fruit is good for you.

Key points sum up all the important facts about a particular area of grammar, to save you time when you are revising and help you focus on the main grammatical points.

Key points

✔ Most Italian adjectives go after the noun.

✔ The meaning of some adjectives changes depending on whether they come before or after the noun.

If you think you would like to continue with your Italian studies to a higher level, look at the **Grammar Extra** sections. These are intended for advanced students who are interested in knowing a little more about the structures they will come across beyond GCSE.

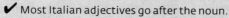

Grammar Extra!

To say that something is getting *better and better, worse and worse, slower and slower*, and so on, use **sempre** with the comparative adverb.

Le cose vanno <u>sempre</u> meglio.	Things are going better and better.
Mio nonno sta <u>sempre</u> peggio.	My grandfather's getting worse and worse.
Cammina <u>sempre</u> più lento.	He's walking slower and slower.

Finally, the supplement at the end of the book contains **Verb Tables**, where 90 important Italian verbs (both regular and irregular) are declined in full. Examples show you how to use these verbs in your own work. If you are unsure of how a verb declines in Italian, you can look up the **Verb Index** on pages 92–96 to find either the conjugation of the verb itself, or a cross-reference to a model verb, which will show you the pattern that verb follows.

Glossary of Grammar Terms

ABSTRACT NOUN a word used to refer to a quality, idea, feeling or experience, rather than a physical object, for example, *size, reason, happiness*. Compare with **concrete noun**.

ACTIVE a form of the verb that is used when the subject of the sentence does the action, for example, *A dog bit him* (subject: *a dog*; active verb: *bit*). Compare with **passive**.

ADJECTIVE a 'describing' word that tells you something about a person or thing, for example, a *blue* shirt, a *big* car, a *good* idea.

ADVERB a word used with verbs to give information on where, when or how an action takes place, for example, *here, today, quickly*. An adverb can also add information to adjectives and other adverbs, for example, *extremely* quick, *very* quickly.

AGREEMENT the matching of words or word endings to the person or thing they refer to. For example, the verb *to be* has different forms for *I, you* and *he*: I *am*, you *are*, he *is*. In Italian you use verbs in the form appropriate to the person doing the action, and articles and adjectives have masculine, feminine and plural forms to match (or *agree* with) the noun they go with.

APOSTROPHE s an ending ('s) added to a noun to show ownership, for example, *Peter's car, the company's headquarters*.

ARTICLE a word such as *the, a,* and *an* which goes with nouns: *the sun, a happy boy, an orange*. See also **definite article**, **indefinite article**.

AUXILIARY VERB a verb such as *be, have* and *do* that is used with a main verb to form tenses, negatives and questions.

BASE FORM the form of the verb that has no ending added to it, for example, *walk, have, be, go*. Compare with **infinitive**.

CARDINAL NUMBER a number used in counting, for example, *one, seven, ninety*. Compare with **ordinal number**.

CLAUSE a group of words containing a verb.

COMPARATIVE an adjective or adverb with *–er* on the end of it or *more* or *less* in front of it that is used to compare things or people, for example, *faster, more important, less interesting*.

COMPOUND NOUN a word for a living being, thing or idea which is made up of two or more words, for example, *prime minister, mobile phone, home truth*.

CONCRETE NOUN a word that refers to a physical object rather than a quality or idea, for example, *ball, school, apples*. Compare with **abstract noun**.

CONDITIONAL a verb form used to talk about things that would happen or would be true under certain conditions, for example, *I would help you if I could*. It is also used in requests and offers, for example, *Could you lend me some money?; I could give you a lift*.

CONJUGATE (to) to give a verb different endings depending on whether its subject is *I, you, he* and so on, and depending on whether you are referring to the present, past or future, for example, *I have, she has, they listened*.

CONJUGATION a group of verbs that has a particular pattern of endings.

CONJUNCTION a word such as *and, but* or *because* that links two words or phrases, or two parts of a sentence, for example, *Diane and I have been friends for years*.

CONSONANT a sound made by letters such as b, g, m, s and t. In English y is sometimes a consonant, as in *year*, and sometimes a vowel, as in *any*. In Italian **i** sometimes has a vowel sound (ee) and sometimes the consonant sound of *y* in *year*, for example, **italiano** (eetalyano). Compare with **vowel**.

CONTINUOUS TENSE a verb form made up of *to be* and the *–ing* form, for example, *I'm thinking; They were quarrelling*. Italian continuous tenses are made with **stare** and the gerund.

DEFINITE ARTICLE the word *the*. Compare with **indefinite article**.

DEMONSTRATIVE ADJECTIVE a word used to point out a particular thing or person. There are four demonstrative adjectives in English: *this, these, that* and *those*.

DEMONSTRATIVE PRONOUN a word used instead of a noun to point out people or things, for example, *That's my brother*. In English the demonstrative pronouns are *this, that, these* and *those*.

DIRECT OBJECT a noun or pronoun used to show who or what is affected by the verb. For example, in the sentence *He sent flowers*, the subject of the verb is *He* (the person who did the sending) and the direct object of the verb is *flowers* (what he sent). Compare with **indirect object**.

DIRECT OBJECT PRONOUN a word such as *me, him, us* and *them* used instead of a noun to show who or what is affected by the action of the verb, for example *His friends helped him*. Compare **indirect object pronoun**.

ENDING something added to the end of a word. In English nouns have plural endings, for example boy → boy<u>s</u>, child → child<u>ren</u> and verbs have the endings *–s, –ed* and *–ing*, for example *walk → walks, walked, walking*. In Italian there are plural endings for nouns, verb endings, and masculine, feminine and plural endings for adjectives and pronouns.

EXCLAMATION a sound, word or sentence that is spoken suddenly by somebody who is surprised, excited or angry, for example *Oh!; Look who's coming!; How dare you!*

FEMININE a noun, pronoun, article or form of adjective used to refer to a living being, thing or idea that is not classed as masculine. For example, **una** (feminine indefinite article) **bella** (adjective with a feminine ending) **casa** (feminine noun).

FUTURE a tense used to talk about something that will happen, or be true in the future, for example *He'll be here soon; I'll give you a call; It will be sunny tomorrow*.

GENDER whether a noun, pronoun or adjective is masculine or feminine.

GERUND in English, a verb form ending in *–ing*, for example, *eating, sleeping*. In Italian the gerund ends in **–ando** or **–endo**.

IMPERATIVE a form of the verb used to give orders and instructions, for example, *Sit down!;Don't go!;Let's start!*

IMPERFECT a tense used to say what was happening, what used to happen and what things were like in the past, for example; *It was sunny at the weekend; They weren't listening; They used to live in Spain*.

IMPERSONAL VERB a verb with the subject *it*, where 'it' does not refer to any specific thing; for example, *It's going to rain; It's nine o'clock*.

INDEFINITE ADJECTIVE one of a small group of adjectives used to give an idea of amounts and numbers, for example, *several, all, every*.

INDEFINITE ARTICLE the word *a* or *an*. Compare with **definite article**.

INDEFINITE PRONOUN a word like *everything, nobody* and *something* which is used to refer to people or things in a non-specific way.

INDIRECT OBJECT a noun or pronoun used to show who benefits or suffers from an action. For example, in the sentence *He sent Claire flowers*, the <u>direct</u> object (what was sent) is *flowers* and the <u>indirect</u> object is *Claire* (the person the flowers were sent to). An indirect object often has *to* in front of it: *He told lies to everyone*; *He told everyone lies*. In both these sentences the direct object is *lies* and the indirect object is *everyone*. Compare with **direct object**.

INDIRECT OBJECT PRONOUN a pronoun such as *to me* (or *me*), *to you* (or *you*) and *to her* (or *her*). In the sentence *He gave the chocolates <u>to me</u> and the flowers <u>to her</u>*, the direct objects are *the chocolates* and *the flowers* (what he gave), and the <u>indirect object pronouns</u> are *to me* and *to her* (who he gave them to). In the sentence *He gave me the chocolates and her the flowers*, the indirect object pronouns are *me* and *her*. Compare with **direct object pronoun**.

INDIRECT QUESTION a more roundabout way of asking a question, for example, instead of *Where are you going?* you can say *Tell me where you are going*, or *I'd like to know where you are going*.

INDIRECT SPEECH the words you use to report what someone has said when you aren't using their actual words, for example, *He said that he was going out*. Also called **reported speech**.

INFINITIVE the base form of the verb, for example, *walk, see, hear*. It is used after other verbs such as *should, must and can*. The infinitive is often used with *to*: *to speak, to eat, to live*. Compare with **base form**.

INTERROGATIVE ADJECTIVE a question word such as *which, what* or *how much* that is used when asking about a noun, for example, *Which colour?*; *What size?*; *How much sugar?*

INTERROGATIVE PRONOUN one of the following: *who, which, whose, whom* and *what*. These words are used without a noun, when asking questions, for example, *What do you want?*

INTRANSITIVE VERB a verb used without a direct object, for example, *The shop is closing; Nothing grows here*. Compare with **transitive verb**.

INVARIABLE the term used to describe an adjective which does not change its form for the feminine or the plural, or a noun which does not change its ending in the plural.

IRREGULAR VERB In Italian, a verb whose forms do not follow one of the three main patterns. Compare with **regular verb**.

MASCULINE a noun, pronoun, article or form of adjective used to refer to a living being, thing or idea that is not classed as feminine. For example, **il** (masculine definite article) **primo** (adjective with a masculine ending) **treno** (masculine noun).

NEGATIVE a question or statement which contains a word such as *not, never* or *nothing*: *Is<u>n't</u> he here?*; *I <u>never</u> eat meat*; *She's doing <u>nothing</u> about it*. Compare with **positive**.

NOUN a naming word for a living being, thing or idea, for example, *woman, Andrew, desk, happiness*.

NUMBER in grammar a verb agrees in number with its subject by being singular with a singular subject and plural with a plural subject, for example, *I <u>am</u> a teacher; they <u>are</u> teachers*.

OBJECT a noun or pronoun that, in English, usually comes after the verb and shows who or what is affected by it, for example, *I* (subject) *want* (verb) *a new car* (object), *They* (subject) *phoned* (verb) *him* (object).

OBJECT PRONOUN one of the following: *me, you, him, her, it, us, them*. They are used instead of nouns after prepositions, for example, *for me, with us* and as the object of verbs, for example, *The company sacked him*; *You'll enjoy it*. Compare **subject pronoun**.

ORDINAL NUMBER an adjective used to show where something comes in numerical order, for example, *first, seventh, ninetieth*. Compare with **cardinal number**.

PART OF SPEECH a word with a particular grammatical function, for example, *noun, adjective, verb, preposition, pronoun*.

PASSIVE a verb form that is used when the subject of the verb is the person or thing the action is done to, for example, *Shaun was bitten by a dog*. Shaun is the subject of the sentence, but he did not do the action. Compare with **active**.

PAST PARTICIPLE a verb form usually ending *–ed*, for example *lived, worked*. Some past participles are irregular, for example, *gone, sat, broken*. Past participles are used to make the perfect, pluperfect and passive, for example *They've gone; They hadn't noticed me; Nobody was hurt*. Past participles are also used as adjectives, for example, *a boiled egg*.

PAST PERFECT see **pluperfect**.

PERFECT a tense used in English to talk about what has or hasn't happened, for example *We've won, I haven't touched it*. Compare **simple past**.

PERSON in grammar one of the following: the first person (*I, we*), the second person (*you*) or the third person (*he, she, it, they*).

PERSONAL PRONOUN a word such as *I, you, he, she, us, them*, which make it clear who you are talking about or talking to.

PLUPERFECT a tense used to talk about what had happened or had been true at a point in the past, for example, *I'd forgotten to send her a card*. Also called **past perfect**.

PLURAL the form of a word which is used to refer to more than one person or thing. In Italian, nouns, adjectives, articles, pronouns and verbs can be plural.

POSITIVE a positive sentence does not contain a negative word such as *not*. Compare with **negative**.

POSSESSIVE ADJECTIVE a word such as *my, your, his* that is used with a noun to show who it belongs to.

POSSESSIVE PRONOUN a word such as *mine, yours, his* that is used instead of a possessive adjective followed by a noun. For example, instead of *My bag is the blue one*, you can say *Mine's the blue one*.

PREPOSITION a word such as *at, for, with, into* or *from*, or a phrase such as *in front of* or *near to*. Prepositions are usually followed by a noun or a pronoun and show how people and things relate to the rest of the sentence, for example, *She's at home; It's for you; You'll get into trouble; It's in front of you*.

PRESENT a verb form used to talk about what is true at the moment, what generally happens and what is happening now; for example, *I'm a student; I travel to college by train; The phone's ringing*.

PRESENT PARTICIPLE a verb form ending in *–ing*, for example, *eating, sleeping*. Compare with **gerund**.

PRONOUN a word you use instead of a noun, when you do not need or want to name someone or something directly, for example, *it, you, somebody*.

PROPER NOUN the name of a person, place or organization. Proper nouns are always written with a capital letter, for example, Kate, New York, the Forestry Commission.

QUESTION WORD a word such as *why, where, who, which* or *how* that is used to ask a question.

REFLEXIVE PRONOUN a word ending in –*self* or –*selves*, such as *myself* and *ourselves*, that is used as the object of a verb, for example *I surprised <u>myself</u>; We're going to treat <u>ourselves</u>*.

REFLEXIVE VERB a verb where the subject and object are the same, and which uses reflexive pronouns such as *myself, yourself* and *themselves*, for example *I've hurt myself; Look after yourself!; They're enjoying themselves*.

REGULAR VERB in Italian, a verb whose forms follow one of the three main patterns. Compare with **irregular verb**.

RELATIVE PRONOUN one of the following: *who, which, that* and *whom*. They are used to specify exactly who or what is being talked about, for example, *<u>The man who has just come in</u> is Anna's boyfriend; <u>The vase that you broke</u> cost a lot of money*.

REPORTED SPEECH see **indirect speech**.

SENTENCE a group of words which usually has a subject and a verb. In writing, a sentence begins with a capital and ends with a full stop, question mark or exclamation mark.

SIMPLE TENSE a verb form made up of one word, for example, *She <u>lives</u> here; They <u>arrived</u> late*. Compare with **continuous tense** and **perfect tense**.

SIMPLE PAST a tense used in English to say when exactly something happened, for example, *We <u>met</u> last summer; I <u>ate</u> it last night; It <u>rained</u> a lot yesterday*. In Italian the perfect tense is used in this kind of sentence.

SINGULAR the form of a word used to refer to one person or thing. Compare with **plural**.

STEM what is left of an Italian verb when you take away the **–are**, **–ere** or **–ire** ending of the infinitive.

STRESSED PRONOUN an object pronoun used in Italian after prepositions and when you want to stress the word for *me, him, them* and so on. Compare **unstressed pronoun**.

SUBJECT a noun or pronoun that refers to the person or thing doing the action or being in the state described by the verb, for example *<u>Pat</u> likes climbing; <u>The bus</u> is late*. Compare with **object**.

SUBJECT PRONOUN a word such as *I, he, she* and *they* used for the person or thing carrying out the action described by the verb. Pronouns replace nouns when it is clear who is being talked about, for example, *My brother's not here at the moment. <u>He</u>'ll be back in an hour*. Compare with **object pronoun**.

SUBJUNCTIVE a verb form often used in Italian to express wishes, thoughts and suppositions. In English the subjunctive is only used occasionally, for example, *If I <u>were</u> you...; So <u>be</u> it; He asked that they <u>be</u> removed*.

SUPERLATIVE an adjective or adverb with –*est* on the end of it or *most* or *least* in front of it that is used to compare things or people, for example, *fastest, most important, least interesting*.

SYLLABLE a unit containing a vowel sound. A word can have one or more syllables, for example, *I, o-pen, ca-the-dral*.

TENSE a particular form of the verb. It shows whether you are referring to the present, past or future.

TRANSITIVE VERB a verb used with a direct object, for example, *Close the door!; They grow wheat*. Compare with **intransitive verb**.

UNSTRESSED PRONOUN an object pronoun used in Italian when you don't want to put any special emphasis on the word for *me, him, them* and so on. Compare **stressed pronoun**.

VERB a word that describes what somebody or something does, what they are, or what happens to them, for example, *play, be, disappear*.

VOWEL one of the sounds made by the letters *a, e, i, o, u*, and sometimes *y*. Compare with **consonant**.

Nouns

> **What is a noun?**
> A **noun** is a naming word for a living being, a thing, or an idea, for example,
> *woman, Andrew, desk, happiness.*

Using nouns

1 The basics

➤ In Italian, all nouns, whether referring to living beings or to things and ideas, are either <u>masculine</u> or <u>feminine</u>. This is their <u>gender.</u>

Masculine		Feminine	
olio	oil	**acqua**	water
uomo	man	**donna**	woman
delfino	dolphin	**tigre**	tiger
concetto	concept	**idea**	idea
armadio	wardrobe	**sedia**	chair

➤ The letter a noun ends with is often a reliable guide to its gender. For instance, words ending in **–o** will nearly always be masculine.

➤ When you use an Italian noun you need to know if it is masculine or feminine so that you can make other words that go with it masculine or feminine too:

- how you translate the words for 'the' or 'a' depends on the noun's gender. For instance, with masculine nouns you use **il** and **un**, and with feminine nouns you use **la** and **una**.

Masculine		Feminine	
<u>il</u> **giorno**	the day	<u>la</u> **notte**	the night
<u>un</u> **gelato**	an ice cream	<u>una</u> **mela**	an apple

- adjectives describing a noun are masculine or feminine in form.

Masculine	Feminine
un *abito* car<u>o</u> – an expensive suit	una *macchina* car<u>a</u> – an expensive car
l'Anti<u>co</u> **Testamento** – the Old Testament	l'anti<u>ca</u> **Roma** - ancient Rome

- words that replace nouns – called <u>pronouns</u> – must also be masculine or feminine. The translation for *Do you want it?* is "**Lo vuoi?**" if you're offering **un gelato** (*an ice cream*), and "**La vuoi?**" if you're referring to **una mela** (*an apple*).

➪ *For more information on **Articles**, **Adjectives** or **Pronouns**, see pages 10, 20 and 40.*

2 Nouns

➤ Just like English nouns, Italian nouns can be singular or plural. Most English nouns add –s in the plural, for example *days, apples*. Most Italian nouns change their final letter from one vowel to another:

Singular		Plural	
giorno	day	**giorni**	days
mela	apple	**mele**	apples
rivoluzione	revolution	**rivoluzioni**	revolutions

Tip

When in doubt, you can find out a noun's gender by looking it up in a dictionary. When you come across a new word it's a good idea to memorize the article that goes with it, to help you remember its gender.

Key points

✔ All nouns in Italian are either masculine or feminine.

✔ This affects the words you use with them.

✔ In most cases it is possible to work out a noun's gender from its ending.

---

2 How to recognize what gender a noun is

➤ There are some simple rules that will enable you to work out the gender of a very large number of Italian nouns from their last letter in the singular:

- nearly all words ending in **–o** are masculine.
- nearly all words ending in **–a** are feminine.
- nearly all words ending in **–à**, **–sione** and **–zione** are feminine.
- nearly all words ending with a consonant are masculine.

i Note that words ending in **–e** are masculine in some cases and feminine in others.

➤ The following are typical masculine nouns ending in **–o**:

il treno	the train
il supermercato	the supermarket
l'aeroporto	the airport
il toro	the bull
un topo	a mouse
un gatto	a (tom) cat
un italiano	an Italian (man)

📖 Note that a few very common nouns ending in **–o** are feminine.

la mano	the hand
una foto	a photo
la radio	the radio
una moto	a motorbike

➤ The following are typical feminine nouns ending in **–a**:

la casa	the house
la macchina	the car
una donna	a woman
una regola	a rule
una gatta	a (she) cat
un'italiana	an Italian (woman)

📖 Note that some very common words ending in **–a** are masculine.

il problema	the problem
il programma	the programme
il sistema	the system
il clima	the climate

● Most words for professions and jobs ending in **–ta** are masculine or feminine, according to whether a male or female is meant.

<u>un</u> **giornalista**	a (male) journalist
<u>una</u> **giornalista**	a (female) journalist
<u>un</u> **dentista**	a (male) dentist
<u>una</u> **dentista**	a (female) dentist

➤ The following are typical feminine nouns ending in **–à**, **–sione**, and **–zione**:

Ending	Example	Meaning
–à	**una difficoltà**	a difficulty
	la realtà	the reality
–sione	**la versione**	the version
	un'occasione	an opportunity
–zione	**una lezione**	a lesson
	una conversazione	a conversation

➤ Nouns ending in a <u>consonant</u> are nearly always masculine.

un film	a film
un bar	a bar
un computer	a computer
BUT	
una Jeep®	a Jeep®

4 Nouns

➤ Nouns ending in **–e** can be masculine in some cases and feminine in others.

un mese	a month
il mare	the sea
la gente	the people
la mente	the mind
il mese di giugno	the month of June
una mente logica	a logical mind

ⓘ Note that the names of languages are always masculine, whether they end in **–e** or in **–o**.

Il giapponese è molto difficile.	Japanese is very difficult.
L'italiano è bellissimo.	Italian is beautiful.

Grammar Extra!

Some words have different meanings depending on whether they are masculine or feminine.

Masculine	Meaning	Feminine	Meaning
il fine	the objective	**la fine**	the end
un posto	a place	**la posta**	the mail
un modo	a way	**la moda**	the fashion
il capitale	capital (money)	**una capitale**	a capital city
un bel posto	a nice place	**posta prioritaria**	first class

---

3 Nouns for males and females

➤ In Italian, just as in English, there are sometimes very different words for male and female people and animals.

un uomo	a man
una donna	a woman
un fratello	a brother
una sorella	a sister
un toro	a bull
una mucca	a cow

➤ In most cases, though, a noun referring to a male can be made to refer to a female by changing the ending:

- Many Italian nouns ending in **–o** can be made feminine by changing the ending to **–a**.

un cuoco	a (male) cook
una cuoca	a (female) cook
un ragazzo	a boy
una ragazza	a girl
un fotografo	a (male) photographer
una fotografa	a (female) photographer
un italiano	an Italian (man)
un'italiana	an Italian (woman)
un gatto	a (tom) cat
una gatta	a (she) cat

- If a noun describing a male ends in **–tore**, the feminine form ends in **–trice**.

un attore	a (male) actor
un'attrice	a (female) actor
un pittore	a (male) painter
una pittrice	a (female) painter
uno scrittore	a (male) writer
una scrittrice	a (female) writer

- Certain nouns describing males ending in **–e** have feminine forms ending in **–essa**.

il professore	the (male) teacher
la professoressa	the (female) teacher
uno studente	a (male) student
una studentessa	a (female) student
un leone	a lion
una leonessa	a lioness

➤ Many nouns ending in **–a** can refer either to males or to females, so there is no change of ending for the feminine.

un turista	a (male) tourist
una turista	a (female) tourist
un collega	a (male) colleague
una collega	a (female) colleague
il mio dentista	my dentist (if it's a man)
la mia dentista	my dentist (if it's a woman)

6 Nouns

➤ Many nouns ending in –e can refer either to males or to females, so there is no change of ending for the feminine.

un nipote	a grandson
una nipote	a granddaughter
un cantante	a (male) singer
una cantante	a (female) singer

Grammar Extra!

A few nouns that are feminine refer both to men and women.

una guida	a guide (male or female)
una persona	a person (male or female)
una spia	a spy (male or female)
una star	a star (male or female)
Sean Connery è ancora una star.	Sean Connery's still a star.

Key points

✔ Most nouns referring to males can be made to refer to females by changing the ending.

✔ Some nouns are the same whether they refer to males or to females, but the words used with them change.

✔ In a few cases the nouns used for male and female are completely different.

Making nouns plural

➤ There are two main ways of making nouns plural in Italian. In most cases you change the ending, but in a few cases the same form as the singular is used. There are also some plurals which are irregular.

1 Nouns which you make plural by changing the ending

➤ In English you usually make nouns plural by adding –s. In Italian you usually do it by changing the ending from one vowel to another:

● Change the –o, –a or –e ending of masculine nouns to –i. Nearly all masculine plurals end in –i.

–o	un anno	one year
	due anni	two years
	un ragazzo	one boy
	due ragazzi	two boys
–a	un ciclista	a (male) cyclist
	due ciclisti	two cyclists
	un problema	a problem
	molti problemi	lots of problems
–e	un mese	one month
	due mesi	two months
	un francese	a Frenchman
	due francesi	two Frenchmen

● Change the –a ending of feminine nouns to –e.

una settimana	one week
due settimane	two weeks
una ragazza	one girl
due ragazze	two girls

● Change the –e ending of feminine nouns to –i.

un'inglese	an Englishwoman
due inglesi	two Englishwomen
la vite	the vine
le viti	the vines

2 Nouns you do not change in the plural

● You do not change feminine nouns ending in –à. You show that they are plural by using the plural word for the, adjectives in the plural, and so on.

la città	the city
le città	the cities
grandi città	great cities

la loro università	their university
le loro università	their universities

⇨ *For more information on* **Articles** *and* **Adjectives**, *see pages 10 and 20.*

- You do not change words ending in a consonant, which are often words borrowed from English and other languages.

il film	the film
i film	the films
il manager	the manager
i manager	the managers
il computer	the computer
i computer	the computers
la Jeep®	the Jeep®
le Jeep®	the Jeeps®

3 Nouns with irregular plurals

➤ A small number of common masculine nouns take the ending **–a** in the plural.

il dito	the finger
le dita	the fingers
un uovo	an egg
le uova	the eggs
il lenzuolo	the sheet
le lenzuola	the sheets

ℹ️ Note that the plural of **uomo** (meaning *man*) is **uomini**. The plural of **la mano** (meaning *hand*) is **le mani**.

➤ All nouns ending in **–ca** and **–ga** add an **h** before the plural ending.

Singular		Plural	
amica	(female) friend	amiche	(female) friends
buca	hole	buche	holes
riga	line	righe	lines
vanga	spade	vanghe	spades

➤ Some nouns ending in **–co** and **–go** also add an **h** before the plural ending.

Singular		Plural	
gioco	game	giochi	games
fuoco	fire	fuochi	fires
luogo	place	luoghi	places
borgo	district	borghi	districts

[i] Note that there are many exceptions: the plurals of **amico** (meaning *friend*) and **psicologo** (meaning *psychologist*) are **amici** and **psicologi**.

⇨ *For more information on **Italian spelling rules**, see page 191.*

4 Plural or singular?

➤ Bear in mind that some words are <u>plural</u> in Italian but <u>singular</u> in English.

i miei capelli	my hair
gli affari	business
le notizie	the news
consigli	advice
i mobili	the furniture
sciocchezze	nonsense

[i] Note that you use the singular of some of these words to refer to *a piece of* something.

un mobile	a piece of furniture
un consiglio	a piece of advice
una notizia	a piece of news

Tip

An important word that is <u>singular</u> in Italian but <u>plural</u> in English is **la gente** (meaning *people*). Remember to use a singular verb with **la gente**.

È gente molto simpatica.   They're very nice people.

Grammar Extra!

When nouns are made by combining two words, such as **pescespada** (meaning *swordfish*), or **capolavoro** (meaning *masterpiece*), the plural is often not formed according to the usual rules. You can check by looking in a dictionary.

Key points

✔ You can make most Italian nouns plural by changing their ending from one vowel to another.

✔ Some nouns are the same in the plural as in the singular.

✔ Some nouns which are singular in English are plural in Italian.

Articles

What is an article?
In English, an **article** is one of the words *the*, *a* and *an* which go with nouns:
<u>the</u> sun, <u>a</u> happy boy, <u>an</u> orange.

Two types of article

➤ There are two types of article: the <u>definite</u> article and the <u>indefinite</u> article.

- The <u>definite</u> article is *the*. You use it to refer to a specified thing or person.

  I'm going to <u>the</u> supermarket.

  That's <u>the</u> woman I was talking to.

- The <u>indefinite</u> article is *a* or *an*. You use it if you are not referring to any particular thing or person.

  Is there <u>a</u> supermarket near here?

  She was talking to <u>a</u> little girl.

For further explanation of grammatical terms, please see pages viii–xii.

The definite article

1 The basics

➤ There are three questions you need to ask yourself to decide which definite article to use in Italian:

- Is the noun masculine or feminine? (This is known as its <u>gender</u>).

- Is it singular or plural?

the child	**il bambino**	(SINGULAR)
the children	**i bambini**	(PLURAL)

- Does the following word begin with a vowel (*a, e, i, o, u*) or with another letter?

➡ *For more information on **Nouns**, see page 1.*

2 Which definite article do you use?

➤ The definite article to use for <u>masculine singular nouns</u> is:

- **il** with most nouns starting with a <u>consonant</u>.

il ragazzo	the boy
il telefonino	the mobile phone

- **lo** with nouns starting with <u>**z**, or **s** + another consonant, **gn**, **pn**, **ps**, **x** or **y**</u>.

lo zio	the uncle
lo studente	the student
lo pneumatico	the tyre
lo psichiatra	the psychiatrist
lo yogurt	the yoghurt

- **l'** with all nouns starting with a <u>vowel</u>.

l'ospedale	the hospital
l'albergo	the hotel

➤ The definite article to use for <u>masculine plural nouns</u> is:

- **i** with most nouns starting with a <u>consonant</u>.

i fratelli	the brothers
i tablet	the tablets

- **gli** with nouns starting with <u>**z**, **s** + another consonant, **gn**, **pn**, **ps**, **x** or **y**</u>.

gli studenti	the students
gli zii	the uncles
gli gnocchi	the gnocchi
gli pneumatici	the tyres
gli yogurt	the yoghurts

- **gli** with all nouns starting with a <u>vowel</u>.

gli amici	the friends
gli orari	the timetables

➤ The definite article to use for <u>feminine singular nouns</u> is:

- **la** with all nouns starting with a <u>consonant</u>.

la ragazza	the girl
la macchina	the car

- **l'** with all nouns starting with a <u>vowel</u>.

l'amica	the (girl)friend
l'arancia	the orange

➤ The definite article to use for <u>feminine plural nouns</u> is:

- **le** with all nouns, whether they start with a <u>consonant</u> or a <u>vowel</u>.

le ragazze	the girls
le amiche	the (girl)friends

Tip

When you're learning vocabulary, remember to learn the article that goes with each noun.

📋 Note that the article you choose depends on the first or first two letters of the following word, which can be an adjective or a noun.

l'amico	the friend
BUT	
il migliore amico	the best friend
lo studente	the student
BUT	
il migliore studente	the best student
gli studenti	the students
BUT	
i migliori studenti	the best students

➡️ *For more information on **Adjectives**, see page 20.*

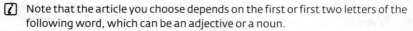

For further explanation of grammatical terms, please see pages viii–xii.

3 | Combining the definite article with other words

➤ In Italian, when you say *at the cinema*, *in the cinema*, and so on, the word for *at* and *in* combines with the article. How this works for **a** (meaning *at* or *to*) is shown below:

a + il = **al**	al cinema	at *or* to the cinema
a + l' = **all'**	all'albergo	at *or* to the hotel
a + lo = **allo**	allo stadio	at *or* to the stadium
a + la = **alla**	alla stazione	at *or* to the station
a + i = **ai**	ai concerti	at *or* to the concerts
a + gli = **agli**	agli aeroporti	at *or* to the airports
a + le = **alle**	alle partite	at *or* to the matches

➤ The other words which combine in the same way are: **da**, **di**, **in** and **su**:

- **da** (meaning *from*)

da + il = **dal**	dal cinema	from the cinema
da + l' = **dall'**	dall'albergo	from the hotel
da + lo = **dallo**	dallo stadio	from the stadium
da + la = **dalla**	dalla stazione	from the station
da + i = **dai**	dai concerti	from the concerts
da + gli = **dagli**	dagli aeroporti	from the airports
da + le = **dalle**	dalle partite	from the matches

- **di** (meaning *of*)

di + il = **del**	del cinema	of the cinema
di + l' = **dell'**	dell'albergo	of the hotel
di + lo = **dello**	dello stadio	of the stadium
di + la = **della**	della stazione	of the station
di + i = **dei**	dei concerti	of the concerts
di + gli = **degli**	degli aeroporti	of the airports
di + le = **delle**	delle partite	of the matches

- **in** (meaning *in*)

in + il = **nel**	nel cinema	in the cinema
in + l' = **nell'**	nell'albergo	in the hotel
in + lo = **nello**	nello stadio	in the stadium
in + la = **nella**	nella stazione	in the station
in + i = **nei**	nei concerti	in the concerts
in + gli = **negli**	negli aeroporti	in the airports
in + le = **nelle**	nelle partite	in the matches

- **su** (meaning *on*)

su + il = <u>sul</u>	sul pavimento	on the floor
su + l' = <u>sull'</u>	sull'orlo	on the edge
su + lo = <u>sullo</u>	sullo scoglio	on the rock
su + la = <u>sulla</u>	sulla spiaggia	on the beach
su + i = <u>sui</u>	sui monti	on the mountains
su + gli = <u>sugli</u>	sugli scaffali	on the bookshelves
su + le = <u>sulle</u>	sulle strade	on the roads

➤ In English, you can use *some* with singular and plural nouns: *some sugar, some students*. One way of expressing the idea of *some* in Italian is to use the word **di** together with the definite article.

<u>del</u> burro	some butter
<u>dell'</u>olio	some oil
<u>della</u> carta	some paper
<u>dei</u> fiammiferi	some matches
<u>delle</u> uova	some eggs
Hanno rotto <u>dei</u> bicchieri.	They broke some glasses.
Ci vuole <u>del</u> sale.	It needs some salt.
Aggiungi <u>della</u> farina.	Add some flour.

---

4 When do you use the definite article?

➤ Italian uses the definite article much more than English does. As a rule of thumb, Italian sentences rarely start with a noun that has no article.

<u>I</u> bambini soffrono.	Children are suffering.
Mi piacciono <u>gli</u> animali.	I like animals.
<u>Le</u> cose vanno meglio.	Things are going better.
<u>Il</u> nuoto è il mio sport preferito.	Swimming is my favourite sport.
Non mi piace <u>il</u> riso.	I don't like rice.
<u>Lo</u> zucchero non fa bene.	Sugar isn't good for you.
<u>La</u> povertà è un grande problema.	Poverty is a big problem.
<u>L'</u>Australia è molto grande.	Australia is very big.
<u>La</u> Calabria è bella.	Calabria is beautiful.

[i] Note that if the name of a country comes after the Italian word **in**, which means *to* or *in*, the article is <u>not</u> used.

Vado in Francia a giugno.	I'm going to France in June.
Lavorano in Germania.	They work in Germany.

For further explanation of grammatical terms, please see pages viii–xii.

> **Tip**
>
> When you translate an English sentence which starts with a noun, don't forget to use the definite article in Italian.
>
> | | |
> |---|---|
> | **Le macchine costano caro.** | Cars cost a lot. |
> | **La frutta fa bene.** | Fruit is good for you. |

➤ In the following cases, the article is used rather differently in Italian from in English:

- When you're talking about <u>parts of the body and bodily actions</u>, use the definite article. The English adjectives *my*, *your*, *his* and so on are not translated.

Dammi <u>la</u> mano.	Give me your hand.
Mi fa male <u>il</u> piede.	My foot is hurting.
Soffiati <u>il</u> naso!	Blow your nose!

- Use the definite article when talking about <u>clothes</u>.

Si è tolto <u>il</u> cappotto.	He took off his coat.
Mettiti <u>le</u> scarpe.	Put your shoes on.

- Use the definite article with the <u>time</u>, <u>dates</u> and <u>years</u>.

<u>all'</u>una	at one o'clock
<u>alle</u> due	at two o'clock
Era <u>l'</u>una.	It was one o'clock.
Sono <u>le</u> due.	It's two o'clock.
Sono nata <u>il</u> primo maggio 2001.	I was born on May 1 2001.
Verranno <u>nel</u> 2017.	They're coming in 2017.

- Use the definite article with words such as *my*, *your*, and *his*.

<u>la</u> mia casa	my house
<u>le</u> sue figlie	her daughters
<u>i</u> vostri amici	your friends

⇨ *For more information on **Possessive adjectives**, see page 34.*

- When you talk about how much something costs <u>per pound</u>, <u>per kilo</u>, and so on; about <u>rates</u>, <u>speeds</u>, and about <u>how often</u> something happens, use the word **a** and the definite article.

Costano 3 euro <u>al</u> chilo.	They cost 3 euro a kilo.
70 km <u>all'</u>ora	70 km an hour
50.000 dollari <u>al</u> mese	50,000 dollars per month
due volte <u>alla</u> settimana	twice a week

- You use the definite article when you are referring to people by using their <u>titles</u>, but NOT when you are speaking to them directly.

<u>La</u> signora Rossi è qui.	Mrs. Rossi is here.
<u>Il</u> dottor Gentile	Doctor Gentile
BUT	
Scusi, signora Rossi.	Excuse me, Mrs. Rossi.

Key points

✔ Definite articles are used much more in Italian than in English.

✔ Italian sentences rarely start with a noun that has no article.

✔ Sometimes the definite article is used very differently from English. For instance, you use it with parts of the body and the time.

The indefinite article

1 The basics

➤ In English the indefinite article is either *a* – *a boy* - or *an* - *an apple*.

➤ In Italian there are four indefinite articles: **un**, **uno**, **una** and **un'**.

➤ Which one you need to choose depends on the gender of the noun it goes with, and the letter the noun starts with.

⇨ *For more information on **Nouns**, see page 1.*

2 Which indefinite article do you use?

➤ The indefinite article to use for <u>masculine nouns</u> is:

- **un** with nouns starting with <u>most consonants</u> and <u>all vowels</u>.

un telefonino	a mobile phone
un uomo	a man

- **uno** with nouns starting with **s** + another consonant, **z**, **gn**, **pn**, **ps**, **x** and **y**.

uno studente	a student
uno zio	an uncle
uno psichiatra	a psychiatrist

➤ The indefinite article to use for <u>feminine nouns</u> is:

- **una** with nouns starting with a <u>consonant</u>.

una ragazza	a girl
una mela	an apple

- **un'** with nouns starting with a <u>vowel</u>.

un'ora	an hour
un'amica	a (girl)friend

[i] Note that the article you choose depends on the first or first two letters of the following word, which can be an adjective or a noun.

<u>un</u> albergo	a hotel
BUT	
<u>uno</u> splendido albergo	a magnificent hotel
<u>uno</u> scultore	a sculptor
BUT	
<u>un</u> bravo scultore	a good sculptor

3 Using the indefinite article

➤ You generally use the indefinite article in Italian when *a* or *an* are used in English.

Era con un'amica.	She was with a friend.
Vuoi un gelato?	Do you want an ice cream?

➤ There are some cases where the article is used in English, but <u>not</u> in Italian:

- with the words **cento** and **mille**

cento volte	a hundred times
mille sterline	a thousand pounds

- when you translate *a few* or *a lot*

qualche parola	a few words
molti soldi	a lot of money

- in exclamations with **che**

Che sorpresa!	What a surprise!
Che peccato!	What a pity!

[*i*] Note that to say what someone's job is you either leave out the article:

È medico.	He's a doctor.
Sono professori.	They're teachers.

Or you use the verb **fare** with the <u>definite</u> article:

Faccio l'ingegnere.	I'm an engineer.
Fa l'avvocato.	She's a lawyer.

4 Plural nouns used without the article

➤ There are some cases where you use plural nouns without any article:

- in negative sentences

Non ha amici.	He hasn't got any friends.
Non ci sono posti liberi.	There aren't any empty seats.

- in questions where *any* is used in English

Hai fratelli?	Have you got any brothers or sisters?
Ci sono problemi?	Are there any problems?

⇨ *For more information on **Negatives** and **Questions**, see pages 149 and 152.*

- in lists

  Ci vogliono patate, cipolle e carote.

  You need potatoes, onions and carrots.

  Vendono giornali, riviste e cartoline.

  They sell newspapers, magazines and postcards.

- when you are not giving details

  Abbiamo visitato castelli e musei.

  We visited castles and museums.

  Ci sono cose da vedere.

  There are things to see.

  Hanno problemi.

  They've got problems.

Key points

✔ You generally use the indefinite article in a very similar way to English.

✔ You do not use it with the numbers **cento** and **mille**, and in exclamations with **che**.

✔ The indefinite article is not used when saying what someone's job is.

Adjectives

What is an adjective?
An **adjective** is a 'describing' word that tells you more about a person or thing, for example, *blue*, *big*, *good*.

Using adjectives

➤ You use adjectives like *nice*, *expensive* and *good* to say something about nouns (living beings, things or ideas). You can also use them with words such as *you*, *he* and *they*. You can use them immediately in front of a noun, or after verbs like *be*, *look* and *feel*.

> a <u>nice</u> girl
> an <u>expensive</u> coat
> a <u>good</u> idea
> He's <u>nice</u>.
> They look <u>expensive</u>.

⇨ *For more information on **Nouns**, see page 1.*

➤ In English, adjectives don't change according to the noun they go with.

> a nice boy
> nice girls

➤ In Italian you have to ask:
  - Is the noun masculine or feminine?
  - Is it singular or plural?

➤ You then choose the adjective ending accordingly. This is called making the adjective agree.

un ragazzo <u>alto</u>	a tall boy
una ragazza <u>alta</u>	a tall girl
ragazzi <u>alti</u>	tall boys
ragazze <u>alte</u>	tall girls

➤ In English you put adjectives <u>IN FRONT OF</u> the noun you're describing, but in Italian you usually put them <u>AFTER</u> it.

> **una casa <u>bianca</u>**   a <u>white</u> house

⇨ *For more information on **Word order with adjectives**, see page 24.*

For further explanation of grammatical terms, please see pages viii–xii.

How to make adjectives agree

1 The basics

➤ When you look up an adjective in a dictionary you find the <u>masculine</u> <u>singular</u> form.

➤ If you want to use an adjective to describe a feminine noun you <u>often</u> have to change the ending.

➤ If you want to use an adjective to describe a plural noun you <u>nearly always</u> have to change the ending.

2 How to make adjectives feminine

➤ If the masculine adjective ends in **–o**, change **–o** to **–a**.

un ragazzo <u>simpatico</u>	a nice boy
una ragazza <u>simpatica</u>	a nice girl
un film <u>italiano</u>	an Italian film
una squadra <u>italiana</u>	an Italian team

➤ You don't change the ending for the feminine:

● if the masculine adjective ends in **–e**

un libro <u>inglese</u>	an English book
una famiglia <u>inglese</u>	an English family
un treno <u>veloce</u>	a fast train
una macchina <u>veloce</u>	a fast car

[*i*] Note that adjectives such as **italiano**, **inglese**, **francese** do not start with a capital letter in Italian.

● in the case of some colours

un calzino <u>rosa</u>	a pink sock
una maglietta <u>rosa</u>	a pink T-shirt
un tappeto <u>blu</u>	a blue rug
una macchina <u>blu</u>	a blue car
un vestito <u>beige</u>	a beige suit
una gonna <u>beige</u>	a beige skirt

[*i*] Note that these adjectives don't change in the plural either.

● if the adjective ends with a consonant

un gruppo <u>pop</u>	a pop group
la musica <u>pop</u>	pop music
un tipo <u>snob</u>	a posh guy
una persona <u>snob</u>	a posh person

[*i*] Note that these adjectives don't change in the plural either.

> *Tip*
>
> If you are female, make sure you always use a feminine adjective when talking about yourself:
>
> | **Sono stanca.** | I'm tired. |
> | **Sono pronta.** | I'm ready. |

3 How to make adjectives plural

➤ If the masculine singular adjective ends in **–o**, change **–o** to **–i**.

un fiore rosso	a red flower
dei fiori rossi	red flowers
un computer nuovo	a new computer
dei computer nuovi	new computers

➤ If the feminine singular adjective ends in **–a**, change **–a** to **–e**.

una strada pericolosa	a dangerous road
delle strade pericolose	dangerous roads
una gonna nera	a black skirt
delle gonne nere	black skirts

➤ If the adjective ends in **–e**, change **–e** to **–i** for both masculine and feminine plural.

un esercizio difficile	a difficult exercise
degli esercizi difficili	difficult exercises
un sito interessante	an interesting site
dei siti interessanti	interesting sites
una storia triste	a sad story
delle storie tristi	sad stories
una valigia pesante	a heavy case
delle valigie pesanti	heavy cases

➤ Some adjectives do not change in the plural.

un paio di guanti rosa	a pair of pink gloves
delle tende blu	blue curtains
dei gruppi pop	pop groups

➤ Adjectives that do not change for the feminine or plural are called <u>invariable</u>, which is abbreviated to *inv* in some dictionaries.

> **Tip**
>
> Remember that **spaghetti**, **ravioli**, **lasagne** and so on are plural nouns in Italian, so you must use plural adjectives with them.
>
> **Sono buoni gli spaghetti?**   Is the spaghetti nice?
> **Le lasagne sono finite.**   The lasagne is all gone.

🛈   Note that when you're describing a couple consisting of a man and a woman or a group of people, use a masculine plural adjective unless the group consists entirely of females.

     Paolo e Loredana sono pronti.   Paolo and Loredana are ready.
     I bambini sono stanchi.   The children are tired.
     Le ragazze sono stanche.   The girls are tired.

4 | Irregular adjectives

➤ There are three very common adjectives which are different from other adjectives – **bello**, **buono** and **grande**.

➤ When the adjective **bello** (meaning *beautiful*) is used in front of a masculine noun it has different forms depending on which letter follows it, just like the definite article.

bello	Masculine Singular	Feminine Singular	Masculine Plural	Feminine Plural
used before a noun	bel	bella	bei	belle
used after a verb or a noun	bello	bella	belli	belle

     bel tempo   beautiful weather
     bei nomi   beautiful names
     Il tempo era bello.   The weather was beautiful.
     I fiori sono belli.   The flowers are beautiful.

➤ **bell'** is used before vowels in the masculine and feminine singular forms.

     un bell'albero   a beautiful tree

➤ **bello** is used in front of **z** and **s** + another consonant in the masculine singular form.

     un bello strumento   a beautiful instrument

➤ **begli** is used in front of vowels, **z** and **s** + another consonant in the masculine plural form.

     begli alberi   beautiful trees
     begli strumenti   beautiful instruments

➤ The adjective **buono** (meaning *good*) is usually shortened to **buon** when it comes before a masculine singular noun.

Buon viaggio!	Have a good journey!
un buon uomo	a good man

➤ The shortened form of **buono** is <u>not</u> used in front of nouns that start with **z** or **s** + another consonant.

un buono studente	a good student

➤ The adjective **grande** (meaning *big*, *large* or *great*) is often shortened to **gran** when it comes before a singular noun starting with a consonant.

la Gran Bretagna	Great Britain
un gran numero di macchine	a large number of cars

Key points

✔ In Italian adjectives agree with the person or thing they are describing.

✔ Adjectives ending in **–o** in the masculine have different endings in the feminine and plural forms.

✔ Some adjectives don't have a different feminine or plural form.

---

5 Where do you put the adjective?

➤ You put most adjectives <u>AFTER</u> the noun.

un gesto <u>spontaneo</u>	a spontaneous gesture
una partita <u>importante</u>	an important match
capelli <u>biondi</u>	blonde hair

🛈 Note that if you have two adjectives you link them with **e** (meaning *and*).

ragazze <u>antipatiche</u> e <u>maleducate</u>	nasty rude girls

➤ The meaning of some adjectives changes depending on whether they come after or before the noun.

gente povera	poor people BUT
Povera Anna!	Poor (meaning *unfortunate*) Anna!
un uomo grande	a big man BUT
una grande sorpresa	a great surprise
una macchina nuova	a new car BUT
la sua nuova ragazza	his new (meaning *latest*) girlfriend

For further explanation of grammatical terms, please see pages viii–xii.

una casa vecchia	an old house BUT
un mio vecchio amico	an old (meaning *long-standing*) friend of mine
una borsa cara	an expensive handbag BUT
un caro amico	a dear friend

[*i*] Note that if you add **molto** (meaning *very*) to an adjective, the adjective always goes after the noun.

una bella casa	a nice house
una casa molto bella	a very nice house

➤ Some types of adjectives always go in front of the noun:

- adjectives that are used to point things out, such as **questo** (meaning *this*) and **quello** (meaning *that*)

<u>Questo</u> telefonino è di mio fratello.	This mobile phone is my brother's.
<u>Quello</u> studente è un mio amico.	That student is a friend of mine.

⇨ *For more information on **Demonstrative adjectives**, see page 30.*

- possessive adjectives such as **mio** (meaning *my*), **tuo** (meaning *your*) and **suo** (meaning *his* or *her*)

<u>mio</u> padre	my father
<u>tuo</u> fratello	your brother
<u>suo</u> marito	her husband

- **ogni** (meaning *each*, *every*), **qualche** (meaning *some*) and **nessuno** (meaning *no*)

<u>ogni</u> giorno	every day
<u>qualche</u> volta	sometimes
Non c'è <u>nessun</u> bisogno di andare.	There's no need to go.

⇨ *For more information on **Indefinite adjectives**, see page 37.*

- question words

<u>Quali</u> programmi hai?	What plans have you got?
<u>Quanto</u> pane hai comprato?	How much bread did you buy?

⇨ *For more information on **Questions**, see page 152.*

Key points

✔ Most Italian adjectives go after the noun.

✔ The meaning of some adjectives changes depending on whether they come before or after the noun.

Comparing people or things

1 Comparative adjectives

> **What is a comparative adjective?**
> In English a **comparative adjective** is one with *–er* on the end, or *more* or *less* in front of it, for example *faster, more important, less interesting*. These adjectives are used when you are comparing people or things.

2 How to make a comparative adjective in Italian

➤ To say that something is *faster, bigger, more important* and so on use **più** in front of the adjective.

una macchina <u>più</u> grande	a bigger car
un film <u>più</u> interessante	a more interesting film
Queste scarpe sono <u>più</u> comode.	These shoes are more comfortable.

➤ To say that something is *less expensive, less interesting* and so on use **meno** in front of the adjective.

un computer <u>meno</u> caro	a less expensive computer
un viaggio <u>meno</u> faticoso	a less tiring journey

3 How to compare one person or thing with another

➤ Put either **più** or **meno** in front of the adjective and use **di** to translate *than*.

Sono <u>più</u> alto <u>di</u> te.	I'm taller than you.
Milano è <u>più</u> grande <u>di</u> Genova.	Milan is bigger than Genoa.
Carlo è <u>più</u> ambizioso <u>di</u> Luca.	Carlo is more ambitious than Luca.
Quello verde è <u>meno</u> caro <u>del</u> nero.	The green one is less expensive than the black one.
La mia borsa è <u>meno</u> pesante <u>della</u> tua.	My bag is less heavy than yours.

i Note that **di** combines with the article to make one word: **di + il = del**, **di + la = della**, and so on.

⇨ *For more information on di, see* **Prepositions** *page 174.*

4 Superlative adjectives

What is a superlative adjective?
In English a **superlative adjective** is one with *–est* on the end, or *most* or *least* in front of it, for example *fastest, most important, least interesting*. The definite article is used with superlative adjectives: *the fastest, the most important, the least interesting*.

5 How to make a superlative adjective in Italian

➤ Making a superlative adjective is very easy: you simply put a definite article in front of the comparative adjective.

il più alto	the tallest
il meno interessante	the least interesting

➤ The definite article must agree with the person or thing you're describing.

Matteo è il più alto.	Matteo is the tallest.
Lidia è la più alta.	Lidia is the tallest.
Queste scarpe sono le più comode.	These shoes are the most comfortable.
Gianni è il meno ambizioso.	Gianni is the least ambitious.

➤ If there is a definite article in front of the noun, do not put a second definite article in front of **più** or **meno**.

il ragazzo più alto	the tallest boy
la banca più vicina	the nearest bank
lo studente più intelligente	the most intelligent student
i voli più economici	the cheapest flights
i suoi film meno interessanti	his least interesting films

⇨ *For more information on the* ***Definite article****, see page 11.*

Tip

In phrases like *the most famous in the world*, and *the biggest in Italy*, use **di** to translate *in*.

lo stadio più grande d'Italia	the biggest stadium in Italy
il ristorante più caro della città	the most expensive restaurant in the town

6 | Irregular comparatives and superlatives

➤ In English the comparatives of *good* and *bad* are irregular: *better, best, worse* and *worst*. In Italian there are regular forms of **buono** and **cattivo**.

Questo è più buono.	This one's better.
I rossi sono i più buoni.	The red ones are the best.
Quello è ancora più cattivo.	That one's even worse.

➤ There are also irregular forms of **buono** and **cattivo**, as there are of **grande**, **piccolo**, **alto** and **basso**:

Adjective	Meaning	Comparative	Meaning	Superlative	Meaning
buono	good	**migliore**	better	**il migliore**	the best
cattivo	bad	**peggiore**	worse	**il peggiore**	the worst
grande	big	**maggiore**	bigger/ older	**il maggiore**	the biggest/ oldest
piccolo	small	**minore**	smaller/ younger	**il minore**	the smallest/ youngest
alto	high	**superiore**	higher	**il superiore**	the highest
basso	low	**inferiore**	lower	**l'inferiore**	the lowest

[*i*] Note that these irregular comparatives and superlatives are adjectives ending in **–e**, so their plural ending is **–i**.

il modo migliore	the best way
il mio fratello minore	my younger brother
le mie sorelle maggiori	my older sisters
il labbro inferiore	the lower lip
Il libro è migliore del film.	The book is better than the film.
Giorgia è la peggiore della classe.	Giorgia is the worst in the class.

7 | as ... as ...

➤ Sometimes you want to say that people or things are similar or the same:
> I'm as tall as you.

➤ In Italian you use **come**, or **quanto** to make this kind of comparison.

Pietro è alto come Michele.	Pietro is as tall as Michele.
La mia macchina è grande come la tua.	My car is as big as yours.
Sono stanca quanto te.	I'm just as tired as you are.

➤ You can make these sentences negative by adding **non**.

    Pietro <u>non</u> è alto come Michele.   Pietro is not as tall as Michele.

    <u>Non</u> sono stanca quanto te.   I'm not as tired as you are.

Grammar Extra!

In English you emphasize adjectives by adding words like *very*, *really* or *terribly*. You do the same in Italian, using **molto**, **veramente** and **terribilmente**.

    Lui è molto ricco.   He's very rich.

    I fiori sono veramente belli.   The flowers are really lovely.

    Sono terribilmente stanca.   I'm terribly tired.

➤ Another way of adding emphasis to Italian adjectives is to replace the **–o** or **–e** ending with **–issimo**.

bello	beautiful
bellissimo	very beautiful
elegante	smart
elegantissimo	very smart

[*i*] Note that these **-issimo** adjectives change their endings for the feminine and the plural.

    Il tempo era bellissimo.   The weather was really beautiful.

    Anna è sempre elegantissima.   Anna is always terribly smart.

    Sono educatissimi.   They're extremely polite.

Key points

✔ You make comparative adjectives in Italian by using **più** and **meno**, and translate *than* by **di**.

✔ You add the definite article to the comparative adjective to make a superlative adjective.

30 Adjectives

Demonstrative adjectives

> **What is a demonstrative adjective?**
> A **demonstrative adjective** is used to point out a particular thing or person. There are four demonstrative adjectives in English: *this*, *these*, *that* and *those*.

1 Using demonstrative adjectives

➤ As in English, Italian demonstrative adjectives go <u>BEFORE</u> the noun. Like other adjectives in Italian, they have to change for the feminine and plural forms.

➤ To say *this*, use **questo**, which has four forms, like any other adjective ending in –**o**.

	Masculine	Feminine	Meaning
Singular	questo	questa	this
Plural	questi	queste	these

Questa gonna è troppo stretta.	This skirt is too tight.
Questi pantaloni mi piacciono.	I like these trousers.
Queste scarpe sono comode.	These shoes are comfortable.

➤ To say *that*, use **quello**, which has several different forms, like the definite article:

- use **quel** with a masculine noun starting with a consonant

quel ragazzo	that boy

- use **quello** with a masculine noun starting with **z** or **s** + another consonant

quello zaino	that rucksack
quello studente	that student

- use **quell'** with nouns starting with a vowel

quell'albero	that tree
quell'amica	that friend

- use **quella** with a feminine noun starting with a consonant

quella ragazza	that girl

- use **quei** with a masculine plural noun starting with a consonant

quei cani	those dogs

- use **quegli** with a masculine plural noun starting with a vowel, with **z** or with **s** + another consonant

quegli uomini	those men
quegli studenti	those students

For further explanation of grammatical terms, please see pages viii–xii.

- use **quelle** before all <u>feminine plural nouns</u>

  quelle macchine   those cars

Tip

When you want to say *this one*, don't translate *one*. Use **questo** if what you're referring to is masculine, and **questa** if it's feminine. The same goes when you want to say *that one*: use **quello**, or **quella**.

  Quale casa? – Questa.   Which house? – This one.
  Quale zaino? – Quello.   Which rucksack? – That one.

Key points

✔ Use **questo** or **questa** for *this*, and **questi** or **queste** for *these*.

✔ Use **quello** for *that*: **quello** behaves like the definite article, **il**.

Interrogative adjectives

> **What is an interrogative adjective?**
> An **interrogative adjective** is a question word such as *which*, *what* or *how much*
> that is used when asking about a noun, for example: *Which colour?*; *What size?*;
> *How much sugar?*

➤ In Italian the interrogative adjectives are **che**, **quale** and **quanto**.

➤ **che** and **quale** are used to ask *which* or *what*:

- Use **che** or **quale** with <u>singular nouns</u>.

<u>Che</u> giorno è oggi?	What day is it today?
A <u>che</u> ora ti alzi?	What time do you get up at?
<u>Quale</u> tipo vuoi?	What kind do you want?
Per <u>quale</u> squadra tifi?	Which team do you support?

- Use **che** or **quali** with <u>plural nouns</u>.

<u>Che</u> gusti preferisci?	Which flavours do you like best?
<u>Quali</u> programmi hai?	What plans have you got?

- Use **quanto** with <u>masculine nouns</u> and **quanta** with <u>feminine nouns</u> to ask *how much*.

<u>Quanto</u> pane hai comprato?	How much bread did you buy?
<u>Quanta</u> minestra vuoi?	How much soup do you want?

- Use **quanti** with <u>masculine nouns</u> and **quante** with <u>feminine nouns</u> to ask *how many*.

<u>Quanti</u> bicchieri ci sono?	How many glasses are there?
<u>Quante</u> uova vuoi?	How many eggs do you want?

➪ *For more information on **Questions**, see page 152.*

Key points

✔ Use **che** with any noun to mean *which* or *what*.

✔ **quale** has the plural form **quali**.

✔ **quanto** has feminine and plural forms.

Adjectives used in exclamations

➤ In Italian **che...!** is often used with a noun where we would say *What a ...!*
in English.

Che peccato!	What a pity!
Che disordine!	What a mess!
Che bella giornata!	What a lovely day!
Che brutto tempo!	What awful weather!

➤ **che** can also be used with an adjective when you're commenting on somebody
or something.

Che carino!	Isn't he sweet!
Che brutti!	They're horrible!

➤ You can also use an Italian adjective by itself when you are commenting on
someone's behaviour.

Furbo!	Cunning devil!
Brava!	Good girl!
Bravi!	Well done!

➤ As in English, you can use an Italian adjective alone when you are commenting on
something you see or taste.

Bello!	Lovely!
Buono!	Nice!

> ## Tip
>
> Remember to make the adjective agree with the person or thing you're
> commenting on.

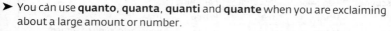

➤ You càn use **quanto**, **quanta**, **quanti** and **quante** when you are exclaiming
about a large amount or number.

Quanto tempo sprecato!	What a waste of time!
Quanta gente!	What a lot of people!
Quanti soldi!	What a lot of money!
Quante storie!	What a fuss!

Possessive adjectives

> **What is a possessive adjective?**
> In English a **possessive adjective** is a word such as *my, your, his* that is used with a noun to show who it belongs to.

How to use possessive adjectives

1 The basics

➤ Unlike English you usually put the <u>definite</u> article (**il**, **la**, **i**, **le**) in front of the possessive adjective.

➤ As with all adjectives ending in **–o**, change the ending to:
- **–a** for the feminine singular
- **–i** for the masculine plural
- **–e** for the feminine plural

il mio indirizzo	my address
la mia scuola	my school
i miei amici	my friends
le mie speranze	my hopes

➪ *For more information on the **Definite article**, see page 11.*

➤ You can also use the <u>indefinite article</u> in front of the possessive adjective in examples like:

una mia amica	a friend of mine
un suo studente	one of her students

➤ You usually put possessive adjectives in front of the noun they describe.

➤ The following table shows all the possessive adjectives:

Singular		Plural		Meaning
Masculine	**Feminine**	**Masculine**	**Feminine**	
il mio	la mia	i miei	le mie	my
il tuo	la tua	i tuoi	le tue	your (belonging to someone you call **tu**)
il suo	la sua	i suoi	le sue	his; her; its; your (belonging to someone you call **Lei**)
il nostro	la nostra	i nostri	le nostre	our
il vostro	la vostra	i vostri	le vostre	your (belonging to people you call **voi**)
il loro	la loro	i loro	le loro	their

➪ *For more information on **Ways of saying 'you' in Italian**, see page 42.*

For further explanation of grammatical terms, please see pages viii–xii.

Dove sono <u>le mie</u> chiavi?	Where are my keys?
Luca ha perso <u>il suo</u> portafoglio.	Luca has lost his wallet.
Ecco <u>i nostri</u> passaporti.	Here are our passports.
Qual è <u>la vostra</u> camera?	Which is your room?
<u>Il tuo</u> amico ti aspetta.	Your friend is waiting for you.

Tip

Possessive adjectives agree with the noun they go with, <u>NOT</u> with the person who is the owner.

Anna ha perso <u>il suo</u> smartphone.	Anna has lost her smartphone.
Marco ha trovato <u>la sua</u> agenda.	Marco's found his diary.
Le ragazze hanno <u>i loro</u> biglietti.	The girls have got their tickets.

i Note that possessive adjectives aren't normally used with parts of the body. You usually use **il**, **la**, and so on (the <u>definite article</u>) instead.

Mi sono fatto male <u>alla</u> gamba.	I've hurt my leg.
Si sta lavando <u>i</u> capelli.	She's washing her hair.

⇨ *For more information on the **Definite article**, see page 11.*

Key points

✔ Italian possessive adjectives agree with the nouns they describe.

✔ Italian possessive adjectives are usually preceded by an article.

✔ Possessive adjectives are not usually used with parts of the body.

2 How to use possessive adjectives when talking about relatives

➤ To say *my mother*, *your father*, *her husband*, *his wife* and so on, use the possessive adjective <u>without</u> the definite article.

mia madre	my mother
tuo padre	your father
suo marito	her husband
sua moglie	his wife
mia sorella	my sister
tuo fratello	your brother

➤ This applies to all family members in the <u>singular</u>, except for the words **mamma** (meaning *mum*) and **babbo** and **papà** (both meaning *dad*).

la mia mamma	my mum
Maria e il suo babbo	Maria and her dad

🛈 Note that if you describe a family member with an adjective, for example *my <u>dear</u> wife, her <u>younger</u> sister*, you DO use the definite article with the possessive.

<u>**il mio caro**</u> **marito**	my dear husband
<u>**il suo**</u> **fratello** <u>**maggiore**</u>	his older brother

➤ You DO use the definite article with the possessive adjective when you're referring to family members in the <u>plural</u>.

Sandro e i suoi fratelli	Sandro and his brothers
Laura e le sue cognate	Laura and her sisters-in-law

Key points

✔ Use the possessive adjective without the definite article when talking about family members in the singular.

✔ Use the possessive adjective with the definite article when talking about family members in the plural.

Indefinite adjectives

> **What is an indefinite adjective?**
> An **indefinite adjective** is one of a small group of adjectives used to give an idea of amounts and numbers, for example, *several*, *all*, *every*.

➤ The indefinite adjectives **ogni** (meaning *each*), **qualche** (meaning *some*) and **qualsiasi** (meaning *any*) are <u>invariable</u>, that is they do not change their form for the feminine or plural.

ogni giorno	every day
ogni volta	every time
fra qualche mese	in a few months
qualche volta	sometimes
in qualsiasi momento	at any time
qualsiasi cosa	anything

➤ The following indefinite adjectives end in **–o**, and change their endings in the normal way.

altro	other
tutto	all
molto	much
parecchio	a lot of
poco	a little
tanto	so much
troppo	too much

➤ Put the indefinite or definite article <u>IN FRONT OF</u> **altro**.

<u>un</u> **altro giorno**	another day
<u>un</u>'**altra volta**	another time
<u>gli</u> **altri studenti**	the other students

➤ Put the definite article <u>AFTER</u> **tutto**, even when there is no article in English.

tutta <u>la</u> **giornata**	all day
tutte <u>le</u> **ragazze**	all the girls

➤ Use **molto** (masculine) and **molta** (feminine) to talk about large amounts.

Non abbiamo <u>molto</u> **tempo.**	We haven't much time.
C'è <u>molta</u> **roba.**	There's a lot of stuff.

➤ Use **molti** (masculine plural) and **molte** (feminine plural) to talk about large numbers.

Abbiamo <u>molti</u> **problemi.**	We've got a lot of problems.
L'ho fatto <u>molte</u> **volte.**	I've done it many times.

➤ You can also use **parecchio** and **parecchia** to talk about quite large amounts, and **parecchi** and **parecchie** to talk about quite large numbers.

Non lo vedo da <u>parecchio</u> tempo.	I haven't seen him for quite some time.
C'era <u>parecchia</u> neve in montagna.	There was quite a lot of snow on the hills.
Ho avuto <u>parecchi</u> guai.	I had quite a few problems.
Ha <u>parecchie</u> amiche inglesi.	She has several English friends.

i Note that the masculine singular ending of **parecchio** changes to a single **–i** in the plural.

➤ Use **poco** and **poca** to talk about small amounts and **pochi** and **poche** to talk about small numbers.

C'è <u>poco</u> tempo.	There's not much time.
Ha <u>pochi</u> amici.	He has few friends.

i Note that the singular endings **–co** and **–ca** change to **–chi** and **–che** in the plural.

➪ *For more information on **Spelling**, see page 191.*

➤ Use **troppo** and **troppa** to say *too much*, and **troppi** and **troppe** to say *too many*.

Questa minestra è <u>troppa</u> per me.	This is too much soup for me.
Ho <u>troppe</u> cose da fare.	I've got too many things to do.

➤ Use **tanto** and **tanta** to talk about very large amounts, and **tanti** and **tante** to talk about very large numbers.

Ho mangiato <u>tanta</u> pasta!	I ate so much pasta!
Abbiamo avuto <u>tanti</u> problemi.	We've had a whole lot of problems.

Grammar Extra!

ciascuno (meaning *each*) and **nessuno** (meaning *no*) have no plural and behave like the indefinite article **uno**.

Before a masculine noun starting with a vowel, or most consonants, use **ciascun** and **nessun**.

<u>ciascun</u> candidato	each candidate
<u>ciascun</u> amico	each friend
<u>nessun</u> irlandese	no Irishman
Non ha fatto <u>nessun</u> commento.	He made no comment.

Before a masculine noun starting with **z** or **s** + another consonant use **ciascuno** and **nessuno**.

<u>ciascuno</u> studente	each student
<u>nessuno</u> spagnolo	no Spanish person

For further explanation of grammatical terms, please see pages viii–xii.

Before a feminine noun starting with a consonant use **ciascuna** and **nessuna**.

<u>**ciascuna**</u> ragazza	each girl
<u>**nessuna**</u> ragione	no reason

Before a feminine noun beginning with a vowel use **ciascun'** and **nessun'**.

<u>**ciascun'**</u>amica	each friend (*female*)
<u>**nessun'**</u>alternativa	no alternative

Key points

✔ **ogni**, **qualche** and **qualsiasi** always have the same form.

✔ **altro**, **tutto**, **molto**, **poco**, **parecchio**, **troppo** and **tanto** change their endings in the feminine and plural.

Pronouns

What is a pronoun?
A **pronoun** is a word you use instead of a noun, when you do not need or want to name someone or something directly, for example, *it, you, somebody, who, that*.

➤ There are many different kinds of pronoun, and all the words underlined in the sentences below are classified as pronouns. As you will see, they are extremely important and versatile words in everyday use.

<u>I</u> liked the black trousers but I couldn't afford <u>them</u>.	(*subject pronoun; direct object pronoun*)
<u>I</u>'m not going to eat it.	(*subject pronoun*)
You know Jack? I saw <u>him</u> at the weekend.	(*direct object pronoun*)
I emailed <u>her</u> my latest ideas.	(*indirect object pronoun*)
It's <u>mine</u>.	(*possessive pronoun*)
<u>Someone</u> came to see you yesterday.	(*indefinite pronoun*)
There's <u>nothing</u> I can do about it.	(*indefinite pronoun*)
<u>This</u> is the book I meant.	(*demonstrative pronoun*)
<u>That's</u> Ian.	(*demonstrative pronoun*)
<u>Who</u>'s he?	(*interrogative pronoun*)
<u>What</u> are those lights over there?	(*interrogative pronoun*)

➤ **Personal pronouns** are words such as *I, you, he, she, us, them*, and so forth, which make it clear who you are talking about or talking to. Personal pronouns replace nouns when it's clear who or what is being referred to, for example,
My brother's not here at the moment. <u>He</u>'ll be back in an hour.

➤ There are two types of personal pronoun:

- <u>subject pronouns</u> for the person or thing performing the action expressed by the verb.

    <u>I</u> like you a lot.
    <u>They</u> always go there on Sundays.

- <u>object pronouns</u> for the person or thing most directly affected by the action.

    I'll help <u>you</u>.
    They sent it to <u>me</u> yesterday.
    He gave <u>us</u> a very warm welcome.

For further explanation of grammatical terms, please see pages viii–xii.

Subject pronouns

➤ Here are the Italian subject pronouns:

Singular	Meaning	Plural	Meaning
io	I	noi	we
tu	you (familiar singular)	voi	you
lui	he	loro	they
lei	she; you (polite singular)		

> **Típ**
>
> You also use **lei** as a polite word for *you*. You will sometimes see it with a capital letter when used in this way.

ⓘ Note that the pronouns **egli** (meaning *he*), **ella** (meaning *she*), **essi** and **esse** (meaning *they*) are used in literary and formal written Italian, so you may well come across them. However, they are not generally used in speaking.

1 When to use subject pronouns in Italian

➤ In English we nearly always put a subject pronoun in front of a verb: <u>I</u> know Paul; <u>they</u>'re nice. Without the pronouns it would not be clear who or what is the subject of the verb.

➤ In Italian the verb ending usually makes it clear who the subject is, so generally no pronoun is necessary.

Conosco Paul.	I know Paul.
Conosci Paul?	Do you know Paul?
Conosciamo Paul.	We know Paul.
Cosa sono? – Sono noci.	What are they? – They're walnuts.

⇨ *For more information on **Verbs**, see page 66.*

➤ You do <u>not</u> use a subject pronoun in Italian to translate *it* at the beginning of a sentence.

Fa caldo.	It's hot.
Sono le tre.	It's three o'clock.
Che cos'è? – È una sorpresa.	What is it? – It's a surprise.

➤ When you do use subject pronouns, it is for one of the following special reasons:

● for emphasis

Tu cosa dici?	What do you think?
Pago io.	I'll pay.
Ci pensiamo noi.	We'll see to it.

[*i*] The subject pronoun can come after the verb:

- for contrast or clarity

Io ci vado, <u>tu</u> fai come vuoi.	I'm going, you do what you like.
Aprilo <u>tu</u>, <u>io</u> non ci riesco.	You open it, I can't.

- after **anche** (meaning *too*) and **neanche** (meaning *neither*)

Vengo anch'<u>io</u>.	I'm coming too.
Prendi un gelato anche <u>tu</u>?	Are you going to have an ice cream too?
Non so perché. – Neanch'<u>io</u>.	I don't know why. – Neither do I.

- when there is no verb in Italian

Chi è il più bravo? – <u>Lui</u>.	Who's the best? – He is.
Viene lui, ma <u>lei</u> no.	He's coming, but she isn't.

Tip

To say *it's me*, for instance when knocking on someone's door, and to say who someone is, you use the subject pronoun.

Chi è? – Sono <u>io</u>.	Who's that? – It's me.
Guarda! È <u>lui</u>.	Look, it's him!

---

2 How to say *you* in Italian

➤ In English we have one way of saying *you*. In Italian, the word you choose depends on:

- whether you're talking to one person or more than one
- how well you know the person concerned.

➤ Use **tu** when you are speaking to a person you know well, or to a child. If you are a student you can call another student **tu**. If you have Italian relations, of course you call them **tu**.

➤ Use **Lei** when speaking to strangers, or anyone you're not on familiar terms with. As you get to know someone better they may suggest that you call each other **tu** instead of **Lei**.

➤ Use **voi** when you are speaking to more than one person, whether you know them well or not.

➤ **tu**, **Lei** and **voi** are subject pronouns. There are also different forms for *you* when it is not a subject. These are explained in the section of this chapter on object pronouns.

For further explanation of grammatical terms, please see pages viii–xii.

[Z] Note that **Lei**, the polite word for *you*, also means *she*. This is rarely confusing, as the context makes it clear – if someone speaks directly to you using **Lei**, the meaning is obviously *you*.

Key points

✔ You don't generally need to use a subject pronoun in Italian. The verb ending makes it clear who is being referred to.

✔ You use subject pronouns in Italian only for emphasis or for contrast.

✔ There are two different ways of saying *you* when talking to one person: **tu** for people you know well; **Lei** for people you don't know.

✔ You use **voi** if you are speaking to more than one person.

Object pronouns

1 What are object pronouns?

➤ Object pronouns are words such as *me, him, us* and *them* used instead of a noun to show who is affected by the action of the verb.

> Do you like Claire? – Yes I like <u>her</u> a lot.
>
> I've lost my purse, have you seen <u>it</u>?
>
> He gave <u>us</u> a fantastic send-off.
>
> Why don't you send <u>them</u> a note?

➤ In English we use object pronouns in two different ways:

- when the person or thing is <u>directly</u> affected by the action:

> I saw <u>them</u> yesterday.
>
> They admire <u>him</u> immensely.

➤ In the above examples, *them* and *him* are called <u>direct objects</u>.

- when the person or thing is <u>indirectly</u> affected by the action. In English you often use *to* with the pronoun in such cases.

> I sent it to <u>them</u> yesterday.
>
> They awarded <u>him</u> a medal.

➤ In the above examples, *them* and *him* are called <u>indirect objects</u>.

➤ For both direct and indirect objects there is one form you use on <u>most</u> occasions. This is called the <u>unstressed</u> form.

2 Unstressed direct object pronouns

➤ Here are the Italian unstressed object pronouns:

mi	me
ti	you (familiar singular)
lo	him, it
la	her, you (polite singular), it
ci	us
vi	you (plural)
li	them (masculine)
le	them (feminine)

➤ Unlike English, you usually put them <u>before</u> the verb.

<u>**Ti**</u> **amo.**	I love you.
<u>**Lo**</u> **invito alla festa.**	I'm inviting him to the party.
Non <u>**lo**</u> **mangio.**	I'm not going to eat it.

<u>La</u> guardava.	He was looking at her.
<u>Vi</u> cercavo.	I was looking for you.
<u>Li</u> conosciamo.	We know them.

➪ *For more information on **Where to place pronouns**, see page 49.*

> ## Tip
> Remember that you use **ti** only when speaking to someone you know
> well.

3 | Lo, la, li and le

➤ You need to pay particular attention to how **lo**, **la**, **li** and **le** are used in Italian.

➤ To translate *it* you need to choose between **lo** or **la**. Use **lo** if the noun referred
to is masculine, and **la** if it's feminine.

Ho <u>un</u> panino, <u>lo</u> vuoi?	I've got a roll, do you want it?
Ho <u>una</u> mela, <u>la</u> vuoi?	I've got an apple, do you want it?

➤ To translate *them* you choose between **li** or **le**. Use **li** if the noun referred to is
masculine, and **le** if it's feminine.

Sto cercando <u>i biglietti</u>. <u>Li</u> hai visti?	I'm looking for the tickets, have you seen them?
Dove sono <u>le caramelle</u>? <u>Le</u> hai mangiate?	Where are the sweets? Have you eaten them?

➤ When **lo** and **la** are followed by **ho**, **hai**, **ha**, **abbiamo**, **avete** and **hanno**, they drop
the vowel and are spelled **l'**.

Non <u>l'</u>ho visto ieri.	I didn't see it yesterday.
<u>L'</u>abbiamo portato con noi.	We took it with us.
<u>L'</u>hanno cercato tutta la giornata.	They looked for it all day.

Grammar Extra!

When you are talking about the past and using the pronouns **lo**, **la**, **li** and **le** you must make the
past participle agree with the noun being referred to. Past participles are just like adjectives
ending in **–o**. You change the **–o** to **–a** for the feminine singular, to **–i** for the masculine plural, and
to **–e** for the feminine plural.

Il suo <u>ultimo</u> film? L'ho vist<u>o</u>.	His new film? I've seen it.
Silvia? L'ho incontra<u>ta</u> ieri.	Silvia? I met her yesterday.
I bigli<u>etti</u>? Li ho già pres<u>i</u>.	The tickets? I've already got them.
Queste scarp<u>e</u>? Le ho compra<u>te</u> anni fa.	These shoes? I bought them years ago.

➪ *For more information on the **Perfect tense**, see page 108.*

> **Key points**
>
> ✔ You generally use the unstressed direct object pronoun.
> ✔ Unstressed direct object pronouns usually come before the verb.
> ✔ You need to pay special attention when translating *it* and *them*.

4 | Unstressed indirect object pronouns

➤ In English some verbs have to be followed by an indirect object pronoun – *explain to him*, *write to him* – but other similar verbs do not: you say *tell him*, *phone him*.

➤ In Italian you have to use indirect object pronouns with verbs such as **dire** (meaning *to tell*) and **telefonare** (meaning *to phone*).

➤ As with direct object pronouns, there are <u>unstressed</u> and <u>stressed</u> indirect object pronouns.

➤ You will generally need to use <u>unstressed</u> pronouns rather than stressed ones.

➤ Here are the unstressed indirect pronouns.

mi	to me, me
ti	to you, you (familiar singular)
gli	to him, him
le	to her, her; to you, you (polite singular)
ci	to us, us
vi	to you, you (plural)
gli, loro	to them, them

➤ Unlike English, you usually put these pronouns <u>before</u> the verb.

➤ Just as in English, when you are telling somebody something, giving somebody something and so on, you use an indirect pronoun for the person concerned.

<u>**Le**</u> **ho detto la verità.**	I told her the truth.
<u>**Gli**</u> **ho dato la cartina.**	I gave him the map.

➤ Indirect pronouns are also generally used with verbs to do with communicating with people.

<u>**Gli**</u> **chiederò il permesso.**	I'll ask him for permission. (*literally, I'll ask to him*)
<u>**Gli**</u> **ho telefonato.**	I phoned him. (*literally, I phoned to him*)
<u>**Le**</u> **scriverò.**	I'll write to her.
Se li vedi chiedi<u>**gli**</u> **di venire.**	If you see them ask them to come. (*literally, ...ask to them...*)

➤ You use indirect object pronouns when you are using verbs such as **piacere**, **importare**, and **interessare** to talk about what people like, care about or are interested in.

<u>Gli</u> piace l'Italia.	He likes Italy.
<u>Le</u> piacciono i gatti.	She likes cats.
Non <u>gli</u> importa il prezzo, sono ricchi.	They don't care about the price, they're rich.
Se <u>gli</u> interessa può venire con me.	If he's interested he can come with me.

Tip

It is worth checking in your dictionary to see if a verb needs a direct or an indirect object. If you look up the verb *to give*, for example, and find the example *to give somebody something*, the **a** in the translation (**dare qualcosa a qualcuno**) shows you that you use an indirect pronoun for the person you give something to.

Gli ho dato il mio numero di telefono.	I gave him my phone number.

Key points

✔ You generally use the unstressed indirect object pronoun.

✔ Unstressed indirect object pronouns are used with many verbs in Italian which do not use them in English such as **chiedere** (meaning *to ask*) and **interessare** (meaning *to interest*).

✔ Unstressed indirect object pronouns usually come before the verb.

---

5 Stressed object pronouns

➤ You use stressed pronouns for special emphasis. They generally go <u>after</u> the verb.

Cercavo proprio <u>voi</u>.	You're just the people I was looking for.
Invitano <u>me</u> e mio fratello.	They're inviting me and my brother.

➤ They are exactly the same as the <u>subject</u> pronouns, except that **me** is used instead of **io** and **te** is used instead of **tu**.

➤ You use the same words for stressed <u>direct</u> and <u>indirect</u> objects. When you use them as indirect objects you put the word **a** (meaning *to*) before them.

DIRECT	
me	me
te	you (*familiar form*)
lui	him
lei/Lei	her, you (*polite singular*)

noi	us
voi	you (*plural*)
loro	them
INDIRECT	
a me	(to) me
a te	(to) you (familiar form)
a lui	(to) him
a lei	(to) her, you (polite singular)
a noi	(to) us
a voi	(to) you (plural)
a loro	(to) them

➤ You use stressed pronouns:

- when you want to emphasize that you mean a particular person and not somebody else, and for contrast:

Amo solo <u>te</u>.	I love only you.
Invito <u>lui</u> alla festa, ma <u>lei</u> no.	I'm inviting him to the party but not her.
Non guardava <u>me</u>, guardava <u>lei</u>.	He wasn't looking at me, he was looking at her.
Ho scritto <u>a lei</u>, <u>a lui</u> no.	I wrote to her, but not to him.
Questo piace <u>a me</u>, ma Luca preferisce l'altro.	I like this one but Luca prefers the other one.

- after a preposition

Vengo con <u>te</u>.	I'll come with you.
Sono arrivati dopo di <u>noi</u>.	They arrived after us.

⇨ *For more information about **Prepositions**, see page 172.*

- after **di** when you're comparing one person with another

Sei più alto di <u>me</u>.	You're taller than me.
Sono più ricchi di <u>lui</u>.	They're richer than him.

Key points

✔ Stressed object pronouns are nearly all the same as subject pronouns.

✔ You use them for emphasis, after prepositions and in comparisons.

✔ You generally put stressed object pronouns after the verb.

✔ You use the same words for direct and indirect objects, but add **a** before them for indirect objects.

For further explanation of grammatical terms, please see pages viii–xii.

6 Before or after the verb?

➤ Unstressed pronouns generally come <u>before</u> the verb.

Mi aiuti?	Could you help me?
Ti piace?	Do you like it?
Ci hanno visto.	They saw us.
Vi ha salutato?	Did he say hello to you?

➤ In some cases, <u>unstressed</u> pronouns come <u>after</u> the verb:

● when you are using the imperative to tell someone to do something. The pronoun is joined onto the verb.

Aiutami!	Help me!
Lasciala stare.	Leave her alone.
Daglielo.	Give it to him (or her).
Arrivano. Non dirgli niente!	They're coming. Don't tell them anything!

i Note that if the verb consists of just one syllable you double the consonant the pronoun starts with, except in the case of **gli**.

Fallo subito!	Do it right away!
Dille la verità!	Tell her the truth!
Dimmi dov'è.	Tell me where it is.
Dacci una mano.	Give us a hand.
Dagli una mano.	Give him a hand.

● when you are using a pronoun with the infinitive (the form of the verb ending in **–re** in Italian). The pronoun is joined onto the verb.

Potresti venire a prendermi?	Could you come and get me?
Non posso aiutarvi.	I can't help you.
Devo farlo?	Do I have to do it?
Dovresti scriverle.	You ought to write to her.
Luigi? Non voglio parlargli.	Luigi? I don't want to talk to him.

i Note that the final **e** of the infinitive is dropped: **prendere** + **mi** becomes **prendermi**, **fare** + **ti** becomes **farti** and so on.

➤ <u>Stressed</u> pronouns often come after the verb.

Amo solo te.	I love only you.
Invito lui alla festa, ma lei no.	I'm inviting him to the party but not her.

7 Using two pronouns together

➤ In English you sometimes use two pronouns together, one referring to the indirect object and the other to the direct object, for example, *I gave him it*.

➤ You often do the same kind of thing in Italian, and must always put the <u>indirect object first</u>.

➤ When you use two pronouns together like this, some of them change:

mi becomes **me**
ti becomes **te**
ci becomes **ce**
vi becomes **ve**

<u>Me</u> li dai?	Will you give me it?
È mia, non <u>te</u> la do.	It's mine, I'm not going to give it to you.
<u>Ce</u> l'hanno promesso.	They promised it to us.
<u>Ve</u> lo mando domani.	I'll send it to you tomorrow.

➤ When you want to use **gli** (meaning *to him* or *to them*) and **le** (meaning *to her*) with **lo**, **la**, **li** or **le**, you add an **–e** to **gli** and join it to **lo**, **la**, and so forth.

gli/le + lo → glielo
gli/le + la → gliela
gli/le + li → glieli
gli/le + le → gliele

<u>Glieli</u> hai promessi.	You promised them to her.
<u>Gliele</u> ha spedite.	He sent them to them.
Carlo? <u>Glielo</u> dirò domani.	Carlo? I'll tell him tomorrow.

➤ When you use two pronouns together to give an order or when using the infinitive (**–re** form of the verb), they join together and are added on to the verb.

Mi piacciono, ma non vuole comprar<u>meli</u>.	I like them but he won't buy me them.
Ecco la lettera di Rita, puoi dar<u>gliela</u>?	Here's Rita's letter, can you give it to her?
Le chiavi? Da<u>gliele</u>.	The keys? Give them to her.
Non abbiamo i biglietti – può mandar<u>celi</u>?	We haven't got the tickets – can you send us them?

> *i* Note that the final **e** of the infinitive is dropped: **prendere** + **mi** + **li** becomes **prendermeli**, **mandare** + **ti** + **le** becomes **mandartele** and so on.

> **Key points**
> ✔ When you use two pronouns together the indirect object comes first.
> ✔ Some indirect objects change when used before a direct object.
> ✔ After orders and the infinitive form, the two pronouns are written as one word and follow the verb.

Grammar Extra!

In English *you* and *one* are used in general statements and questions such as *You don't do it like that; Can you park here?; One has to be careful.*

Use **si** and the reflexive form of the verb in Italian for these kinds of statements and questions.

Si fa così.	This is how you do it.
Si può nuotare qui?	Can you swim here?
Non si sa mai.	You never know.

➡ *For more information on **Reflexive Verbs**, see page 87.*

Possessive pronouns

> **What is a possessive pronoun?**
> In English the **possessive pronouns** are *mine, yours, his, hers, ours* and *theirs*.
> You use them instead of a possessive adjective followed by a noun. For example,
> instead of saying *My bag is the blue one*, you say *Mine's the blue one*.

➤ Here are the Italian possessive pronouns; they are exactly the same as Italian
possessive adjectives, but with the definite article in front of them.

⇨ *For more information on **Possessive adjectives** and the **Definite article**, see pages 34
and 11.*

Singular		Plural		Meaning
Masculine	**Feminine**	**Masculine**	**Feminine**	
il mio	la mia	i miei	le mie	mine
il tuo	la tua	i tuoi	le tue	yours (*familiar*)
il suo	la sua	i suoi	le sue	his, hers, yours (*polite*)
il nostro	la nostra	i nostri	le nostre	ours
il vostro	la vostra	i vostri	le vostre	yours
il loro	la loro	i loro	le loro	theirs

> ## Tip
> There are three ways of saying *yours*, because there are three words for
> *you* – **tu**, **lei** and **voi**.

Questa borsa non è <u>la mia</u>, è <u>la tua</u>.	This bag's not mine, it's yours.
Non è <u>il mio</u>, è <u>il suo</u>, signore.	It's not mine, it's yours, sir.
La nostra casa è piccola, <u>la vostra</u> è grande.	Our house is small, yours is big.
I miei genitori e <u>i suoi</u> si conoscono.	My parents and hers know each other.

[*i*] Note that **i miei**, **i tuoi** and **i suoi** are used to refer to someone's parents.

Vivo con <u>i miei</u>.	I live with my parents.
Cosa hanno detto <u>i tuoi</u>?	What did your parents say?
Lucia è venuta con <u>i suoi</u>.	Lucia came with her parents.

➤ In Italian, possessive pronouns agree with the noun they're used instead of.
For example **il mio** can only be used to refer to a masculine singular noun.

Key points

✔ Italian possessive pronouns are the same as Italian possessive adjectives.

✔ They are masculine or feminine, singular or plural, depending on what they refer to.

ne and ci

➤ **ne** and **ci** are two extremely useful pronouns which have no single equivalent in English. There are some phrases where you have to use them in Italian.

| 1 | **ne** |

ne is a pronoun with several meanings.

➤ It can refer to amounts and quantities.

- It means *some*, and can be used without a noun, just like English.

| **Ne** vuoi? | Would you like some? |
| **Vuoi del pane? – Ne** ho grazie. | Would you like some bread? – I've got some, thanks. |

➤ In English, when talking about amounts and quantities, you can say *How much do you want of it?*, or *How much do you want?* and *How many do you want of them?*, or *How many do you want?* **Ne** translates *of it* and *of them* but it is <u>not</u> optional. So you need to remember to use it in sentences of the kind shown below.

Ne ho preso la metà.	I've taken half (of it).
Ne vuoi la metà?	Do you want half (of it/of them)?
Quanti **ne** vuole?	How many (of them) do you want?
Ne voglio pochi.	I don't want many (of them).

➤ **Ne** also means *about it/them*, *of it/them*, *with it/them*, and so on, when used with Italian adjectives or verbs which are followed by **di**, for example **contento di** (meaning *happy about*), **stufo di** (meaning *fed up with*), **aver paura di** (meaning *to be afraid of*), **scrivere di** (meaning *to write about*).

Ne è molto contenta.	She's very happy about it.
Ne sono conscio.	I'm aware of it.
Ne erano stufi.	They were fed up with it.
Ne sei sicura?	Are you sure (of it)?
Ne hai paura?	Are you afraid of it?
Ne ha scritto sul giornale.	She's written about it in the paper.
Non se **ne** accorge.	He doesn't realize it.

➤ With adjectives and verbs followed by **di**, **ne** can be used to refer to nouns that have already been mentioned.

| Parliamo **del** futuro. – Sì, parli**amone** | Let's talk about the future. Yes, let's talk about it. |
| Hai bisogno **della** chiave? – No, non **ne** ho più bisogno. | Do you need the key? No, I don't need it any more. |

➡ *For more information on **di**, see **Prepositions** page 174.*

➤ **Ne** usually comes <u>before</u> the verb, except when the verb is an order or the infinitive (the **–re** form of the verb).

➤ When it comes after the verb the final **–e** of the infinitive is dropped.

Volevo parlar<u>ne</u>.	I wanted to talk about it.

➤ It follows any other pronoun and is written as one word with it and the verb form.

D<u>amme</u>ne uno per favore.	Give me one of them please.
D<u>aglie</u>ne due rossi.	Give him two red ones.

ⓘ Note that when joined to **ne**, **mi** becomes **me**, **ti** becomes **te**, **ci** becomes **ce**, **vi** become **ve** and **gli** and **le** become **glie**.

Key points

✔ **ne** can be used to mean *some*.

✔ **ne** can also be used to mean *of it* or *of them* when talking about amounts and quantities. Unlike English, it is not optional.

✔ **ne** is used to mean *about it* or *about them* and so forth with verbs and adjectives followed by **di**.

✔ **ne** usually comes before the verb.

---

2 ci

➤ **Ci** is used with certain verbs to mean *it* or *about it*.

Ripensando<u>ci</u> mi sono pentito.	When I thought it over I was sorry.
Non <u>ci</u> credo per niente.	I don't believe it at all.
<u>Ci</u> penserò.	I'll think about it.
Non <u>ci</u> capisco niente.	I can't understand it at all.
Non so che far<u>ci</u>.	I don't know what to do about it.

➤ **Ci** is often used with Italian verbs which are followed by **a**, for example:

● **credere <u>a</u> qualcosa** to believe something, to believe in something

Non <u>ci</u> credo.	I don't believe it.

● **pensare <u>a</u> qualcosa** to think about something

Non voglio nemmeno pensar<u>ci</u>.	I don't even want to think about it.

● **far caso <u>a</u> qualcosa** to notice something

Non <u>ci</u> ho fatto caso.	I didn't notice.

ⓘ Note that the equivalent English verb may not be followed by any preposition at all.

➤ With verbs followed by **a**, **ci** can be used to refer to nouns that have already been mentioned.

I fantasmi, non ci credi?	Ghosts – don't you believe in them?
Non pensi mai al futuro? –	Don't you ever think about the
Ci penserò quando sarò più	future? – I'll think about it when
vecchio.	I'm older.

➤ **ci** is used with the verb **entrare** in some common idiomatic phrases.

Cosa c'entra?	What's that got to do with it?
Io non c'entro.	It's nothing to do with me.

➤ Like **ne**, **ci** usually comes <u>before</u> the verb, except when the verb is an order, the infinitive (the **–re** form of the verb) or the –ing form.

Key points

✔ **ci** is used to mean *it* or *about it*.

✔ **ci** is used with verbs which can be followed by the preposition **a**.

✔ **ci** usually comes before the verb.

Indefinite pronouns

> **What is an indefinite pronoun?**
> An **indefinite pronoun** is a word like *everything*, *nobody* and *something* which is used to refer to people or things in a non-specific way.

➤ Some Italian indefinite pronouns always keep the same form:

- **chiunque** anyone
  Attacca discorso con <u>chiunque</u>.   She'll talk to anyone.

- **niente** nothing
  Cosa c'è? – <u>Niente</u>.   What's wrong? – Nothing.

🔟 Note that **niente** and **nulla** mean exactly the same, but **niente** is used more often.

- **nulla** nothing
  Che cos'hai comprato? – <u>Nulla</u>.   What did you buy? – Nothing.

- **qualcosa** something, anything
  Ho <u>qualcosa</u> da dirti.   I've got something to tell you.
  Ha bisogno di <u>qualcosa</u>?   Do you need anything?
  Voglio <u>qualcos</u>'altro.   I want something else.

⇨ *For more information on **Negatives**, see page 149.*

➤ Other indefinite pronouns are masculine singular words, with a feminine form ending in **–a**:

- **ciascuno, ciascuna** each
  Ne avevamo uno per <u>ciascuno</u>.   We had one each.
  Le torte costano dieci euro <u>ciascuna</u>.   The cakes cost ten euros each.

- **nessuno, nessuna** nobody, anybody; none
  Non è venuto <u>nessuno</u>.   Nobody came.
  Hai visto <u>nessuno</u>?   Did you see anybody?
  <u>Nessuna</u> delle ragazze è venuta.   None of the girls came.

- **ognuno, ognuna** each
  <u>ognuno</u> di voi   each of you

- **qualcuno, qualcuna** somebody; one
  Ha telefonato <u>qualcuno</u>.   Somebody phoned.
  Chiedilo a <u>qualcun</u> altro.   Ask somebody else.
  Conosci <u>qualcuna</u> delle ragazze?   Do you know any of the girls?

- **uno, una** somebody
  Ho incontrato <u>uno</u> che ti conosce.   I met somebody who knows you.

C'è <u>una</u> che ti cerca.	There's somebody (*meaning a woman*) looking for you.

● **alcuni** and **alcune** (meaning *some*) are always used in the plural.

Ci sono posti liberi? – Sì, <u>alcuni</u>.	Are there any empty seats? – Yes, some.
Ci sono ancora delle fragole? – Sì, <u>alcune</u>.	Are there any strawberries left? – Yes, some.

➤ The following pronouns can be singular or plural, masculine or feminine:

● **altro, altra, altri, altre** the other one; another one; other people

L'<u>altro</u> è meno caro.	The other one is cheaper.
Preferisco l'<u>altra</u>.	I prefer the other one.
Non m'interessa quello che dicono gli <u>altri</u>.	I don't care what other people say.
Le <u>altre</u> sono partite.	The others have gone.
Prendine un altro.	Take another one.

[*i*] Note that **altro** can also mean *anything else*.

Vuole <u>altro</u>?	Do you want anything else?

● **molto, molta, molti, molte** a lot, lots

Ne ha <u>molto</u>.	He's got lots.
<u>molti</u> di noi	a lot of us

● **parecchio, parecchia, parecchi, parecchie** quite a lot

C'è ancora del pane? – Sì, <u>parecchio</u>.	Is there any bread left? – Yes, quite a lot.
Avete avuto problemi? – Sì, <u>parecchi</u>.	Did you have problems? – Yes, a lot.

● **poco, poca, pochi, poche** not much, not many

C'è pane? – <u>Poco</u>.	Is there any bread? – Not much.
Ci sono turisti? – <u>Pochi</u>.	Are there any tourists? – Not many.

● **tanto, tanta, tanti, tante** lots, so much, so many

Hai mangiato? – Sì, <u>tanto</u>!	Have you eaten? – Yes, lots!
Sono <u>tanti</u>!	There are so many of them!

● **troppo, troppa, troppi, troppe** too much, too many

Quanto hai speso? – <u>Troppo</u>!	How much have you spent? – Too much!
Ci sono errori? – Sì, <u>troppi</u>.	Are there any mistakes? – Yes, too many.

● **tutti, tutte** everybody, all

Vengono <u>tutti</u>.	Everybody is coming.
Sono arrivate <u>tutte</u>.	They've all arrived (*they're all women*).

For further explanation of grammatical terms, please see pages viii–xii.

i Note that in English you can say *Everybody is coming*; *They're all coming*, or *All of them are coming*. All three sentences are translated into Italian in the same way, using **tutti** and a plural verb. **tutti** cannot be followed by **di**, so don't try to translate *all of them* – translate *they all*.

- **tutto** everything, all

  Va <u>tutto</u> bene?   Is everything okay?

  L'ho finito tutto.   I've finished it all.

Key points

✔ Some indefinite pronouns always have the same form.

✔ Other indefinite pronouns can be masculine or feminine, singular or plural.

Relative pronouns

1 | What is a relative pronoun?

➤ In English the relative pronouns are *who, which, that* and *whom*. They are used to specify exactly who or what is being talked about, for example, *The man who has just come in is Anna's boyfriend; The vase that you broke cost a lot of money.*

➤ Relative pronouns can also introduce an extra piece of information, for example, *Peter, who is a brilliant painter, wants to study art; Their house, which was built in 1890, needs a lot of repairs.*

2 | che

➤ In English *who, whom* and *that* are used to talk about people and *which* and *that* are used to talk about things. In Italian you use **che** for all of these.

quella signora <u>che</u> ha il piccolo cane nero	that lady who has the little black dog
Mio padre, <u>che</u> ha sessant'anni, va in pensione.	My father, who's sixty, is retiring.
una persona <u>che</u> detesto	a person whom I detest
l'uomo <u>che</u> hanno arrestato	the man that they've arrested
la squadra <u>che</u> ha vinto	the team which or that won
il dolce <u>che</u> hai fatto	the pudding you made

➤ In English you can miss out the relative pronoun: *a person I detest; the man they've arrested*. You can <u>never</u> miss out **che**.

the person I admire most → **la persona <u>che</u> ammiro di più**

the money you lent me → **i soldi <u>che</u> mi hai prestato**

➤ Prepositions are sometimes used with relative pronouns: *the man <u>to</u> whom she was talking/the man that she was talking <u>to</u>; the girl who he's going out <u>with</u>*. In English the preposition often goes <u>at the end</u> of the phrase.

➤ In Italian, when you use a preposition with a relative pronoun, use **cui** instead of **che**, and put the preposition in front of it.

la ragazza <u>di cui</u> ti ho parlato	the girl that I told you about
gli amici <u>con cui</u> andiamo in vacanza	the friends who we go on holiday with
la persona <u>a cui</u> si riferiva	the person he was referring to
il quartiere <u>in cui</u> abito	the area in which I live
il film <u>di cui</u> parlavo	the film which I was talking about

> **Tip**
>
> In English *who* is used both as a question word, and as a relative pronoun. In Italian: **chi** is used in questions, and **che** is used as a relative pronoun:
>
> **Chi** va al concerto?   Who's going to the concert?
> la ragazza <u>che</u> hai visto   the girl (that) you saw

➤ In English you often use *which* to refer to a fact or situation that you've just mentioned. In Italian use **il che**.

Loro non pagano nulla, <u>il che</u> non mi sembra giusto.	They don't pay anything, which doesn't seem fair to me.
Dice che non è colpa sua, <u>il che</u> è vero.	She says it's not her fault, which is true.

Grammar Extra!

You may come across **il quale** used to mean *who, which, that* and *whom*. **il quale** is more formal than **che**. **il quale** has feminine and plural forms: **la quale**, **i quali** and **le quali**.

suo padre, **il quale** è avvocato	his father, who is a lawyer
le sue sorelle, **le quali** studiano a Roma	his sisters, who study in Rome

il quale, **la quale**, **i quali** and **le quali** are used most often with prepositions.

l'albergo <u>al quale</u> ci siamo fermati	the hotel that we stayed at
la signora <u>con la</u> quale parlavi	the lady you were talking to
gli amici <u>ai quali</u> mando questa cartolina	the friends I'm sending this card to
la medicina <u>della quale</u> hanno bisogno	the medicine they need

⇨ *For more information about **Prepositions**, see page 172.*

---

3 | quello che

➤ In English you can put *the one* or *the ones* in front of a relative pronoun such as *who, which, that* and *whom*. For example, *That's the one that I'd like; They're the ones we need.*

➤ To say *the one* in Italian use **quello** to refer to masculine nouns or **quella** to refer to feminine nouns. The relative pronoun is **che**.

È <u>quello</u> che non funziona.	That's the one which isn't working.
È <u>quello</u> che preferisco.	That's the one I prefer.
È <u>quella</u> che parla di più.	She's the one who talks most.

➤ To say *the ones* in Italian use **quelli** for masculine nouns or **quelle** for feminine nouns. The relative pronoun is **che**.

Sono <u>quelli</u> che sono partiti senza pagare.	They're the ones who left without paying.
Queste scarpe sono <u>quelle</u> che ha ordinato.	These shoes are the ones you ordered.

➤ With a preposition use **cui** instead of **che**. Put the preposition in front of **cui**.

È quello a <u>cui</u> parlavo.	He's the one I was talking to.
Sono quelli a <u>cui</u> ti riferivi?	Are they the ones to whom you were referring?
Sono quelli di <u>cui</u> abbiamo bisogno.	They're the ones we need.

[*i*] Note that in English the relative pronoun can be left out, for example, *That's the one I want* instead of *That's the one that I want*. In Italian the relative pronoun **che** can <u>never</u> be left out.

Key points

✔ **che** can refer to both people and things in Italian.

✔ The relative pronouns *who*, *which* and *that* can be left out in English, but **che** must always be used.

✔ Use **cui** instead of **che** after a preposition.

✔ **quello**, **quella**, **quelli** and **quelle** are used to say *the one* or *the ones*. They are used with **che**.

Interrogative pronouns

> **What is an interrogative pronoun?**
> In English the **interrogative pronouns** are *who...?*, *which...?*, *whose...?*, *whom...?* and *what...?*. They are used without a noun, to ask questions.

1 The interrogative pronouns in Italian

➤ These are the interrogative pronouns in Italian:

Chi?	Who? Whom?
Che?	What?
Cosa?	What?
Che cosa?	What?
Quale?	Which? Which one? What?
Quanto?	How much?
Quanti?	How many?

➤ **Chi**, **che**, **cosa**, and **che cosa** never change their form.

<u>Chi</u> è?	Who is it?
<u>Chi</u> sono?	Who are they?
<u>Che</u> vuoi?	What do you want?
<u>Cosa</u> vuole?	What does he want?
<u>Che cosa</u> vogliono?	What do they want?

> *i* Note that there is no difference between **che**, **cosa** and **che cosa**.

➤ **Quale** is used for the masculine and feminine singular, and **quali** is used for masculine and feminine plural.

Conosco sua sorella. – <u>Quale</u>?	I know his sister. – Which one?
Ho rotto dei bicchieri. – <u>Quali</u>?	I broke some glasses. – Which ones?

⇨ *For more information on **Question words**, see page 155.*

➤ **Quanto** and **quanti** have feminine forms.

Farina? Quanta ce ne vuole?	Flour? How much is needed?
Quante di loro passano la sera a leggere?	How many of them spend the evening reading?

2 | che cos'è or qual è?

➤ **che cos'è?** and **qual è?** both mean *what is?* but are used in different ways:

- Use **che cos'è?** or **che cosa sono?** when you're asking someone to explain or identify something.

Che cos'è questo?	What's this?
Che cosa sono questi? –	What are these? –
Sono funghi.	They're mushrooms.

- Use **qual è?** or **quali sono?**, not **che**, when you ask *what is?*, or *what are?* to find out a particular detail, number, name, and so on.

Qual è il suo indirizzo?	What's her address?
Qual è la capitale della Finlandia?	What's the capital of Finland?
Quali sono i loro indirizzi?	What are their addresses?

📖 Note that **quale** becomes **qual** in front of a vowel.

3 | chi?

➤ Use **chi** for both *who* and *whom*.

Chi ha vinto?	Who won?
Chi hai visto?	Whom did you see?

➤ When there is a preposition in your question put it <u>in front of</u> **chi.**

A chi l'hai dato?	Who did you give it to?
Con chi parlavi?	Who were you talking to?
A chi si riferiva?	To whom was he referring?

➤ Use **di chi è?** or **di chi sono?** to ask who things belong to.

Di chi è questa borsa?	Whose is this bag?
Di chi sono queste chiavi?	Whose are these keys?

Key points

✔ **chi**, **che cosa**, **quale** and **quanto** are the interrogative pronouns in Italian.

✔ Use **chi** for both *who* and *whom*.

Demonstrative pronouns

> **What is a demonstrative pronoun?**
> In English the **demonstrative pronouns** are *this, that, these* and *those*. They are used instead of a noun to point out people or things, for example, *That's my brother*.

1 Using demonstrative pronouns

➤ These are the demonstrative pronouns in Italian:

	Masculine	Feminine	Meaning
Singular	questo quello	questa quella	this, this one that, that one
Plural	questi quelli	queste quelle	these, these ones those, those ones

➤ The demonstrative pronoun <u>must</u> agree with the noun it is replacing.

<u>Questo</u> è mio marito.	This is my husband.
<u>Questa</u> è camera mia.	This is my bedroom.
<u>Questi</u> sono i miei fratelli.	These are my brothers.
Quali scarpe ti metti? – <u>Queste</u>.	Which shoes are you going to wear? – These ones.
Qual è la sua borsa? – <u>Quella</u>.	Which bag is yours? – That one.
<u>Quelli</u> quanto costano?	How much do those cost?

(i) Note that **quello** and **quella** can also be used to mean *that man* and *that woman*.

Dice sempre bugie <u>quello</u>.	That man is always telling lies.
Conosci <u>quella</u>?	Do you know that woman?

➡ *For more information on **Demonstrative adjectives**, see page 30.*

Key points

✔ The demonstrative pronouns in Italian are **questo** and **quello**.

✔ **Questo** and **quello** have masculine, feminine, singular and plural forms.

✔ They agree with the nouns they replace.

Verbs

> **What is a verb?**
> A **verb** is a word which describes what somebody or something does, what they are, or what happens to them, for example, *play*, *be*, *disappear*.

Overview of verbs

➤ Verbs are frequently used with a noun or with somebody's name, for example <u>Children</u> like stories; <u>Jason</u>'s playing football. In English, pronouns such as *I, you* and *she* often come in front of verbs, for example, <u>She</u> knows my sister.

➤ Verbs can relate to the present, the past or the future; this is called their <u>tense</u>.

➡️ *For more information on* **Nouns** *and* **Pronouns***, see pages 1 and 40.*

➤ Verbs are either:
  ● <u>regular</u>: their forms follow the normal rules
  OR
  ● <u>irregular</u>: their forms do not follow the normal rules

➤ Almost all verbs have a form called the <u>infinitive</u> that isn't present, past or future, (for example, *walk, see, hear*). It is used after other verbs, for example, *You should <u>walk</u>; You can <u>see</u>; Kirsty wants <u>to come</u>*. In English, the infinitive is usually shown with the word *to*, for example, *to speak, to eat, to live*.

➤ In Italian the infinitive is always just one word that in most cases ends in either –**are**, –**ere** or –**ire**: for example, **parl<u>are</u>** (meaning *to speak*), **cred<u>ere</u>** (meaning *to believe*) and **dorm<u>ire</u>** (meaning *to sleep*).

➤ Regular English verbs can add three endings to the infinitive: *–s* (*walks*), *–ing* (*walking*) and *–ed* (*walked*).

➤ Italian verbs add endings to the verb <u>stem</u>, which is what is left of the verb when you take away the –**are**, –**ere** or –**ire** ending of the infinitive. This means the stem of **parlare** is **parl-**, the stem of **credere** is **cred-**, and the stem of **dormire** is **dorm-**.

➤ Italian verb endings change according to who or what is doing the action. The person or thing that does the action is called the <u>subject</u> of the verb.

➤ In English you nearly always put a noun or a pronoun in front of a verb to show who is doing the action, for example <u>Jack</u> speaks Italian; <u>She</u>'s playing tennis.

For further explanation of grammatical terms, please see pages viii–xii.

➤ In Italian, <u>nouns</u> are used as the subject of verbs just as they are in English, but <u>pronouns</u> are used much less often. This is because the ending of an Italian verb often shows you who the subject is.

> **<u>Mia sorella</u> gioca a tennis.**   My sister is playing tennis.
> **<u>Gioca</u> bene.**   She plays well.

⇨ *For more information on **Subject pronouns**, see page 41.*

➤ Italian verb forms also change depending on whether you are talking about the present, past or future: **credo** means I *believe*, **cred<u>evo</u>** means I *believed* and **cred<u>erò</u>** means I *will believe*.

➤ In English some verbs are <u>irregular</u>, for example, you do not add *–ed* to *speak*, *go*, or *see* to make the past tense. In the same way, some Italian verbs do not follow the usual patterns. These irregular Italian verbs include some very important and common verbs such as **andare** (meaning *to go*), **essere** (meaning *to be*) and **fare** (meaning *to do* or *to make*).

⇨ *For **Verb tables**, see middle section.*

Key points

✔ Italian verbs have different endings depending on their subject and their tense.

✔ Endings are added to the verb stem.

✔ You often do not need to use a pronoun before a verb in Italian.

The present tenses

> **What are the present tenses?**
> The present tenses are the verb forms that are used to talk about what is true at the moment, what generally happens and what is happening now; for example, *I'm a student; I travel to college by train; The phone's ringing*.

➤ In English there are two tenses you can use to talk about the present:

- the <u>present simple</u> tense
  I <u>live</u> here.
  They always <u>get up</u> early.

- the <u>present continuous</u> tense
  He <u>is eating</u> an apple.
  You <u>aren't</u> <u>listening</u>.

➤ In Italian there is also a <u>present simple</u> and a <u>present continuous</u> tense.

➤ As in English, the <u>present simple</u> tense in Italian is used to talk about:

- things that are generally true

  D'inverno <u>fa</u> freddo.   It'<u>s</u> cold in winter.

- what people and things usually do

  Giulia non <u>mangia</u> la carne.   Giulia <u>doesn't</u> eat meat.

  Queste macchine <u>consumano</u>   These cars <u>use</u> a lot of petrol.
  molta benzina.

  <u>Andiamo</u> spesso al cinema.   We often <u>go</u> to the cinema.

➤ Unlike in English, the <u>present simple</u> tense in Italian can be used to talk about:

- what is happening right now

  Piove.   It'<u>s raining</u>.

  Cosa <u>fai</u>?   What <u>are</u> you <u>doing</u>?

➤ In Italian the <u>present continuous</u> is also used to talk about things that are happening right now.

  Ci <u>sto pensando</u>.   I'<u>m thinking</u> about it.

➡ *For more information on the use of the **Present tenses**, see pages 69 and 81.*

> *Tip*
>
> You can use the Italian present simple to translate both the English simple present and the English present continuous.
>
> **Piove.**   It's raining.
> **Piove molto.**   It rains a lot.
>
> ➡ *For more information on **How to use the present simple tense**, see page 77.*

The present simple tense

1 How to make the present simple tense of regular –are verbs

➤ Verbs that have an infinitive ending in **–are**, such as **parlare**, **abitare** and **studiare** have a particular pattern of endings.

➤ To make the present simple tense of regular **–are** verbs take off the **–are** ending to get the <u>stem</u> of the verb.

Infinitive	Meaning	Stem (without –are)
parlare	*to speak*	**parl-**
abitare	*to live*	**abit-**
studiare	*to study*	**studi-**

➤ Then add the correct ending for the person you're talking about.

➤ Here are the present simple endings for regular **–are** verbs:

Present simple endings	Present simple of parlare	Meaning: *to speak*
–o	(io) parl<u>o</u>	I speak/am speaking
–i	(tu) parl<u>i</u>	you speak/are speaking
–a	(lui/lei) parl<u>a</u> (Lei) parl<u>a</u>	he/she/it speaks/is speaking you speak/are speaking
–iamo	(noi) parl<u>iamo</u>	we speak/are speaking
–ate	(voi) parl<u>ate</u>	you speak/are speaking
–ano	(loro) parl<u>ano</u>	they speak/are speaking

Parli inglese?	Do you speak English?
Chi parla?	Who's speaking?
Parlano bene italiano.	They speak good Italian.

> *Tip*
>
> When you are talking about a male, a female or a thing, or are using **lei** as the polite word for *you*, you use the same verb form.
>
> ➪ For more information on **Ways of saying 'you' in Italian**, see page 42.

ℹ️ Note that in Italian there's often no need to use a subject pronoun such as **io** (meaning *I*) or **tu** (meaning *you*) because the verb ending makes it clear who is doing the action. However, when you're talking about people you can use the pronouns **lui**, **lei** or **loro** with the verb for the sake of emphasis or to make things clearer.

Parla italiano <u>lui</u>?	Does he speak Italian?
<u>**Lei**</u> **parla bene inglese, ma lui no.**	She speaks good English, but he doesn't.
<u>**Loro**</u> **non parlano mai.**	They never speak.

When you're talking about things you <u>ALWAYS</u> use the verb by itself, with no pronoun.

Vedi l'*autobus***? – Sì, <u>arriva</u>.**	Can you see the bus? – Yes, it's coming.
Vuole queste? – No, <u>costano</u> troppo.	Do you want these? – No, they cost too much.

➪ For more information on **Subject pronouns**, see page 41.

Key points

✔ If you take the **–are** ending off the infinitive of a regular verb you get the stem.

✔ You add one of these endings to the stem: **–o**, **–i**, **–a**, **–iamo**, **–ate** or **–ano**.

✔ You only use a pronoun with the verb for emphasis or to be specially clear, but only when talking about people.

---

2 How to make the present simple tense of regular –ere verbs

➤ Verbs that have an infinitive ending in **–ere**, such as **credere**, **ricevere** and **ripetere** have their own pattern of endings.

➤ To make the present simple tense of regular **–ere** verbs take off the **–ere** ending to get the <u>stem</u> and then add the correct ending for the person you're talking about.

Infinitive	Meaning	Stem (without –ere)
credere	*to believe*	**cred-**
ricevere	*to receive*	**ricev-**
ripetere	*to repeat*	**ripet-**

➤ The **io**, **tu** and **noi** endings you add to the stem of **–ere** verbs are the same as **–are** verb endings. The other endings are different.

➤ Here are the present simple endings for regular **–ere** verbs:

Present simple endings	Present simple of credere	Meaning: *to believe*
–o	(io) cred<u>o</u>	I believe
–i	(tu) cred<u>i</u>	you believe
–e	(lui/lei) cred<u>e</u> (Lei) cred<u>e</u>	he/she believes you believe
–iamo	(noi) cred<u>iamo</u>	we believe
–ete	(voi) cred<u>ete</u>	you believe
–ono	(loro) cred<u>ono</u>	they believe

Non ci credo.	I don't believe it.
Credi ai fantasmi?	Do you believe in ghosts?
Lo credono tutti.	They all believe it.

Típ

When you are talking about a male, a female or a thing, or are using **Lei** as the polite word for *you*, you use the same verb form.

ℹ️ Note that in Italian there's often no need to use a subject pronoun such as **io** (meaning *I*) or **tu** (meaning *you*) because the verb ending makes it clear who is doing the action. However, when you're talking about people you can use the pronouns **lui**, **lei** or **loro** with the verb for the sake of emphasis or to make things clearer.

<u>Lui</u> **non ci crede.**	He doesn't believe it.
<u>Lei</u> **crede ai fantasmi, io no.**	She believes in ghosts, I don't.
<u>Loro</u> **lo credono tutti.**	They all believe it.

When you're talking about things you <u>ALWAYS</u> use the verb by itself, with no pronoun.

La minestra? Non <u>sa</u> di nulla.	The soup? It doesn't taste of anything.
Le piante? <u>Crescono</u> bene.	The plants? They're growing well.

⇨ *For more information on **Subject pronouns**, see page 41.*

72 Verbs

> **Tip**
>
> Remember that you never use a pronoun in Italian to translate *it* at the beginning of a sentence.
>
> | **Dipende.** | It depends. |
> | **Piove.** | It's raining. |

Key points

✔ If you take the **–ere** ending off the infinitive of a regular verb you get the stem.

✔ You add one of these endings to the stem: **–o**, **–i**, **–e**, **–iamo**, **–ete** or **–ono**.

✔ You only use a pronoun with the verb for emphasis or to be specially clear, but only when talking about people.

---

3 | How to make the present simple tense of regular –ire verbs

➤ Most verbs that have an infinitive ending in **–ire**, such as **finire** (meaning *to finish*), **pulire** (meaning *to clean*) and **capire** (meaning *to understand*) follow one pattern of endings in the present. Some common verbs such as **dormire** and **servire** have a different pattern.

➤ To make the present simple tense of <u>all</u> **–ire** verbs take off the **–ire** ending to get the <u>stem</u> of the verb.

Infinitive	Meaning	Stem (without –ire)
finire	*to finish*	**fin-**
pulire	*to clean*	**pul-**
capire	*to understand*	**cap-**
dormire	*to sleep*	**dorm-**
servire	*to serve*	**serv-**

➤ Here are the present simple endings for regular **–ire** verbs:

Present simple endings	Present simple of finire	Meaning: *to finish*
–isco	**(io) fin<u>isco</u>**	I finish/am finishing
–isci	**(tu) fin<u>isci</u>**	you finish/are finishing
–isce	**(lui/lei) fin<u>isce</u>**	he/she/it finishes/ is finishing
	(Lei) fin<u>isce</u>	you finish/are finishing
–iamo	**(noi) fin<u>iamo</u>**	we finish/are finishing
–ite	**(voi) fin<u>ite</u>**	you finish/are finishing
–iscono	**(loro) fin<u>iscono</u>**	they finish/are finishing

For further explanation of grammatical terms, please see pages viii–xii.

Il film fin**isce** alle dieci.	The film finishes at ten.
Fin**iscono** il lavoro.	They're finishing the work.
Non pul**isco** mai la macchina.	I never clean the car.
Prefer**isci** l'altro?	Do you prefer the other one?
Non cap**iscono**.	They don't understand.

[*i*] Note that in Italian there's often no need to use a subject pronoun such as **io** (meaning *I*) or **tu** (meaning *you*) because the verb ending makes it clear who is doing the action. However, when you're talking about people you can use the pronouns **lui**, **lei** or **loro** with the verb for the sake of emphasis or to make things clearer.

Lui non pulisce mai la macchina.	He never cleans the car.
Lei mi capisce sempre.	She always understands me.
Loro preferiscono l'altro.	They prefer the other one.

When you're talking about things you <u>ALWAYS</u> use the verb by itself, with no pronoun.

Il primo treno? – **Parte** alle cinque.	The first train? It goes at five.
Le lezioni quando fin**iscono**? –	When do lessons finish?
Fin**iscono** alle quattro.	They finish at four.

➤ Some common **–ire** verbs do not add **–isc–** to the stem. The most important ones are **dormire** (meaning *to sleep*), **servire** (meaning *to serve*), **aprire** (meaning *to open*), **partire** (meaning *to leave*), **sentire** (meaning *to hear*) and **soffrire** (meaning *to suffer*).

➤ The endings of these verbs are as follows:

Present simple endings	Present simple of dormire	Meaning: *to sleep*
–o	(io) dorm**o**	I sleep/am sleeping
–i	(tu) dorm**i**	you sleep/are sleeping
–e	(lui/lei) dorm**e** (Lei) dorm**e**	he/she/it sleeps/is sleeping you sleep/are sleeping
–iamo	(noi) dorm**iamo**	we sleep/are sleeping
–ite	(voi) dorm**ite**	you sleep/are sleeping
–ono	(loro) dorm**ono**	they sleep/are sleeping

[*i*] Note that these endings are the same as **–ere** verb endings, except for the second person plural (**voi**).

Dorm**o** sempre bene.	I always sleep well.
A che cosa serv**e**?	What's it for?
Quando part**ite**?	When are you leaving?
Soffr**ono** molto.	They are suffering a lot.

> **Tip**
>
> When you are talking about a male, a female or a thing, or are using **Lei** as the polite word for *you*, you use the same verb form.

Key points

✔ Take the **–ire** ending off the infinitive of a regular verb to get the stem.

✔ For most **–ire** verbs the endings you add to the stem are: **–isco**, **–isci**, **–isce**, **–iamo**, **–ite** or **–iscono**.

✔ A few common **–ire** verbs add these endings to the stem: **–o**, **–i**, **–e**, **–iamo**, **–ite**, **–ono**.

✔ You only use a pronoun with the verb for emphasis or to be specially clear, but only when talking about people.

---

4 | Infinitives that end in –rre

➤ All regular verbs have infinitives ending in **–are**, **-ere**, or **–ire**.

➤ A few common irregular verbs have infinitives ending in **–rre**. For example:

comporre	to compose	**condurre**	to lead
porre	to put	**produrre**	to produce
proporre	to propose	**ridurre**	to reduce
supporre	to suppose	**tradurre**	to translate

➤ Here are the present simple forms of **comporre**

	Present simple of comporre	Meaning: *to compose*
(io)	compongo	I compose/I am composing
(tu)	componi	you compose/you are composing
(lui/lei) (Lei)	compone	he/she/it composes/is composing you compose/are composing
(noi)	componiamo	we compose/are composing
(voi)	componete	you compose/are composing
(loro)	compongono	they compose/are composing

➤ Here are the present simple forms of **produrre**:

	Present simple of produrre	Meaning: *to produce*
(io)	produco	I produce/I am producing
(tu)	produci	you produce/you are producing
(lui/lei) (Lei)	produce	he/she/it produces/is producing you produce/are producing
(noi)	produciamo	we produce/are producing
(voi)	producete	you produce/are producing
(loro)	producono	they produce/are producing

The present tense of all verbs ending in **–porre** follow the pattern of **comporre**, and all verbs ending in **–durre** follow the pattern of **produrre**.

| 5 | **Where to put the stress when saying the infinitive**

➤ When you say the infinitives of **–are** and **–ire** verbs the stress goes on the **a**, or **i** of the ending:

| **Non vuole parlare.** | He doesn't want to speak. |
| **Non riesco a dormire.** | I can't sleep. |

➤ When you say the infinitive of most **–ere** verbs the stress goes on the syllable that comes <u>before</u> the ending.

| **Devono vendere la casa.** | They've got to sell their house. |
| **Può ripetere?** | Could you repeat that? |

➤ However, there are a number of very important irregular **–ere** verbs which have the stress on the first **e** of the ending.

–ere verb	Meaning
avere	*to have*
cadere	*to fall*
dovere	*to have to*
persuadere	*to persuade*
potere	*to be able*
rimanere	*to remain*
vedere	*to see*

| **Fa' attenzione a non cadere.** | Mind you don't fall. |
| **Non puoi avere il mio.** | You can't have mine. |

⇨ *For more information on the **Infinitive**, see page 138.*

6 How to make the present simple tense of common irregular verbs

➤ There are many verbs that do not follow the usual patterns. These include some very common and important verbs such as **avere** (meaning *to have*), **fare** (meaning *to do* or *to make*) and **andare** (meaning *to go*).

➤ Here are the present simple forms of **avere**:

	Present simple of avere	Meaning: *to have*
(io)	ho	I have/have got
(tu)	hai	you have
(lui/lei) (Lei)	ha	he/she/it has you have
(noi)	abbiamo	we have
(voi)	avete	you have
(loro)	hanno	they have

<u>Ho</u> due sorelle.	I've got two sisters.
<u>Hai</u> abbastanza soldi?	Have you got enough money?
<u>Abbiamo</u> tempo.	We've got time.
<u>Hanno</u> i capelli biondi.	They have blonde hair.

➤ Here are the present simple forms of **fare**:

	Present simple of fare	Meaning: *to do, to make*
(io)	faccio	I do/am doing, I make/am making
(tu)	fai	you do/are doing, you make/are making
(lui/lei) (Lei)	fa	he/she/it does/is doing, he/she/it makes/is making you do/are doing, you make/are making
(noi)	facciamo	we do/are doing, we make/are making
(voi)	fate	you do/are doing, you make/are making
(loro)	fanno	they do/are doing, they make/are making

<u>Faccio</u> troppi errori.	I make too many mistakes.
Cosa <u>fai</u> stasera?	What are you doing this evening?
<u>Fa</u> caldo.	It's hot.
<u>Fanno</u> quello che possono.	They're doing what they can.

➤ Here are the present simple forms of **andare**:

	Present simple of andare	Meaning: *to go*
(io)	**vado**	I go/am going
(tu)	**vai**	you go/are going
(lui/lei) **(Lei)**	**va**	he/she/it goes/is going you go/are going
(noi)	**andiamo**	we go/are going
(voi)	**andate**	you go/are going
(loro)	**vanno**	they go/are going

    Ci <u>vado</u> spesso.   I often go there.

    Dove <u>vai</u>?   Where are you going?

    <u>Va</u> bene.   That's okay.

    <u>Vanno</u> tutti al concerto.   They're all going to the concert.

⇨ *For other irregular verbs in the present simple tense, see **Verb tables** in the middle section.*

7 | How to use the present simple tense in Italian

➤ The present simple tense is often used in Italian in the same way as in English, but there are also some important differences.

➤ As in English, you use the Italian present simple to talk about:

- things that are generally true
  La frutta <u>fa</u> bene.   Fruit is good for you.

- current situations
  <u>Vivono</u> in Francia.   They live in France.

- what people and things usually do
  <u>Litigano</u> sempre.   They always quarrel.
  <u>Si blocca</u> spesso.   It often jams.

- fixed arrangements
  <u>Comincia</u> domani.   It starts tomorrow.

➤ Unlike in English, the Italian present simple is used to talk about:

- what is happening right now
  <u>Arrivo</u>!   I'm coming!
  Non <u>mangi</u> niente.   You're not eating anything.

- what you are going to do
  È rotto, lo <u>butto</u> via.   It's broken, I'm going to throw it away.
  Ci <u>penso</u> io.   I'll see to it.

- predictions

  Se fai così lo <u>rompi</u>.   If you do that you'll break it.

- offers

  <u>Pago</u> io.   I'll pay.

➤ In English the <u>perfect</u> tense is used to say how long someone has been doing something, or how long something has been happening. In Italian you use **da** and the <u>present simple</u> tense for this kind of sentence.

    <u>Aspetto</u> da tre ore.   I've been waiting for three hours.

    Da quanto tempo <u>studi</u>   How long have you been learning
    l'italiano?   Italian?

⇨ *For more information on the use of tenses with **da**, see page 174.*

Key points

✔ The present simple tense in Italian is used as in English, and has a few additional uses.

✔ Use the present simple with **da** to talk about how long something has been going on.

---

essere and stare

➤ In Italian there are two irregular verbs, **essere** and **stare**, that both mean *to be*. In the present tense they follow the patterns shown below:

Pronoun	essere	stare	Meaning: *to be*
(io)	sono	sto	I am
(tu)	sei	stai	you are
(lui/lei) (Lei)	è	sta	he/she/it is you are
(noi)	siamo	stiamo	we are
(voi)	siete	state	you are
(loro)	sono	stanno	they are

➤ **essere** is the verb generally used to translate *to be*:

Cosa <u>sono</u>?	What are they?
<u>È</u> italiana.	She's Italian.
<u>Sono</u> io.	It's me.
<u>È</u> un problema.	It's a problem.
<u>Siete</u> pronti?	Are you ready?

➤ However, **stare** is used for *to be* in some common contexts:

- to say or ask how someone is

Come <u>stai</u>?	How are you?
<u>Sto</u> bene, grazie.	I'm fine thanks.
Mio nonno <u>sta</u> male.	My grandfather isn't well.

- to say where someone is

Luigi <u>sta</u> a casa.	Luigi's at home.
<u>Starò</u> a Roma due giorni.	I'll be in Rome for two days.

- to say where something is situated

La casa <u>sta</u> sulla collina.	The house is on the hill.

- with the adjectives **zitto** and **solo**

Vuole <u>stare</u> solo.	He wants to be alone.
<u>Sta'</u> zitto!	Be quiet!

- to make continuous tenses

<u>Sta</u> studiando.	He's studying.
<u>Stavo</u> andando a casa.	I was going home.

➪ *For more information on the **Present continuous**, see page 81.*

Key points

✔ *essere* is generally used to translate *to be*.

✔ **stare** is used to talk about health, where people and things are and with some adjectives.

✔ **stare** is also used to make continuous tenses.

The present continuous tense

➤ In Italian the <u>present continuous</u> is used instead of the <u>present simple</u> to talk about what is happening at the moment, when you want to emphasize that it's happening <u>right now</u>.

Arrivano.	They are coming.
Stanno arrivando!	They're coming!

➤ The Italian present continuous is made with the present tense of **stare** and the <u>gerund</u> of the verb. The gerund is a verb form that ends in **–ando** (for **–are** verbs), or **–endo** (for **–ere** and **–ire** verbs) and is the same as the *–ing* form of the verb in English, for example, *walking, swimming*.

<u>**Sto cercando**</u> il mio passaporto.	I'm looking for my passport.
<u>**Sta scrivendo**</u>.	He's writing.
<u>**Stanno dormendo**</u>.	They're sleeping.
Cosa <u>**stai facendo**</u>?	What are you doing?

➡️ *For more information on **stare**, see page 79.*

➤ To make the gerund of an **–are** verb, take off the ending and add **–ando**, for example, **mangiando** (meaning *eating*), **cercando** (meaning *looking for*). To make the gerund of an **–ere** or **–ire** verb, take off the ending and add **–endo**, for example, **scrivendo** (meaning *writing*), **partendo** (meaning *leaving*).

➡️ *For more information on the **Gerund**, see page 123.*

Tip

Only use the Italian present continuous to talk about things that are happening at this very minute. Use the present simple tense to talk about things that are continuing, but not necessarily happening at this minute.

Studio medicina.	I'm studying medicine.

➡️ *For more information on the **Present simple tense**, see page 69.*

Key points

✔ Only use the present continuous in Italian for actions that are happening right now.

✔ To make the present continuous, use the present tense of **stare** and the gerund of the main verb.

The imperative

> **What is the imperative?**
> An **imperative** is the form of the verb used to give orders and instructions,
> for example, *Sit down!*; *Don't go!*; *Let's start!*

1 Using the imperative

➤ In Italian, you use a different form of the imperative depending on whether
you are:

- telling someone to do something
- telling someone not to do something
- speaking to one person or more than one person
- speaking to someone you call **tu**
- speaking formally

➤ The pronouns **tu**, **Lei** (the formal way of saying *you*) and **voi** all have their own
forms of the imperative, although you don't actually use these pronouns
when giving orders and instructions. There is also a formal plural form of the
imperative.

- You can also use a form of the imperative to make suggestions. This form
is like *let's* in English.

2 How to tell someone to do something

➤ You make the imperative of regular verbs by adding endings to the verb <u>stem</u>,
which is what is left when you take away the **–are**, **–ere** or **–ire**. There are different
endings for **–are**, **–ere** and **–ire** verbs:

- The endings for **–are** verb imperatives are **–a** (**tu** form), **–i** (**lei** form),
–iamo (*let's*), **–ate** (**voi** form) and **–ino** (polite plural). For example,
aspettare → aspett- → aspetta.

Imperative of aspettare	Example	Meaning: *to wait*
aspetta!	**Aspetta, Marco!**	Wait, Marco!
aspetti!	**Aspetti, signore!**	Wait, Sir!
aspettiamo	**Aspettiamo qui.**	Let's wait here.
aspettate!	**Aspettate, ragazzi!**	Wait, children!
aspettino!	**Aspettino un attimo, signori!**	Wait a moment, ladies and gentlemen!

- The endings for **–ere** verb imperatives are **–i** (**tu** form), **–a** (**lei** form), **–iamo** (*let's*), **–ete** (**voi** form) and **–ano** (polite plural).
  For example, **prendere** → prend- → **prendi**.

Imperative of prendere	Example	Meaning: *to take*
prend**i**	**Prendi quello, Marco!**	Take that one, Marco!
prend**a**	**Prenda quello, signore!**	Take that one, Sir!
prend**iamo**	**Prendiamo quello.**	Let's take that one.
prend**ete**	**Prendete quelli, ragazzi!**	Take those ones, children!
prend**ano**	**Prendano quelli, signori!**	Take those ones, ladies and gentlemen!

- The endings for most **–ire** verb imperatives are **–isci** (**tu** form), **–isca** (**lei/Lei** form), **–iamo** (*let's*), **–ite** (**voi** form) and **–iscano** (polite plural).
  For example, **finire** → fin- → **finisci**.

[*i*] Note that **sci** is pronounced like *she*; **sca** is pronounced *ska*.

Imperative of finire	Example	Meaning: *to finish*
fin**isci**	**Finisci l'esercizio, Marco!**	Finish the exercise, Marco!
fin**isca**	**Finisca tutto, signore!**	Finish it all, Sir!
fin**iamo**	**Finiamo tutto.**	Let's finish it all.
fin**ite**	**Finite i compiti, ragazzi!**	Finish your homework, children!
fin**iscano**	**Finiscano tutto, signori!**	Finish it all, ladies and gentlemen!

➤ The endings for verbs that do not add **–isc** to the stem, such as **partire** (meaning *to leave*), **dormire** (meaning *to sleep*) **aprire** (meaning *to open*) and **sentire** (meaning *to listen*) are **–i**, **–a**, **–iamo**, **–ite** and **–ano**.

    Dormi, Giulia!   Go to sleep, Giulia!
    Partiamo.   Let's go.

⇨ *For more information on **Regular –ire verbs**, see page 72.*

➤ Some of the commonest verbs in Italian have irregular imperative forms. Here are the forms for some important verbs:

	dare	dire	essere	fare	andare
(tu)	da'! *or* dai!	di'!	sii!	fa'! *or* fai!	va'! *or* vai!
(lei/lui/Lei)	dia!	dica!	sia!	faccia!	vada!
(noi)	diamo	diciamo	siamo	facciamo	vadano!
(voi)	date!	dite!	siate!	fate!	andate!
(loro)	diano!	dicano!	siano!	facciano!	vadano!

Sii bravo, Paolo!	Be good, Paolo!
Faccia pure, signore!	Carry on, sir!
Dite la verità, ragazzi!	Tell the truth, children!

➪ *For more information on the imperatives of Irregular verbs, see* **Verb tables** *in the middle section.*

Key points

✔ There are familiar and polite forms of the imperative.

✔ The **–iamo** form is used to translate *let's*.

---

3 Where do pronouns go?

➤ In English, pronouns such as *me*, *it* and *them* always come after the imperative, for example *Watch me!; Take it!; Give them to me!*

➤ In Italian pronouns come <u>AFTER</u> the imperative in the **tu** and **voi** forms:

● The pronoun joins with the imperative to make one word.

Guardami, mamma!	Look at me, mum!
Aspettateli!	Wait for them!

● When the imperative is only one syllable **mi** becomes **–mmi**, **ti** becomes **–tti**, **lo** becomes **–llo** and so on.

Dimmi!	Tell me!
Fallo subito!	Do it immediately!

● When the pronouns **mi**, **ti**, **ci** and **vi** are followed by another pronoun they become **me-**, **te-**, **ce-** and **ve-**, and **gli** and **le** become **glie-**.

Mandameli.	Send me them.
Daglielo.	Give it to him.

Tip

In Italian you <u>always</u> put the indirect object pronoun first.

➪ *For more information on* **Indirect object pronouns**, *see page 46.*

➤ Pronouns also come <u>AFTER</u> the **–iamo** form of the imperative, joining onto it to make one word.

Proviamo<u>lo</u>!	Let's try it!
Mandiamo<u>gliela</u>!	Let's send it to them.

➤ Pronouns come <u>BEFORE</u> the **lei** form of the imperative and the polite plural form.

<u>Mi</u> dia un chilo d'uva, per favore.	Give me a kilo of grapes please.
<u>La</u> prenda, signore.	Take it, sir.
<u>Ne</u> assaggino un po', signori!	Try a bit, ladies and gentlemen!
<u>Si</u> accomodi!	Take a seat!

⇨ *For more information on **Reflexive verbs**, see page 87.*

Key points

✔ Pronouns come after the **tu**, **voi** and **–iamo** forms of the imperative.

✔ Pronouns which come after the imperative join onto it to make one word.

✔ Pronouns come before the polite imperative, and do not join onto it.

---

4 | How to tell someone NOT to do something

➤ When you are telling someone you call **tu** <u>NOT</u> to do something:

● use **non** with the <u>infinitive</u> (the **–are**, **–ere**, **–ire** form) of the verb

Non <u>dire</u> bugie Andrea!	Don't tell lies Andrea!
Non <u>dimenticare</u>!	Don't forget!

⇨ *For more information on the **Infinitive**, see page 138.*

● if there is also a pronoun, join it onto the infinitive, or put it in front

Non tocca<u>rlo</u>! OR	
Non <u>lo</u> toccare!	Don't touch it!
Non dir<u>glielo</u>! OR	
Non <u>glielo</u> dire!	Don't tell him about it!
Non far<u>mi</u> ridere! OR	
Non <u>mi</u> far ridere!	Don't make me laugh!
Non preoccupar<u>ti</u>! OR	
Non <u>ti</u> preoccupare!	Don't worry!
Non bagnar<u>ti</u>! OR	
Non <u>ti</u> bagnare!	Don't get wet!

ℹ Note that the infinitive usually drops the final **e** when the pronoun joins onto it.

➤ In all other cases, to tell someone not to do something:

- use **non** with the imperative

Non dimenticate, ragazzi.	Don't forget, children.
Non abbia paura, signora.	Don't be afraid, madam.
Non esageriamo!	Don't let's go too far!

- join pronouns onto <u>the end of</u> the **voi** and **–iamo** forms of the imperative

Non guard*a*teli!	Don't look at them.
Non ditemelo!	Don't say it to me!
Non mangi*a*moli tutti.	Don't let's eat them all.
Non di*a*moglielo.	Don't let's give it to them.

- put pronouns <u>in front of</u> the **lei** and polite plural forms of the imperative

Non li guardi, signora.	Don't look at them, madam.
Non si preoccupino, signori.	Don't worry, ladies and gentlemen.

Key points

✔ To tell a person you call **tu** not to do something, use **non** with the infinitive.

✔ To tell all other people not to do something use **non** with the imperative.

✔ To say *Let's not* use **non** with the **–iamo** form.

Reflexive verbs

> **What is a reflexive verb?**
> **Reflexive verbs** in English are ones where the subject and object are the same, and which use reflexive pronouns such as *myself, yourself* and *themselves*, for example *I've hurt myself; Look after yourself!; They're enjoying themselves.*

1 Using reflexive verbs

The basics

➤ There are more reflexive verbs in Italian than in English. The infinitive form of a reflexive verb has **–si** joined onto it, for example, **divertirsi** (meaning *to enjoy oneself*). This is the way reflexive verbs are shown in dictionaries. **si** is a <u>reflexive pronoun</u> and means *himself, herself, itself, themselves* and *oneself*.

➤ Verbs that are reflexive in English, such as *to hurt oneself* or *to enjoy oneself* are reflexive in Italian. In addition, many verbs that include *get*, for example *to get up, to get dressed, to get annoyed, to get bored, to get tanned*, are reflexive verbs in Italian. Here are some important Italian reflexive verbs:

accomodarsi	to sit down; to take a seat
addormentarsi	to go to sleep
alzarsi	to get up
annoiarsi	to get bored; to be bored
arrabbiarsi	to get angry
chiamarsi	to be called
chiedersi	to wonder
divertirsi	to enjoy oneself; to have fun
farsi male	to hurt oneself
fermarsi	to stop
lavarsi	to wash; to get washed
perdersi	to get lost
pettinarsi	to comb one's hair
preoccuparsi	to worry
prepararsi	to get ready
ricordarsi	to remember
sbrigarsi	to hurry
svegliarsi	to wake up
vestirsi	to dress; to get dressed

<u>**Si accomodi**</u>!	Take a seat!
<u>**Mi alzo**</u> alle sette.	I get up at seven o'clock.
Come <u>**ti chiami**</u>?	What are you called?
Non <u>**vi preoccupate**</u>!	Don't worry!
<u>**Sbrigati**</u>!	Hurry up!

Ci prepariamo.	We're getting ready.
Matteo si annoia.	Matteo is getting bored.
Lucia si è fatta male.	Lucia hurt herself.
I bambini si divertono.	The children are enjoying themselves.

[i] Note that in English, you can often add a reflexive pronoun to verbs if you want to, for example, you can say *Don't worry yourself!* or *He didn't hurry himself*. Whenever you can do this in English, the Italian equivalent is likely to be a reflexive verb.

➤ Some Italian verbs can be used both as reflexive verbs, and as ordinary verbs with no reflexive pronoun. If you are talking about getting yourself ready you use **prepararsi**; if you are talking about gettting the dinner ready you use **preparare**.

Mi preparo alla maratona.	I'm getting ready for the marathon.
Sto preparando il pranzo.	I'm getting lunch ready.
Mi chiedo cosa stia facendo.	I wonder what he's doing.
Chiedi a Lidia perché piange.	Ask Lidia why she's crying.

[i] Note that **chiedersi** literally means *to ask oneself*.

Grammar Extra!

Some reflexive verbs in Italian add the pronoun **ne** after the reflexive pronoun. The most important of these verbs is **andarsene** (meaning *to go away, to leave*).

Me ne vado.	I'm leaving.
Vattene!	Go away!
Ce ne andiamo.	Let's be off.
Se ne sono andati.	They've left.

The pronouns **mi**, **ti**, **si**, **ci** and **vi** become **me**, **te**, **se**, **ce** and **ve** when they are followed by another pronoun, such as **ne**.

---

2 How to make the present tense of reflexive verbs

➤ First, decide which reflexive pronoun to use. You can see how the reflexive pronouns correspond to the subject pronouns in the following table:

Subject pronoun	Reflexive pronoun	Meaning
(io)	mi	myself
(tu)	ti	yourself
(lui), (lei), (Lei), (loro)	si	himself, herself, itself, yourself, themselves
(noi)	ci	ourselves
(voi)	vi	yourselves

For further explanation of grammatical terms, please see pages viii–xii.

Mi alzo presto.	I get up early.
Mia sorella si veste.	My sister's getting dressed.
Si lamentano sempre.	They're always complaining.

➤ The present tense forms of a reflexive verb are just the same as those of an ordinary verb, except for the addition of the reflexive pronoun in front of the verb.

⇨ For more information on the **Present tense**, see page 68.

➤ The following table shows the reflexive verb **divertirsi** in full.

Reflexive forms of divertirsi	Meaning
mi diverto	I'm enjoying myself
ti diverti	you're enjoying yourself
si diverte	he is enjoying himself she is enjoying herself you are enjoying yourself
ci divertiamo	we're enjoying ourselves
vi divertite	you're enjoying yourselves
si divertono	they're enjoying themselves

3 | Where to put reflexive pronouns

➤ The reflexive pronoun usually goes in front of the verb, but there are some exceptions. The pronoun goes in front if the verb is:

● an ordinary tense, such as the present simple

| **Si** diverte signora? | Are you enjoying yourself madam? |
| **Mi** abituo al lavoro. | I'm getting used to the work. |

⇨ For more information on the **Present simple tense**, see page 69.

● the polite imperative

| **Si** avvicini, signore. | Come closer, sir. |

⇨ For more information on the **Imperative**, see page 82.

● an imperative telling someone NOT to do something

| Non **vi** avvicinate troppo, ragazzi. | Don't come too close, children. |
| Non **si** lamenti, dottore. | Don't complain, doctor. |

➤ The pronoun comes after the verb if it is the **tu** or **voi** form of the imperative, used positively:

| Svegliati! | Wake up! |
| Divertitevi! | Enjoy yourselves! |

➤ In the case of the infinitive, used with **non** to tell someone NOT to do something, the pronoun can either:

- go <u>in front of</u> the infinitive

OR

- join onto the end of the infinitive

Non <u>ti</u> bruciare! OR **Non bruciar<u>ti</u>!**	Don't burn yourself!
Non <u>ti</u> preoccupare! OR **Non preoccupar<u>ti</u>!**	Don't worry!

ⓘ Note that, when telling someone not to do something, you use **non** with the <u>infinitive</u> for people you call **tu**.

➤ There are also two options when you use the infinitive of a reflexive verb after a verb such as *want, must, should* or *can't*. The pronoun can either:

- go in front of the main verb

OR

- join onto the end of the infinitive

<u>Mi</u> voglio abbronzare. OR **Voglio abbronzar<u>mi</u>.**	I want to get a tan.
<u>Ti</u> devi alzare. OR **Devi alzar<u>ti</u>.**	You must get up.
<u>Vi</u> dovreste preparare. OR **Dovreste preparar<u>vi</u>.**	You ought to get ready.
Non <u>mi</u> posso fermare molto. OR **Non posso fermar<u>mi</u> molto.**	I can't stop for long.

➤ In the same way, in <u>continuous tenses</u>, the reflexive pronoun can either:

- go in front of the verb **stare**

OR

- join onto the gerund

<u>Ti</u> stai annoiando? OR **Stai annoiando<u>ti</u>?**	Are you getting bored?
<u>Si</u> stanno alzando? OR **Stanno alzando<u>si</u>?**	Are they getting up?

ⓘ Note that the pronoun is always joined onto the gerund when it is not used in a continuous tense.

Incontrando<u>ci</u> per caso, **abbiamo parlato molto.**	Meeting by chance, we had a long talk.
Pettinando<u>mi</u> ho trovato un **capello bianco.**	When I combed my hair I found a white hair.

For further explanation of grammatical terms, please see pages viii–xii.

4 | **Using reflexive verbs with parts of the body and clothes**

➤ In Italian you often talk about actions to do with your body or your clothing using a reflexive verb.

Mi lavo i capelli ogni mattina.	I wash my hair every morning.
Mettiti il cappotto!	Put your coat on!
Si è rotta la gamba.	She's broken her leg.

ℹ️ Note that you do not use possessive adjectives in this kind of sentence. Instead you use the definite article **il**, **la**, **i** and so on with the noun, and a reflexive verb.

    Mi lavo le mani.   I'm washing my hands.

⇨ *For more information on **Articles**, see page 10.*

5 | **How to use reflexive verbs in the perfect tense**

➤ The English perfect tense, for example, I _have burnt_ myself, and the English simple past, for example I _burnt_ myself yesterday, are both translated by the Italian perfect tense.

⇨ *For more information about the **Perfect tense**, see page 108.*

➤ The perfect tense of reflexive verbs is always made with the verb **essere** and the past participle.

    Mi sono fatto male.   I've hurt myself.

➤ The past participle used in the perfect tense of reflexive verbs has to agree with the subject of the sentence. You change the **–o** ending of the participle to **–a** if the subject is feminine. The masculine plural ending is **–i**, and the feminine plural is **–e**.

Silvia si è alzata tardi stamattina.	Silvia got up late this morning.
Vi siete divertiti, ragazzi?	Did you have a nice time, children?
Le mie sorelle si sono abbronzate.	My sisters have got suntanned.

Tip

If you are female always use a feminine adjective when you are talking about yourself, and always make the past participle feminine when you are talking about what you have done.

Mi sono svegliata, mi sono alzata e mi sono vestita.	I woke up, got up and got dressed.

---

6 Other uses of reflexive pronouns

➤ **ci**, **vi** and **si** are used to mean *each other* and *one another*.

Ci vogliamo molto bene.	We love each other very much.
Si vede che si odiano.	You can see they hate one another.
Vi conoscete?	Do you know each other?

Tip

Remember that when *you* is used to mean people in general, it is often translated by **si**.

Si fa così.	You do it this way.
Non si tocca!	You can't touch them!
Come si dice "genitori" in inglese?	How do you say "genitori" in English?

Key points

✔ The perfect tense of reflexive verbs is made with **essere**, and the past participle agrees with the subject of the verb.

✔ Reflexive verbs are used with the definite article to talk about washing your hair, breaking your leg, putting on your coat, and so on.

For further explanation of grammatical terms, please see pages viii–xii.

The future tense

> **What is the future tense?**
> The **future tense** is a tense used to talk about something that will happen, or will be true in the future, for example *He'll be here soon; I'll give you a call; It will be sunny tomorrow.*

1 Using the present tense to talk about the future

➤ Sometimes, both in Italian and in English, you use the <u>present tense</u> to refer to the future.

Il corso <u>comincia</u> domani.	The course <u>starts</u> tomorrow.
Quando <u>partite</u>?	When <u>are you leaving</u>?

➤ In the following cases the <u>present tense</u> is used in Italian, while the <u>future</u> is used in English:

- to say what you're about to do

<u>Pago</u> io.	<u>I'll pay</u>.
<u>Prendo</u> un espresso.	<u>I'll have</u> an espresso.

- to ask for suggestions

Dove lo <u>metto</u>?	Where <u>shall I</u> put it?
Cosa <u>facciamo</u>?	What <u>shall we</u> do?

➪ *For more information on the **Present simple**, see page 69.*

➤ In Italian the <u>future tense</u> is used after **quando** in cases where *when* is followed by the <u>present</u> in English.

Quando <u>finirò</u>, verrò da te.	When I <u>finish</u> I'll come to yours.
Lo comprerò quando <u>avrò</u> abbastanza denaro.	I'll buy it when <u>I've got</u> enough money.

2 How to make the future tense

➤ In English we make the future tense by putting *will*, *'ll* or *shall* in front of the verb. In Italian you change the verb endings: **parlo** (meaning *I speak*), becomes **parlerò** (meaning *I will speak*) in the future.

➤ To make the future of regular **–are** and **–ere** verbs take the <u>stem</u>, which is what is left of the verb when you take away the **–are**, **–ere** or **–ire** ending of the infinitive and add the following endings:

- -erò, -erai, -erà, -eremo, -erete, -eranno
  For example, **parlare → parl- → parlerò**.

➤ The following tables show the future tenses of **parlare** (meaning *to speak*) and **credere** (meaning *to believe*).

Pronoun	Future tense of parlare	Meaning: *to speak*
(io)	parler**ò**	I'll speak
(tu)	parler**ai**	you'll speak
(lui/lei) (Lei)	parler**à**	he/she'll speak you'll speak
(noi)	parler**emo**	we'll speak
(voi)	parler**ete**	you'll speak
(loro)	parler**anno**	they'll speak

Gli parlerò domani.   I'll speak to him tomorrow.

Pronoun	Future tense of credere	Meaning: *to speak*
(io)	creder**ò**	I'll believe
(tu)	creder**ai**	you'll believe
(lui/lei) (Lei)	creder**à**	he/she'll believe you'll believe
(noi)	creder**emo**	we'll believe
(voi)	creder**ete**	you'll believe
(loro)	creder**anno**	they'll believe

Non ti crederanno.   They won't believe you.

ⓘ Note that there are accents on the first and third person singular forms, to show that you stress the last vowel.

➤ To make the future of regular **–ire** verbs take the stem and add the following endings:

● **-irò, -irai, -irà, -iremo, -irete, -iranno**
For example, **finire → fin- → finirò**.

➤ The following table shows the future tense of **finire** (meaning *to finish*).

Pronoun	Future tense of finire	Meaning: *to finish*
(io)	fin**irò**	I'll finish
(tu)	fin**irai**	you'll finish
(lui/lei) (Lei)	fin**irà**	he/she'll finish you'll finish
(noi)	fin**iremo**	we'll finish
(voi)	fin**irete**	you'll finish
(loro)	fin**iranno**	they'll finish

Quando finirai il lavoro?   When will you finish the work?

For further explanation of grammatical terms, please see pages viii–xii.

➤ Some verbs do not have a vowel before the **r** of the future ending. Their endings are:

- **-rò, -rai, -rà, -remo, -rete, -ranno**

➤ The following table shows the future tense of some of these verbs which you should learn.

Verb	Meaning	io	tu	lui/lei/Lei	noi	voi	loro
andare	to go	andrò	andrai	andrà	andremo	andrete	andranno
cadere	to fall	cadrò	cadrai	cadrà	cadremo	cadrete	cadranno
dire	to say	dirò	dirai	dirà	diremo	direte	diranno
dovere	to have to	dovrò	dovrai	dovrà	dovremo	dovrete	dovranno
fare	to do/ make	farò	farai	farà	faremo	farete	faranno
potere	to be able	potrò	potrai	potrà	potremo	potrete	potranno
sapere	to know	saprò	saprai	saprà	sapremo	saprete	sapranno
vedere	to see	vedrò	vedrai	vedrà	vedremo	vedrete	vedranno
vivere	to live	vivrò	vivrai	vivrà	vivremo	vivrete	vivranno

Andrò con loro. — I'll go with them.

Pensi che <u>diranno</u> la verità? — Do you think they'll tell the truth?

Non credo che <u>farà</u> bel tempo. — I don't think the weather will be nice.

Lo <u>sapremo</u> domani. — We'll know tomorrow.

➤ Some verbs have no vowel before the future ending, and they also change their stem, for example:

Verb	Meaning	io	tu	lui/lei/Lei	noi	voi	loro
rimanere	to remain	rimarrò	rimarrai	rimarrà	rimarremo	rimarrete	rimarranno
tenere	to hold	terrò	terrai	terrà	terremo	terrete	terranno
venire	to come	verrò	verrai	verrà	verremo	verrete	verranno
volere	to want	vorrò	vorrai	vorrà	vorremo	vorrete	vorranno

➤ Verbs with infinitives that end in **–ciare** and **–giare**, for example, **parcheggiare** (meaning *to park*), **cominciare** (meaning *to start*), **mangiare** (meaning *to eat*) and **viaggiare** (meaning *to travel*) drop the **i** from the stem in the future. For example, **mangiare → mang- → mangerò**.

Comin<u>cerò</u> domani. — I'll start tomorrow.

Mang<u>eranno</u> alle otto. — They'll eat at eight o'clock.

➤ Verbs with infinitives that end in **–care** and **–gare**, for example **cercare** (meaning *to look for, to try*), **seccare** (meaning *to annoy*), **pagare** (meaning *to pay*) and **spiegare** (meaning *to explain*) add an **h** before the future ending in the future. For example, **pagare → pagh- → pagherò**.

<u>Cercherò</u> di aiutarvi.	I'll try to help you.
Mi <u>pagheranno</u> sabato.	They'll pay me on Saturday.

⇨ *For more information on **Spelling**, see page 191.*

Tip

You use **vero** to translate *will it?* and **vero** or **no** to translate *won't it?* and so on at the end of sentences.

Non costerà molto, vero?	It won't cost much, will it?
Arriveranno fra poco, no?	They'll be here soon, won't they?
OR **vero?**	

Grammar Extra!

Will you is used in English to ask someone to do something: *Will you hurry up?*; *Will you stop talking!* You use the Italian imperative, or the verb **volere** (meaning *to want*) to translate this sort of request.

Sta' zitto!	Will you be quiet!
Vuoi smetterla!	Will you stop that!

---

3 | The future tense of *essere* and avere

➤ **essere** (meaning *to be*) and **avere** (meaning *to have*) have irregular future forms.

Pronoun	Future tense of essere	Meaning	Future tense of avere	Meaning
(io)	sarò	I'll be	avrò	I'll have
(tu)	sarai	you'll be	avrai	you'll have
(lui/lei) (Lei)	sarà	he/she/it will be you'll be	avrà	he/she/it will have you'll have
(noi)	saremo	we'll be	avremo	we'll have
(voi)	sarete	you'll be	avrete	you'll have
(loro)	saranno	they'll be	avranno	they'll have

Sarà difficile.	It'll be difficult.
Non ne **sarai** deluso.	You won't be disappointed by it.
Non **avrò** tempo.	I won't have time.
Lo **avrai** domani.	You'll have it tomorrow.

Grammar Extra!

In English we sometimes use *will* or *'ll* to say what we think must be true, for example, *You'll be tired after that long journey; It'll be about three miles from here to the town centre.*

The future tense in Italian is used in the same way.

Saranno venti chilometri.	It'll be twenty kilometres.
Avrà cinquant'anni.	He'll be fifty.

Key points

✔ The future endings of regular **–are** and **–ere** verbs are **–erò, –erai, –erà, –eremo, –erete, –eranno**.

✔ The future endings of regular **–ire** verbs are **–irò, –irai, –irà, –iremo, –irete, –iranno**.

The conditional

> **What is the conditional?**
> The **conditional** is used to talk about things that would happen or would be true under certain conditions, for example, *I would help you if I could.*
> It is also used in requests and offers, for example, *Could you lend me some money?*; *I could give you a lift.*

1 Using the conditional

➤ In English, when you're talking about what would happen in certain circumstances, or saying what you could or would like to do, you use *would*, *'d* or *could* with the infinitive (the base form of the verb).

  I would pay the money back as soon as possible.

  If you asked him he'd probably say yes.

  You could stay here for a while.

➤ In Italian the conditional is used in this kind of sentence. Like the present and the future tenses, you make it by adding endings to the verb stem, which is what is left of the verb when you take away the **–are**, **–ere** or **–ire** ending of the infinitive.

➤ You use the conditional of any Italian verb to say what would happen or would be true.

Sarebbe difficile.	It would be difficult.
Farebbe finta di capire.	He'd pretend to understand.
Mia madre non me lo permetterebbe.	My mother wouldn't let me.

➤ You use the conditional of the verbs **potere** (meaning *to be able*) and **dovere** (meaning *to have to*) to say what could or should happen or could or should be true.

Potremmo andare in Spagna il prossimo anno.	We could go to Spain next year.
Dovresti studiare di più.	You should study more.

2 How to make the conditional

➤ To make the conditional of regular **–are** and **–ere** verbs take the stem and add the following endings: **–erei**, **–eresti**, **–erebbe**, **–eremmo**, **–ereste**, **–erebbero**.

➤ The following table shows the conditional of **parlare** (meaning *to speak*) and **credere** (meaning *to believe*).

For further explanation of grammatical terms, please see pages viii–xii.

	Conditional of parlare	Meaning	Conditional of credere	Meaning
(io)	parlerei	I'd speak	crederei	I'd believe
(tu)	parleresti	you'd speak	crederesti	you'd believe
(lui/lei) (Lei)	parlerebbe	he/she'd speak you'd speak	crederebbe	he/she'd believe you'd believe
(noi)	parleremmo	we'd speak	crederemmo	we'd believe
(voi)	parlereste	you'd speak	credereste	you'd believe
(loro)	parlerebbero	they'd speak	crederebbero	they'd believe

Con chi parleresti?   Who would you speak to?

Non ti crederebbe.   He wouldn't believe you.

[i] Note that the same form of the verb is used for the pronouns **lui**, **lei** and **Lei**.

➤ To make the conditional of regular **–ire** verbs take the <u>stem</u> and add the following endings: **–irei**, **–iresti**, **–irebbe**, **–iremmo**, **–ireste**, **–irebbero**.

➤ The following table shows the conditional of **finire** (meaning *to finish*).

(io)	finirei	I'd finish
(tu)	finiresti	you'd finish
(lui/lei) (Lei)	finirebbe	he/she'd finish you'd finish
(noi)	finiremmo	we'd finish
(voi)	finireste	you'd finish
(loro)	finirebbero	they'd finish

Non finiremmo in tempo.   We wouldn't finish in time.

[i] Note that the same form of the verb is used for the pronouns **lui**, **lei** and **Lei**.

3 | The conditionals of volere, potere and dovere

➤ You use the <u>conditional</u> of the verb **volere** (meaning *to want*) to say what you <u>would like</u>.

Vorrei un'insalata.   I'd like a salad.

➤ You use the conditional of **volere** with an infinitive to say what you <u>would like</u> to do.

Vorremmo venire con voi.   We'd like to come with you.

Vorrebbero rimanere qui.   They'd like to stay here.

Tip

In Italian there are two ways of saying *I'd like to*: **vorrei** and **mi piacerebbe**.

Vorrei vedere quel film. OR   I'd like to see that film.
Mi piacerebbe vedere quel film.

➤ The conditional of **volere** is irregular:

	Conditional of volere	Meaning
(io)	**vorrei**	I'd like
(tu)	**vorresti**	you'd like
(lui/lei) (Lei)	**vorrebbe**	he/she'd like you'd like
(noi)	**vorremmo**	we'd like
(voi)	**vorreste**	you'd like
(loro)	**vorrebbero**	they'd like

Tip

In English, the conditional *What would you like?* is more polite than *What do you want?* In Italian there is no difference in politeness.

Vuoi un gelato?   Would you like OR
                                       Do you want an ice cream?

Vuole altro, signora?   Would you like anything else,
                                       madam?

➤ You use the conditional of the verb **potere** (meaning *to be able*) with an infinitive.

● to say what <u>could</u> be the case, or <u>could</u> happen.

<u>Potresti</u> **avere ragione.**   You could be right.
<u>Potrebbe</u> **essere vero.**   It could be true.
<u>Potrebbero</u> **vendere la casa.**   They could sell the house.

● to ask if somebody <u>could</u> do something.

<u>Potresti</u> **chiudere la finestra?**   Could you close the window?

For further explanation of grammatical terms, please see pages viii–xii.

➤ The conditional of **potere** is as follows:

	Conditional of potere	Meaning
(io)	potrei	I could
(tu)	potresti	you could
(lui/lei) (Lei)	potrebbe	he/she/it could you could
(noi)	potremmo	we could
(voi)	potreste	you could
(loro)	potrebbero	they could

➤ You use the conditional of **dovere** (meaning *to have to*):

- to say what you or somebody else <u>should</u> do

Dovrei fare un po' di ginnastica.	I should do some exercise.
Dovresti telefonare ai tuoi.	You should phone your parents.

- to talk about what <u>should</u> be the case, or <u>should</u> happen.

Dovrebbe arrivare verso le dieci.	He should arrive at around ten.
Dovrebbe essere bello.	This should be good.

➤ The conditional of **dovere** is as follows:

	Conditional of dovere	Meaning
(io)	dovrei	I should
(tu)	dovresti	you should
(lui/lei) (Lei)	dovrebbe	he/she/it should you should
(noi)	dovremmo	we should
(voi)	dovreste	you should
(loro)	dovrebbero	they should

4 Irregular conditionals

➤ Some common verbs do not have a vowel before the **r** of the conditional ending, their endings are **rei, resti, rebbe, remmo, reste, rebbero**.

Verb	Meaning	io	tu	lui/lei/Lei	noi	voi	loro
andare	to go	andrei	andresti	andrebbe	andremmo	andreste	andrebbero
cadere	to fall	cadrei	cadresti	cadrebbe	cadremmo	cadreste	cadrebbero
sapere	to know	saprei	sapresti	saprebbe	sapremmo	sapreste	saprebbero
vedere	to see	vedrei	vedresti	vedrebbe	vedremmo	vedreste	vedrebbero
vivere	to live	vivrei	vivresti	vivrebbe	vivremmo	vivreste	vivrebbero

Non so se <u>andrebbe</u> bene.	I don't know if it would be okay.
<u>Sapreste</u> indicarmi la strada per la stazione?	Could you tell me the way to the station?
Non <u>vivrei</u> mai in un paese caldo.	I'd never live in a hot country.

➤ Some verbs have no vowel before the conditional ending, <u>and</u> change their stem, for example, **rimanere, tenere, venire**:

Verb	Meaning	io	tu	lui/lei/Lei	noi	voi	loro
rimanere	to remain	rimarrei	rimarresti	rimarrebbe	rimarremmo	rimarreste	rimarrebbero
tenere	to hold	terrei	terresti	terrebbe	terremmo	terreste	terrebbero
venire	to come	verrei	verresti	verrebbe	verremmo	verreste	verrebbero

➪ *For more information on **Verbs which change their stem**, see page 76.*

➤ Verbs such as **cominciare** (meaning *to start*) and **mangiare** (meaning *to eat*), which end in **–ciare** or **–giare**, and which drop the **i** in the future tense also drop the **i** in the conditional.

Quando <u>comincerebbe</u>?	When would it start?
<u>Mangeresti</u> quei funghi?	Would you eat those mushrooms?

➪ *For more information on the **Future tense**, see page 93.*

➤ Verbs such as **cercare** (meaning *to look for*) and **pagare** (meaning *to pay*), which end in **–care** or **–gare**, and which add an **h** in the future tense also add an **h** in the conditional.

Probabilmente <u>cercherebbe</u> una scusa.	He'd probably look for an excuse.
Quanto mi <u>pagheresti</u>?	How much would you pay me?

➪ *For more information on **Spelling**, see page 191.*

5 | The conditional of essere and avere

➤ **essere** (meaning *to be*) and **avere** (meaning *to have*) have irregular conditionals.

	Conditional of essere	Meaning	Conditional of avere	Meaning
(io)	sarei	I'd be	avrei	I'd have
(tu)	saresti	you'd be	avresti	you'd have
(lui/lei) (Lei)	sarebbe	he/she/ it would be you would be	avrebbe	he/she/ it would have you would have
(noi)	saremmo	we'd be	avremmo	we'd have
(voi)	sareste	you'd be	avreste	you'd have
(loro)	sarebbero	they'd be	avrebbero	they'd have

Sarebbe bello.	It would be lovely.
Non so se <u>sarei</u> capace di farlo.	I don't know if I'd be able to do it.
Non <u>avremmo</u> tempo.	We wouldn't have time.
<u>Avresti</u> paura?	Would you be frightened?

Key points

✔ The Italian conditional is often the equivalent of a verb used with *would* in English.

✔ *would like*, *could* and *should* are translated by the conditionals of **volere**, **potere** and **dovere**.

Grammar Extra!

The conditional we have looked at so far is the <u>present conditional</u>. There is also the <u>perfect conditional</u>, which is used to talk about what would have happened in the past.

The perfect conditional is made up of the conditional of **avere** or **essere**, and the past participle. Verbs which form their perfect tense with **avere**, such as **fare** (meaning *to do*) and **pagare** (meaning *to pay*) also form their perfect conditional with **avere**. Those forming their perfect with **essere**, such as **andare** (meaning *to go*) also form their perfect conditional with **essere**.

➡ *For more information about the **Perfect tense** and the **Past participle**, see pages 108-109.*

Non <u>l'avrei fatto</u> così.	I wouldn't have done it like that.
Non <u>l'avrebbero pagato</u>.	They wouldn't have paid it.
<u>Ci saresti</u> andato?	Would you have gone?

In Italian, unlike in English, the <u>perfect conditional</u> is used to report what somebody said in the past.

Ha detto che mi <u>avrebbe aiutato</u>.	He said he would help me.
Hanno detto che <u>sarebbero venuti</u>.	They said they would come.

The imperfect tense

> **What is the imperfect tense?**
> The **imperfect** is a tense used to say what was happening, what used to happen in the past and what things were like in the past, for example, I _was speaking_ to my mother.

1 When to use the imperfect tense

➤ In English various tenses are used to talk about what things were like in the past, for example, It _was raining_; I _used to like_ her; I _didn't know_ what to do. In Italian the imperfect is the tense you use to translate the verbs in all three of these sentences.

➤ Use the Italian imperfect tense:

- to describe what things were like, what people were doing and how people felt in the past.

Faceva caldo.	It was hot.
Aspettavano impazienti.	They were waiting impatiently.
Eravamo tutti felici.	We were all happy.
Avevo fame.	I was hungry.

- to say what people knew, thought or meant in the past.

Non **sapevo** cosa **volevi dire**.	I didn't know what you meant.
Pensavo che fosse lui.	I thought it was him.

- to say what used to happen or what people used to do in the past.

Ci **trovavamo** ogni venerdì.	We met every Friday.
Vendevano le uova al mercato.	They used to sell eggs in the market.

- to describe what was going on when an event took place.

Guardavamo la partita quando è entrato lui.	We were watching the match when he came in.
È successo mentre **dormivano**.	It happened while they were asleep.
Mentre **parlavi** mi sono ricordato di qualcosa.	While you were talking I remembered something.

Grammar Extra!

The imperfect continuous is made with the imperfect tense of **stare** and the gerund. The imperfect continuous is used to describe what was going on at a particular moment.

Che **stavano facendo**?	What were they doing?
Non **stava studiando**, dormiva.	He wasn't studying, he was asleep.

⇨ For more information on the **Gerund**, see page 123.

For further explanation of grammatical terms, please see pages viii–xii.

2 | How to make the imperfect tense

➤ You make the imperfect tense of regular **–are**, **–ere** and **–ire** verbs by knocking off the **–re** from the infinitive to form the <u>stem</u> of the verbs and adding **–vo**, **–vi**, **–va**, **–vamo**, **–vate**, **–vano**.

➤ The following tables show the imperfect tense of three regular verbs: **parlare** (meaning *to speak*), **credere** (meaning *to believe*) and **finire** (meaning *to finish*).

	Imperfect tense of parlare	Meaning	Imperfect tense of credere	Meaning
(io)	parla<u>vo</u>	I was speaking	crede<u>vo</u>	I believed
(tu)	parla<u>vi</u>	you were speaking	crede<u>vi</u>	you believed
(lui/lei) (Lei)	parla<u>va</u>	he/she was speaking you were speaking	crede<u>va</u>	he/she believed you believed
(noi)	parla<u>vamo</u>	we were speaking	crede<u>vamo</u>	we believed
(voi)	parla<u>vate</u>	you were speaking	crede<u>vate</u>	you believed
(loro)	parla<u>vano</u>	they were speaking	crede<u>vano</u>	they believed

	Imperfect tense of finire	Meaning
(io)	fini<u>vo</u>	I was finishing
(tu)	fini<u>vi</u>	you were finishing
(lui/lei) (Lei)	fini<u>va</u>	he/she was finishing you were finishing
(noi)	fini<u>vamo</u>	we were finishing
(voi)	fini<u>vate</u>	you were finishing
(loro)	fini<u>vano</u>	they were finishing

Con chi <u>parlavi</u>?	Who were you talking to?
<u>Credevamo</u> di aver vinto.	We thought we'd won.
Loro si <u>divertivano</u> mentre io <u>lavoravo</u>.	They had fun while I was working.
Una volta <u>costava</u> di più.	It used to cost more.

3 | Perfect tense or imperfect tense?

➤ The Italian <u>perfect tense</u> is used for what happened on one occasion.

Oggi <u>ho giocato</u> male.	I played badly today.
<u>Ha finto</u> di non conoscermi.	He pretended not to recognize me.

➤ The Italian <u>imperfect tense</u> is used for repeated actions or for a continuing state of affairs.

Da studente <u>giocavo</u> a c*a*lcio.	When I was a student I played football.
<u>Fingevano</u> sempre di avere capito tutto.	They always pretended they'd understood everything.
Mi <u>sentivo</u> male solo a pensarci.	I felt ill just thinking about it.
Non <u>sorrideva</u> mai.	She never smiled.
Ci <u>credevi</u>?	Did you believe it?

4 Verbs with an irregular imperfect tense

➤ The imperfect of **essere** (meaning *to be*) is irregular:

(io)	ero	I was
(tu)	eri	you were
(lui/lei) (Lei)	era	he/she/it was you were
(noi)	eravamo	we were
(voi)	eravate	you were
(loro)	*e*rano	they were

<u>Era</u> un ragazzo molto simp*a*tico.	He was a very nice boy.
<u>Eravamo</u> in It*a*lia.	We were in Italy.
<u>Erano</u> le quattro.	It was four o'clock.

➤ **bere** (meaning *to drink*), **dire** (meaning *to say*), **fare** (meaning *to do, to make*) and **tradurre** (meaning *to translate*) are the most common verbs which have the normal imperfect endings added onto a stem which is irregular. You just have to learn these.

Verb	(io)	(tu)	(lui/lei/Lei)	(noi)	(voi)	(loro)
bere	bevevo	bevevi	beveva	bevevamo	bevevate	bev*e*vano
dire	dicevo	dicevi	diceva	dicevamo	dicevate	dic*e*vano
fare	facevo	facevi	faceva	facevamo	facevate	fac*e*vano
tradurre	traducevo	traducevi	traduceva	traducevamo	traducevate	traduc*e*vano

Di s*o*lito <u>bev*e*vano</u> solo acqua.	They usually only drank water.
Cosa <u>dicevo</u>?	What was I saying?
<u>Faceva</u> molto freddo.	It was very cold.
<u>Traducevo</u> la l*e*ttera.	I was translating the letter.

Grammar Extra!

The Italian imperfect tense is used to translate sentences such as *How long <u>had they known</u> each other?*; *They <u>had been going out</u> together for a year when they got engaged*; *He <u>had been</u> ill since last year.* The words *for* and *since* are translated by **da**.

A quel punto <u>aspettava</u> già da tre ore.	By then he'd already been waiting for three hours.
<u>Guidavo</u> dalle sei di mattina.	I'd been driving since six in the morning.
Da quanto tempo <u>stava</u> male?	How long had he been ill?

➩ *For more information on **da**, see page 174.*

Key points

✔ You make the imperfect tense of regular verbs by knocking off the final **–re** of the infinitive and adding endings: **–vo, –vi, –va, –vamo, –vate, –vano**.

✔ The imperfect is used for actions and situations that continued for some time in the past.

The perfect tense

> **What is the perfect tense?**
> In English the **perfect tense** is used to talk about what has or hasn't happened, for example *We've won*, *I haven't touched it*.

1 Using the perfect tense

➤ In English the perfect tense is made up of the verb *to have* followed by a <u>past participle</u>, such as *done, broken, worked, arrived*. It is used to talk about:
  ● what you've done at some time in the past, for example, *We've been to Australia*.
  ● what you've done so far, for example, *I've eaten half of it*.

➤ In English the <u>simple past</u>, not the <u>perfect</u> is used to say when exactly something happened, for example, *We met last summer; I ate it last night; It rained a lot yesterday*.

➤ In Italian there are two ways of making the perfect tense:
  ● the present tense of **avere** (meaning *to have*) followed by a past participle
  ● the present tense of **essere** (meaning *to be*), followed by a past participle.

⇨ *For more information on the **Present tense of avere and essere**, see pages 109 and 112.*

➤ The Italian perfect tense is used to say:
  ● what you've done at some time in the past.

Ho già **visto** quel film.	I've already seen that film.
Sono uscita con lui un paio di volte.	I've been out with him a couple of times.

  ● what you've done so far.

Finora **abbiamo fatto** solo il presente dei verbi.	So far we've only done the present tense.

➤ Unlike in English, the Italian perfect tense is <u>ALSO</u> used to say what you did at some particular time, or when exactly something happened.

Ho visto quel film sabato scorso.	I saw that film last Saturday.
Sono uscita con lui ieri sera.	I went out with him last night.
È successo ieri.	It happened yesterday.

> ## Tip
> Do not use the perfect tense to say since when, or how long you've been doing something – **da** and the present tense is used for this in Italian.
>
> ⇨ *For more information on **da**, see page 174.*

2 How to make the past participle

➤ The past participle is <u>always</u> part of the perfect tense.

➤ To make the past participle of a regular **–are** verb, take off the **–are** of the infinitive and add **–ato**.

parlare (meaning *to speak*) → **parlato** (*spoken*)

➤ To make the past participle of a regular **–ere** verb, take off the **–ere** of the infinitive and add **–uto**.

credere (meaning *to believe*) → **creduto** (*believed*)

➤ To make the past participle of a regular **–ire** verb, take off the **–ire** of the infinitive and add **–ito**.

finire (meaning *to finish*) → **finito** (*finished*)

3 How to make the perfect tense with avere .

➤ To make the perfect tense with **avere**:

- choose the present tense form of **avere** that matches the subject of the sentence.
- add the past participle. <u>Do not</u> change the ending of the participle to make it agree with the subject.

➤ The perfect tense of **parlare** (meaning *to speak*) is as follows:

	Present tense of avere	Past participle of parlare	Meaning
(io)	ho	parlato	I spoke *or* have spoken
(tu)	hai	parlato	you spoke *or* have spoken
(lui/lei) (Lei)	ha	parlato	he/she spoke *or* has spoken you spoke *or* have spoken
(noi)	abbiamo	parlato	we spoke *or* have spoken
(voi)	avete	parlato	you spoke *or* have spoken
(loro)	hanno	parlato	they spoke *or* have spoken

Non gli <u>ho</u> mai <u>parlato</u>.   I've never spoken to him.
Roberta gli <u>ha parlato</u> ieri.   Roberta spoke to him yesterday.

4 Verbs with irregular past participles

➤ As in English, some very common verbs have irregular past participles. These are some of the most important ones:

aprire (*to open*)	→	**aperto** (*opened*)
ALSO **coprire** (*to cover*)	→	**coperto** (*covered*)
chiudere (*to close*)	→	**chiuso** (*closed*)
decidere (*to decide*)	→	**deciso** (*decided*)
dire (*to say*)	→	**detto** (*said*)
fare (*to do, to make*)	→	**fatto** (*done, made*)
friggere (*to fry*)	→	**fritto** (*fried*)
leggere (*to read*)	→	**letto** (*read*)
mettere (*to put*)	→	**messo** (*put*)
ALSO **promettere** (*to promise*)	→	**promesso** (*promised*)
morire (*to die*)	→	**morto** (*died*)
offrire (*to offer*)	→	**offerto** (*offered*)
prendere (*to take*)	→	**preso** (*taken*)
ALSO **sorprendere** (*to surprise*)	→	**sorpreso** (*surprised*)
rispondere (*to reply*)	→	**risposto** (*replied*)
ALSO **spendere** (*to spend*)	→	**speso** (*spent*)
rompere (*to break*)	→	**rotto** (*broken*)
scegliere (*to choose*)	→	**scelto** (*chosen*)
scrivere (*to write*)	→	**scritto** (*written*)
vincere (*to win*)	→	**vinto** (*won*)
ALSO **convincere** (*to convince*)	→	**convinto** (*convinced*)
vedere (*to see*)	→	**visto** (*seen*)

[*i*] Note that, as in English, some Italian past participles are also used as adjectives. When they are adjectives they <u>agree</u> with the noun they go with.

patate fritte	fried potatoes
È aperta la banca?	Is the bank open?

⇨ *For more information on* **Adjectives**, *see page 20.*

5 When to make the perfect tense with avere

➤ You use **avere** to make the perfect tense of most verbs.

<u>Ho preso</u> il treno delle dieci.	I <u>got</u> the ten o'clock train.
<u>L'hai messo</u> in frigo?	<u>Have you put</u> it in the fridge?
Perché <u>l'hai fatto</u>?	Why <u>did you do</u> it?
Carlo <u>ha speso</u> più di me.	Carlo <u>spent</u> more than me.
<u>Abbiamo comprato</u> una macchina.	<u>We've bought</u> a car.
Dove <u>avete parcheggiato</u>?	Where <u>did you park</u>?
Non <u>hanno voluto</u> aiutarmi.	They <u>didn't want</u> to help me.

For further explanation of grammatical terms, please see pages viii–xii.

➤ You <u>do not</u> use **avere** to make the perfect tense of:

- reflexive verbs
- certain verbs that do not take a direct object, such as **andare** (meaning *to go*), **venire** (meaning *to come*) and **diventare** (meaning *to become*).

[i] Note that in English the verb *to have* can be used on its own in replies such as *No, he hasn't*, and question phrases such as *haven't you?* – **avere** <u>cannot</u> be used in this way in Italian.

Te l'ha detto? – No.	Has he told you? – No, he hasn't.
Lo hai fatto, vero?	You've done it, haven't you?

⇨ *For more information on* ***Questions***, *see page 152.*

For more information on ***Questions***, *see page 152.*

6 | When to make the past participle agree

➤ When you make the perfect tense with **avere**, the past participle <u>never</u> agrees with the <u>subject</u>.

➤ You <u>must</u> make the past participle agree with the <u>object pronouns</u> **lo** and **la** (meaning *him, her* and *it*) when they come in front of the verb.

Hai visto Marco? – Sì, <u>l'ho visto</u>.	Have you seen Marco? – Yes, I've seen him.
È un bel film, <u>l'hai visto</u>?	It's a good film, have you seen it?
Hai visto Lucia? – Non <u>l'ho vista</u>.	Have you seen Lucia? – No, I haven't seen her.

➤ You <u>must</u> make the past participle agree with the object pronouns **li** and **le** (meaning *them*) when they come in front of the verb.

I fiammiferi? Non <u>li ho presi</u>.	The matches? I haven't taken them.
Le fragole? <u>Le ho mangiate</u> tutte.	The strawberries? I've eaten them all.

Key points

✔ The Italian perfect tense is used to translate both the English perfect, and the English simple past.

✔ The Italian perfect tense is made with **avere** or ***essere*** and the past participle.

✔ The past participle does not agree with the subject when the perfect tense is made with **avere**, except when certain object pronouns come in front of the verb.

7 How to make the perfect tense with *essere*

➤ To make the perfect tense with **essere**:

- choose the present tense form of **essere** that matches the subject of the sentence.
- add the past participle. Make the ending of the participle <u>agree</u> with the subject.

➤ The perfect tense of **andare** (meaning *to go*) is as follows:

	Present tense of *essere*	Past participle of andare	Meaning
(io)	sono	**andato** *or* **andata**	I went *or* have gone
(tu)	sei	**andato** *or* **andata**	you went *or* have gone
(lui)	è	**andato**	he/it went *or* has gone
(lei)	è	**andata**	she/it went *or* has gone
(Lei)	è	**andato** *or* **andata**	you went *or* have gone
(noi)	siamo	**andati** *or* **andate**	we went *or* have gone
(voi)	siete	**andati** *or* **andate**	you went *or* have gone
(loro)	sono	**andati** *or* **andate**	they went *or* have gone

---

Tip

You make past participles agree when they follow the verb **essere**, in the same way that you make adjectives agree.

Sei pronta, Maria?   Are you ready Maria?

Sei andata anche tu, Maria?   Did you go too, Maria?

⇨ *For more information on **Adjectives**, see page 20.*

---

8 When to make the perfect tense with *essere*

➤ Use **essere** to make the perfect tense of certain verbs that <u>do not</u> take a direct object.

⇨ *For more information on **Direct objects**, see page 44.*

➤ The most important of these verbs are:

andare	to go	**arrivare**	to arrive
diventare	to become	**entrare**	to come in
partire	to leave	**rimanere**	to stay
riuscire	to succeed, manage	**salire**	to go up, get on
scendere	to go down	**succedere**	to happen
stare	to be	**tornare**	to come back
uscire	to go out	**venire**	to come

<u>È rimasta</u> a casa tutto il giorno.	She stayed at home all day.
<u>Siamo riusciti</u> a convincerla.	We managed to persuade her.
<u>Sei</u> mai <u>stata</u> a Bologna, Tina?	Have you ever been to Bologna, Tina?
Le tue amiche <u>sono arrivate</u>.	Your friends have arrived.
Cos'<u>è successo</u>?	What happened?

[*i*] Note that **essere** is used to make the perfect tense of **piacere** (meaning literally *to please*). The past participle agrees with the <u>subject</u> of the Italian verb, and not with the subject of the English verb *to like*.

<u>La musica</u> ti è <u>piaciuta</u>, Roberto?	Did you like the music, Robert?
<u>I cioccolatini</u> mi sono <u>piaciuti</u> molto.	I liked the chocolates very much.
<u>Le foto</u> sono <u>piaciute</u> a tutti.	Everyone liked the photos.

➤ Use **essere** to make the perfect tense of all reflexive verbs.

I miei fratelli si <u>sono alzati</u> tardi.	My brothers got up late.
Le ragazze si <u>sono alzate</u> alle sei.	The girls got up at six.

➪ *For more information on **Reflexive verbs**, see page 87.*

Key points

✔ When the perfect tense is made with **essere** the past participle agrees with the subject of the sentence.

✔ **essere** is used to make the perfect tense of some very common verbs that do not take a direct object.

✔ **essere** is used to make the perfect tense of all reflexive verbs.

The past historic

> **What is the past historic?**
> The **past historic** is equivalent to the English simple past, except that it is only used in written Italian. In spoken Italian the <u>perfect</u> tense is used to talk about the past.

Recognizing the past historic

➤ You do not need to learn the past historic (**il passato remoto**), since you will never need to use it. However, you may come across it in written Italian. To help you recognize it, here are the past historic forms of **essere** (meaning *to be*), **avere** (meaning *to have*), **parlare** (meaning *to speak*), **credere** (meaning *to believe*), and **partire** (meaning *to leave*).

	Past historic of essere	Meaning	Past historic of avere	Meaning
(io)	fui	I was	ebbi	I had
(tu)	fosti	you were	avesti	you had
(lui/lei) (Lei)	fu	he/she was you were	ebbe	he/she had you had
(noi)	fummo	we were	avemmo	we had
(voi)	foste	you were	aveste	you had
(loro)	furono	they were	ebbero	they had

Ci <u>fu</u> un improvviso silenzio quando entrai nella stanza.

There was a sudden silence when I came into the room.

Non <u>ebbero</u> nessuna speranza.

They had no hope.

	Past historic of parlare	Meaning	Past historic of credere	Meaning
(io)	parlai	I spoke	credei *or* credetti	I believed
(tu)	parlasti	you spoke	credesti	you believed
(lui/lei) (Lei)	parlò	he/she spoke you spoke	credé *or* credette	he/she believed you believed
(noi)	parlammo	we spoke	credemmo	we believed
(voi)	parlaste	you spoke	credeste	you believed
(loro)	parlarono	they spoke	crederono *or* credettero	they believed

	Past historic of partire	Meaning
(io)	partii	I left
(tu)	partisti	you left
(lui/lei) (Lei)	partì	he/she left you left
(noi)	partimmo	we left
(voi)	partiste	you left
(loro)	partirono	they left

Parlò piano. He spoke slowly.

Non lo credettero. They did not believe it.

Partì in fretta. He left hastily.

Key points

✔ You will come across the past historic in written Italian.

✔ It is translated by the English simple past.

The pluperfect or past perfect tense

> **What is the pluperfect tense?**
> The **pluperfect tense** is used to talk about what had happened or had been true at a point in the past, for example, *I'd forgotten to send her a card.*

1 Using the pluperfect tense

➤ When talking about the past we sometimes refer to things that had already happened previously. In English we use *had* followed by a <u>past participle</u> such as *done, broken, worked, arrived* to do this. This tense is called the <u>pluperfect</u> or <u>past perfect</u>.

➤ The Italian pluperfect tense is used in a similar way, but like the perfect tense, it can be made with either **avere** or **essere**, and the past participle.

⇨ *For more information on **Past participles**, see page 109.*

Avevamo già **mangiato** quando è arrivato.	We'd already eaten when he arrived.
Ovviamente <u>erano</u> <u>riusciti</u> a risolvere il problema.	They'd obviously managed to solve the problem.

2 How to make the pluperfect tense with avere

➤ To make the pluperfect tense with **avere**:

- choose the <u>imperfect</u> form of **avere** that matches the subject of the sentence.
- add the past participle. <u>Do not</u> change the ending of the participle to make it agree with the subject.

⇨ *For more information on the **Imperfect tense of avere** and **Past participles**, see pages 106 and 109.*

➤ The pluperfect tense of **parlare** (meaning *to speak*) is as follows:

	Imperfect tense of avere	Past participle of parlare	Meaning
(io)	avevo	parlato	I had spoken
(tu)	avevi	parlato	you had spoken
(lui/lei) (Lei)	aveva	parlato	he/she had spoken you had spoken
(noi)	avevamo	parlato	we had spoken
(voi)	avevate	parlato	you had spoken
(loro)	avevano	parlato	they had spoken

For further explanation of grammatical terms, please see pages viii–xii.

Non gli <u>avevo</u> mai <u>parlato</u> prima.   I'd never spoken to him before.
Sara gli <u>aveva parlato</u> il giorno   Sara had spoken to him the day
prima.   before.

[i] Note that you use the same form of **avere** for **lui**, **lei** and **Lei**.

⇨ *For more information on **Verbs with irregular past participles**, see page 110.*

> ## Tip
>
> Do not use the pluperfect tense to say since when, or how long you had
> been doing something – **da** and the imperfect tense is used for this in Italian.
>
> **Abitavamo lì dal 1990.**   We'd lived there since 1990.
>
> ⇨ *For more information on **da**, see **Prepositions** page 174.*

3 When to make the pluperfect tense with avere

➤ As with the perfect tense, you use **avere** to make the <u>pluperfect</u> tense of most
verbs.

➤ You do <u>not</u> use **avere** to make the pluperfect tense of:

- reflexive verbs
- certain verbs that do not take a direct object, such as **andare** (meaning *to go*),
  venire (meaning *to come*), **diventare** (meaning *to become*).

  Ovviamente <u>avevo</u> <u>sbagliato</u>.   I'd obviously made a mistake.
  <u>Avevano</u> <u>lavorato</u> molto il giorno   They'd worked hard the day before.
  prima.

[i] Note that, as with the perfect tense, the past participle agrees with the
<u>object</u> <u>pronouns</u> **lo** and **la**, (meaning *him, her* and *it*) and **li** and **le** (meaning
them) when they come before the verb.

  Non <u>l'avevo vista</u>.   I hadn't seen her.
  Le lettere? Non <u>le aveva</u> mai <u>lette</u>.   The letters? He'd never read them.

⇨ *For more information on **Object pronouns** and the **Perfect tense**, see pages 44 and 108.*

> ### Key points
>
> ✔ The pluperfect tense is used to talk about what had already happened in
> the past.
> ✔ The Italian pluperfect tense is made with the imperfect of **avere** or
> **essere**, and the past participle.
> ✔ **avere** is used to make the pluperfect tense of most verbs.

4 | How to make the pluperfect tense with *essere*

➤ To make the pluperfect tense with **essere**:
- choose the <u>imperfect</u> form of **essere** that matches the subject of the sentence.
- add the past participle. Make the ending of the participle <u>agree</u> with the subject.

➤ The pluperfect tense of **andare** (meaning *to go*) is as follows:

	Imperfect tense of *essere*	Past participle of andare	Meaning
(io)	ero	andato *or* andata	I had gone
(tu)	eri	andato *or* andata	you had gone
(lui)	era	andato	he/it had gone
(lei)	era	andata	she/it had gone
(Lei)	era	andato *or* andata	you had gone
(noi)	eravamo	andati *or* andate	we had gone
(voi)	eravate	andati *or* andate	you had gone
(loro)	erano	andati *or* andate	they had gone

Silvia <u>era andata</u> con loro. Silvia had gone with them.

Tutti i miei amici <u>erano andati</u> alla festa. All my friends had gone to the party.

5 | When to make the pluperfect tense with *essere*

➤ When **essere** is used to make the perfect tense of a verb, you also use **essere** to make the pluperfect.

⇨ *For more information on* **Making the perfect tense with essere**, *see page* 112.

➤ Use **essere** to make the pluperfect of all reflexive verbs, and of certain verbs that do not take a direct object, such as **andare** (meaning *to go*), **venire** (meaning *to come*), **riuscire** (meaning *to succeed*), **diventare** (meaning *to become*) and **piacere** (meaning *to like*).

Ovviamente non gli <u>erano piaciuti</u> i quadri. He obviously hadn't liked the pictures.

Sono arrivata alle cinque, ma <u>erano</u> già <u>partiti</u>. I arrived at five, but they'd already gone.

Fortunatamente non si <u>era fatta</u> male. Luckily she hadn't hurt herself.

Key points

✔ Verbs that make their perfect tense with **essere** also make their pluperfect tense with **essere**.

✔ When the pluperfect tense is made with **essere** the past participle agrees with the subject of the sentence.

✔ **essere** is used to make the pluperfect tense of reflexive verbs and certain verbs that do not take a direct object.

The passive

> **What is the passive?**
> The **passive** is a verb form that is used when the subject of the verb is the person or thing that is affected by the action, for example, *Everyone was shocked by the incident; Two people were hurt; The house is being demolished.*

1 Using the passive

➤ Verbs can be <u>active</u> or <u>passive</u>.

➤ In a sentence with an <u>active verb</u> the subject of the sentence does the action:

Subject	Active verb	Object
She	does	most of the work.
A dog	bit	him.

➤ In a sentence with a <u>passive</u> verb the action is done by someone or something that is not the subject of the sentence.

Subject	Passive verb	Who/what the action is done by
Most of the work	is done	by her.
He	was bitten	by a dog.

➤ To show who or what is responsible for the action in a passive sentence you use *by* in English.

➤ You use passive rather than active verbs:

- when you want to focus on the person or thing <u>affected</u> by the action
   <u>John</u> was injured in an accident.

- when you don't know who is responsible for the action
   My car was stolen last week.

2 How to make the passive

➤ In English we use the verb *to be* with a <u>past participle</u> (*is done, was bitten*) to make the passive.

➤ In Italian the passive is made in exactly the same way, using **essere** (meaning *to be*) and a <u>past participle</u>.

⇨ *For more information on the **Past participle**, see page 109.*

Siamo invitati ad una festa a casa loro.	We're invited to a party at their house.
L'elettricità **è stata tagliata** ieri.	The electricity was cut off yesterday.
La partita **è stata rinviata**.	The match has been postponed.
È stato costretto a ritirarsi dalla gara.	He was forced to withdraw from the competition.

➤ When you say who or what is responsible for the action you use **da** (meaning *by*).

I ladri **sono stati catturati** dalla polizia.	The thieves were caught by the police.

📋 Note that the past participle agrees with the subject of the verb **essere** in the same way an adjective would.

⇨ *For more information on **Adjectives**, see page 20.*

➤ Here is the perfect tense of the **–are** verb **invitare** (meaning *to invite*) in its passive form.

(Subject pronoun)		Perfect tense of *essere*	Past Participle	Meaning
(io)	– masculine	**sono stato**	**invitato**	I was, have been invited
	– feminine	**sono stata**	**invitata**	
(tu)	– masculine	**sei stato**	**invitato**	you were, have been invited
	– feminine	**sei stata**	**invitata**	
(lui)		**è stato**	**invitato**	he was, has been invited
(lei)		**è stata**	**invitata**	she was, has been invited
(Lei)	– masculine	**è stato**	**invitato**	you were, have been invited
	– feminine	**è stata**	**invitata**	you were, have been invited
(noi)	– masculine	**siamo stati**	**invitati**	we were, have been invited
	– feminine	**siamo state**	**invitate**	we were, have been invited
(voi)	– masculine	**siete stati**	**invitati**	you were, have been invited
	– feminine	**siete state**	**invitate**	you were, have been invited
(loro)	– masculine	**sono stati**	**invitati**	they were, have been invited
	– feminine	**sono state**	**invitate**	they were, have been invited

For further explanation of grammatical terms, please see pages viii–xii.

➤ You can change the tense of the verb **essere** to make whatever passive tense you want.

> **Sarete** tutti invitati.   You'll all be invited.
>
> Non so se **sarebbe** invitata.   I don't know if she would be invited.

➤ Some past participles are irregular.

⇨ *For more information on **Irregular past participles**, see page 110.*

Grammar Extra!

venire (meaning *to come*) and **rimanere** (meaning *to remain*) are sometimes used instead of **essere** to make the passive.

venire is used in the present, imperfect, future and conditional to make passives, but not in the perfect or pluperfect.

> Quando **vengono cambiate**?   When <u>are they changed</u>?
>
> **Venivano controllati** ogni sei mesi.   They <u>were checked</u> every six months.
>
> **Verrà criticato** da tutti.   He'<u>ll be criticized</u> by everyone.
>
> **Verrebbe scoperto**.   It <u>would be</u> discovered.

rimanere is used very often with **ferito** (meaning *injured*), and with participles describing emotion, such as **stupefatto** (meaning *amazed*) and **deluso** (meaning *disappointed*).

> <u>**È rimasto ferito**</u> in un incidente stradale.   He <u>was injured</u> in a car accident.
>
> <u>**È rimasta stupefatta**</u> dalla scena.   She <u>was amazed</u> by the scene.

---

3 Avoiding the passive

➤ Passives are not as common in Italian as they are in English. In many cases, where we would use a passive verb, one of the following alternatives would be used in Italian:

- an active construction

  > Due persone sono morte.   Two people were killed.
  >
  > Mi hanno rubato la macchina la settimana scorsa.   My car was stolen last week.
  >
  > C'erano delle microspie nella stanza.   The room was bugged.
  >
  > Dicono che sia molto ambizioso.   He's said to be very ambitious.

- an ordinary verb made passive by having **si** put in front (this is known as the **si passivante**)

  > Qui <u>si vende</u> il pane.   Bread is sold here.
  >
  > <u>Si parla</u> inglese.   English spoken.
  >
  > Dove <u>si trovano</u> i migliori vini?   Where are the best wines to be found?

In Italia il prosciutto <u>si mangia</u> col melone.	In Italy ham is eaten with melon.
Gli spaghetti non <u>si mangiano</u> con le dita!	Spaghetti should not be eaten with one's fingers!
"comodo" <u>si scrive</u> con una sola m.	**"comodo"** is spelled with only one m.

📖 Note that wherever the subject comes in the sentence the verb has to agree with it.

- an impersonal construction with **si**

| **Si dice che non vada molto bene.** | It's said not to be going very well. |
| **Non si fa così.** | That's not how it's done. |

Tip

When you want to say something like *I was told*, or *She was given* use an active construction in Italian: **Mi hanno detto** (meaning *they told me*); **Le hanno dato** (meaning *they gave her*).

Key points

✔ The passive is made using **essere** with the past participle

✔ The past participle must agree with the subject of **essere**.

✔ Alternatives to the passive are often used in Italian.

The gerund

> **What is a gerund?**
> In English the gerund is a verb form ending in –ing which is used to make continuous tenses, for example, What are you doing? It can also be used as a noun or an adjective, for example, I love swimming; a skating rink.

1 Using the gerund

➤ In Italian the gerund is a verb form ending in **–ando** or **–endo**. It is used to make continuous tenses.

Sto <u>lavorando</u>.	I'm working.
Cosa stai <u>facendo</u>?	What are you doing?

● The gerund follows the present tense of **stare** to make the <u>present continuous</u>.

<u>Sto scrivendo</u> una lettera.	I'm writing a letter.
<u>Stai cercando</u> lavoro?	Are you looking for a job?

➪ For more information on the **Present continuous**, see page 81.

● The gerund follows the imperfect tense of **stare** to make the <u>past continuous.</u>

Il bambino <u>stava piangendo</u>.	The little boy was crying.
<u>Stavo lavando</u> i piatti.	I was washing the dishes.

🛈 Note that the Italian <u>past participle</u> is sometimes used where the gerund is used in English: **essere disteso** means to be lying; **essere seduto** means to be sitting and **essere appoggiato** means to be leaning.

<u>Era disteso</u> sul divano.	He was lying on the sofa.
<u>Era seduta</u> accanto a me.	She was sitting next to me.
La scala <u>era appoggiata</u> al muro.	The ladder was leaning against the wall.

➤ The gerund can be used by itself:

● to say when something happened

<u>Entrando</u> ho sentito odore di pesce.	When I came in I could smell fish.
<u>Ripensandoci</u>, credo che non fosse colpa sua.	Thinking about it, I don't reckon it was his fault.

● to say why something happened

<u>Sentendomi</u> male sono andato a letto.	Because I felt ill I went to bed.
<u>Vedendolo</u> solo, è venuta a parlargli.	Seeing that he was on his own she came to speak to him.

- to say in what circumstances something could happen

> **Volendo, potremmo comprarne un altro.**
>
> If we wanted to, we could buy another one.

Tip

The gerund never changes its form to agree with the subject of the sentence.

2 How to make the gerund

➤ To make the gerund of **-are** verbs, take off the **-are** ending of the infinitive to get the stem, and add **-ando**.

Infinitive	Stem	Gerund	Meaning
lavorare	lavor-	lavorando	working
andare	and-	andando	going
dare	d-	dando	giving
stare	st-	stando	being

i Note that the only **-are** verb that does not follow this rule is **fare**, and verbs made of **fare** with a prefix, such as **rifare** (meaning *to do again*) and **disfare** (meaning *to undo*). The gerund of **fare** is **facendo**.

➤ To make the gerund of **-ere** and **-ire** verbs, take off the **-ere** or **-ire** ending of the infinitive to get the stem, and add **-endo**.

Infinitive	Stem	Gerund	Meaning
credere	cred-	credendo	believing
essere	ess-	essendo	being
dovere	dov-	dovendo	having to
finire	fin-	finendo	finishing
dormire	dorm-	dormendo	sleeping

i Note that the only **-ire** verb that does not follow this rule is **dire** (and verbs made of **dire** with a prefix, such as **disdire** (meaning *to cancel*) and **contraddire** (meaning *to contradict*). The gerund of **dire** is **dicendo**.

For further explanation of grammatical terms, please see pages viii–xii.

3 | When not to use the gerund

➤ In English the –*ing* form can follow other verbs, for example, *She started crying; He insisted on paying; They continued working.*

➤ In Italian the gerund is not used in this way. A construction with a preposition and the infinitive is used instead.

Ha cominciato <u>a ridere</u>.	She started laughing.
Hai finito <u>di mangiare</u>?	Have you finished eating?

⇨ *For more information on **Prepositions after verbs**, see page 143.*

➤ In English we often use –*ing* forms as nouns, for example, *driving, skating, cleaning.*

➤ In Italian you cannot use the **–ando** and **–endo** forms like this. When talking about activities and interests you use nouns, such as **il giardinaggio** (meaning *gardening*), **la pulizia** (meaning *cleaning*) and **il fumo** (meaning *smoking*).

A mia madre piace molto <u>il giardinaggio</u>.	My mother loves gardening.
Facciamo un po' di <u>pulizia</u>.	Let's do a bit of cleaning.
<u>Il fumo</u> fa male.	Smoking is bad for you.

➤ In English you can put an -*ing* noun in front of another noun, for example, *skating rink.*

➤ In Italian you can never put one noun in front of another noun .

- Often you link two words together with a preposition:

calzoncini <u>da</u> bagno	swimming trunks
una borsa <u>per</u> la spesa	a shopping bag
un istruttore <u>di</u> guida	a driving instructor

- Sometimes there is one word in Italian for two English words:

la <u>patente</u>	the <u>driving licence</u>
una <u>piscina</u>	a <u>swimming pool</u>

Tip

When you want to translate this kind of English two-word combination it's a good idea to look it up in a dictionary.

4 Where to put pronouns used with the gerund

➤ Pronouns are usually joined onto the end of the gerund.

Vedendoli è scoppiata in lacrime.	When she saw them she burst into tears.
Ascoltandolo mi sono addormentato.	Listening to him, I fell asleep.
Incontrandosi per caso sono andati al bar.	Meeting each other by chance, they went to a café.

➤ When the gerund is part of a continuous tense the pronoun can either come before **stare** or be joined onto the gerund.

Ti sto parlando OR **Sto parlandoti.**	I'm talking to you.
Si sta vestendo OR **Sta vestendosi.**	He's getting dressed.
Me lo stavano mostrando OR **Stavano mostrandomelo.**	They were showing me it.

Key points

✔ Use the gerund in continuous tenses with **stare**, and by itself to say when or why something happened.

✔ *-ing* forms in English are not always translated by the gerund.

Impersonal verbs

> **What is an impersonal verb?**
> In English an impersonal verb has the subject *it*, but this '*it*'does not refer to any specific thing; for example, *It's going to rain; It's nine o'clock.*

1 Verbs that are always impersonal

➤ Verbs such as **piovere** (meaning *to rain*) and **nevicare** (meaning *to snow*), are always impersonal because there is no person, animal or thing doing the action.

➤ They are used only in the '*it*' form, the infinitive, and as a gerund (the *–ing* form of the verb).

Piove.	It's raining.
Sta piovendo?	Is it raining?
Ha iniziato a piovere.	It started to rain.
Nevicava da due giorni.	It had been snowing for two days.
Pensi che nevicherà?	Do you think it'll snow?

[i] Note that the perfect and pluperfect tenses of verbs to do with the weather such as **piovere**, **nevicare**, **grandinare** (meaning *to hail*) and **tuonare** (meaning *to thunder*) can be made either with **avere** or **essere**.

<u>Ha</u> piovuto or <u>è</u> piovuto molto ieri.	It rained a lot yesterday.
<u>Aveva</u> nevicato or <u>era</u> nevicato durante la notte.	It had snowed during the night.

2 Verbs that are sometimes impersonal

➤ **fare** is used impersonally to talk about the weather and time of day:

<u>Fa</u> caldo.	It's hot.
<u>Fa</u> freddo.	It's cold.
<u>Faceva</u> bel tempo.	It was good weather. OR The weather was good.
<u>Fa</u> sempre brutto tempo.	The weather's always bad.
<u>Fa</u> notte.	It's getting dark.

> ## *Tip*
> **Fa niente** means *It doesn't matter*.

➤ **è**, and other tenses of **essere** are used impersonally, like *it's* and other tenses of *to be* in English.

È tardi.	It's late.
Era presto.	It was early.
È da tre ore che aspettano.	It's three hours now that they've been waiting.
Era Pasqua.	It was Easter.
Non era da lei fare così.	It wasn't like her to act like that.

> ## Tip
> Just use the verb by itself when talking about the time or the weather.
> There is no Italian equivalent for "*it*".

➤ **essere** is used in impersonal constructions with adjectives, for example:

- with an adjective followed by an infinitive

È facile capire che qualcosa non va.	It's easy to see that something's wrong.
Mi è impossibile andar via adesso.	It's impossible for me to leave now.
È stato stupido buttarli via.	It was stupid to throw them away.
Sarebbe bello andarci.	It would be nice to go there.

- with an adjective followed by **che**

È vero che sono stato impaziente.	It's true that I've been impatient.
Era bello che ci fossimo tutti.	It's nice that we were all there.

Grammar Extra!

When an impersonal construction with **che** is used to refer to something that is a possibility rather than a fact, the following verb must be in the <u>subjunctive</u>.

The following impersonal expressions refer to what might, should, or could be the case, rather than what <u>is</u> the case, and therefore they are always followed by the subjunctive:

- **È possibile che...**
  È possibile che abbia sbagliato tu.

  It's possible that...
  It's possible that you made a mistake.

- **Non è possibile che...**
  Non è possibile che sappiano.

  It's impossible that...
  It's impossible that they should know. OR They can't possibly know.

- **È facile che...**
  È facile che piova.

  It's likely that...
  It's likely that it'll rain. OR It'll probably rain.

- **È difficile che...**
  È difficile che venga.

  It's unlikely that...
  It's unlikely that he'll come.

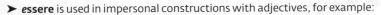 *For more information on the **Subjunctive**, see page 130.*

For further explanation of grammatical terms, please see pages viii–xii.

➤ **parere** and **sembrare** (both meaning *to seem*) are often used impersonally.

Sono contenti? – <u>Pare</u> di sì.	Are they happy? – It seems so.
L'ha creduto? – <u>Pare</u> di no.	Did he believe it? – Apparently not.
Forse va tutto bene, ma non <u>sembra</u>.	Maybe everything's okay, but it doesn't look like it.
<u>Pare</u> che sia stato lui.	Apparently it was him.
<u>Sembra</u> che tu abbia ragione.	Seemingly you're right.

ⓘ Note that the Italian construction with a verb can often be translated by the adverbs *apparently* and *seemingly*.

➤ Other verbs used impersonally are **bastare** (meaning *to be enough*), **bisognare** and **occorrere** (both meaning *to be necessary*), **importare** (meaning *to be important*).

Basta?	Is that enough?
Bisogna prenotare?	Is it necessary to or do you have to book?
Bisogna arrivare un'ora prima.	You have to get there an hour before.
Occorre farlo subito.	It should be done at once.
Oggi o domani, non importa.	Today or tomorrow, it doesn't matter.

ⓘ Note that these verbs can be replaced by impersonal constructions with **essere** and an adjective.

È necessario prenotare?	Is it necessary to book?
Sarebbe opportuno farlo subito.	It would be best to do it at once.

Tip

può darsi (meaning *it's possible*), can be used like **forse** (meaning *maybe*).

Vieni? – Può darsi.	Are you coming? – Maybe.
Può darsi che vincano.	It's possible *or* maybe they'll win.

Key points

✔ Impersonal verbs and expressions can only be used in the 'it' form, the infinitive and the gerund.

✔ Impersonal verbs are often used when talking about the weather.

The subjunctive

> **What is the subjunctive?**
> The **subjunctive** is a verb form that is often used in Italian to express wishes,
> thoughts and beliefs. In English the subjunctive is only used occasionally, mainly
> in formal language, for example, *If I <u>were</u> you...; So <u>be</u> it; He asked that they <u>be</u>
> removed*.

1 Using the subjunctive

➤ If you have the word **che** (meaning *that*) in an Italian sentence you often have
to use the subjunctive.

➤ The subjunctive is used after **che**:

● following verbs such as **pensare** (meaning *to think*), **credere** (meaning
to believe/think) and **sperare** (meaning *to hope*).

Penso che <u>sia</u> giusto.	I think it's fair.
Credo che <u>partano</u> domani.	I think they're leaving tomorrow.
Spero che Luca <u>arrivi</u> in tempo.	I hope Luca arrives in time.

> *Tip*
> Whereas in English you can say either *I think...* or *I think <u>that</u>...* in Italian you
> <u>always</u> say **che**.

● following the verb **volere** (meaning *to want*).

Voglio che i miei ragazzi <u>siano</u> felici.	I want my children to be happy.
Vuole che la <u>aiuti</u>.	She wants me to help her.

2 How to make the present subjunctive

➤ To make the present subjunctive of most verbs, take off the **–o** ending of the
io form and add endings.

➤ For **–are** verbs the endings are **–i**, **–i**, **–i**, **–iamo**, **–iate**, **–ino**.

➤ For **–ere** and **–ire** verbs the endings are **–a**, **–a**, **–a**, **–iamo**, **–iate**, **–ano**.

ⓘ Note that in the case of **–ire** verbs which add **–isc** in the **io** form, for example
finisco (meaning *I finish*) and **pulisco** (meaning *I clean*), **–isc** is <u>not</u> added in
the **noi** and **voi** forms.

For further explanation of grammatical terms, please see pages viii–xii.

Tip

The **io**, **tu**, **lui** and **lei** forms of the present subjunctive are all the same. The **noi** form of the present subjunctive is the same as the present simple.

➡️ *For more information on the **Present simple**, see page 69.*

➤ The following table shows the present subjunctive of three regular verbs: **parlare** (meaning *to speak*), **credere** (meaning *to believe*) and **finire** (meaning *to finish*).

Infinitive	io, tu, lui, lei, Lei	noi	voi	loro
parlare	parli	parliamo	parliate	parlino
credere	creda	crediamo	crediate	credano
finire	finisca	finiamo	finiate	finiscano

Non voglio che mi <u>parlino</u>.	I don't want them to speak to me.
Può darsi che non ti <u>creda</u>.	Maybe she doesn't believe you.
È meglio che lo <u>finisca</u> io.	It'll be best if I finish it.

➤ Some common verbs that are irregular in the ordinary present tense also have irregular present subjunctives:

Infinitive	io, tu, lui, lei, Lei	noi	voi	loro
andare *to go*	vada	andiamo	andiate	vadano
avere *to have*	abbia	abbiamo	abbiate	abbiano
dare *to give*	dia	diamo	diate	diano
dire *to say*	dica	diciamo	diciate	dicano
dovere *to have to*	debba	dobbiamo	dobbiate	debbano
essere *to be*	sia	siamo	siate	siano
fare *to do/make*	faccia	facciamo	facciate	facciano
potere *to be able*	possa	possiamo	possiate	possano
scegliere *to choose*	scelga	scegliamo	scegliate	scelgano
stare *to be*	stia	stiamo	stiate	stiano
tenere *to hold*	tenga	teniamo	teniate	tengano
tradurre *to translate*	traduca	traduciamo	traduciate	traducano
uscire *to go out*	esca	usciamo	usciate	escano
venire *to come*	venga	veniamo	veniate	vengano
volere *to want*	voglia	vogliamo	vogliate	vogliano

È meglio che tu te ne <u>vada</u>.	You'd better leave.
Vuoi che lo <u>traduca</u>?	Do you want me to translate it?
È facile che <u>scelgano</u> quelli rossi.	They'll probably choose those red ones.
Spero che tua madre <u>stia</u> meglio ora.	I hope your mother is better now.
Credi che <u>possa</u> essere vero?	Do you think it can be true?

> ### Key points
> ✔ When you express a wish, hope, or belief with a verb + **che**, the verb following **che** should be in the subjunctive.
> ✔ **che** cannot be missed out in Italian.

3 | When to use the present subjunctive

➤ Use the present subjunctive when you're saying what you think, feel or hope.

➤ The following are common verbs and expressions used to express opinions and hopes. They are used with **che** followed by the subjunctive:

● **pensare che** to think (that)

Pensano <u>che abbia</u> ragione io.	They think I'm right.
Pensi <u>che sia</u> giusto?	Do you think that's fair?

● **credere che** to believe/think (that)

Crede <u>che sia stata</u> una macchina rossa.	He thinks it was a red car.

● **supporre che** to suppose (that)

Suppongo <u>che</u> quello <u>sia</u> il padre.	I suppose he's the father.

● **sperare che** to hope (that)

Spero <u>che vada</u> bene.	I hope it'll be okay.

● **essere contento che** to be glad (that)

Sono contento <u>che faccia</u> bel tempo.	I'm glad the weather's nice.

● **mi dispiace che** I'm sorry (that)

Mi dispiace <u>che</u> non <u>vengano</u>.	I'm sorry they're not coming.

● **è facile che** it's likely (that)

È facile <u>che piova</u>.	It'll probably rain.

For further explanation of grammatical terms, please see pages viii–xii.

- **può darsi che** it's possible (that)

  Può darsi <u>che</u> non <u>venga</u>.　　　It's possible that he won't come.

- **è un peccato che** it's a pity (that)

  È un peccato <u>che</u> non <u>sia potuto</u> <u>venire</u>.　　　It's a pity he couldn't come.

Tip

It is best to learn the irregular subjunctives of common verbs such as **avere** (meaning *to have*), **essere** (meaning *to be*), **andare** (meaning *to go*) and **fare** (meaning *to make* or *do*).

➤ **che** is not always followed by the subjunctive. Use the ordinary present, future and so on, when you're saying what you know, or are sure of.

  So che <u>è</u> tuo.　　　I know it's yours.
  Sa che <u>vale</u> la pena.　　　She knows it's worth it.
  Sono certo che <u>verrà</u>.　　　I'm sure she'll come.

Key points

✔ Use the present subjunctive + **che** to say what you think, feel or hope.
✔ Do not use the subjunctive + **che** to say what you know or are sure of.

Grammar Extra!

Verbs and verbal expressions that express thoughts and hopes are followed by **di** + the infinitive, instead of **che** + the subjunctive if the subject of the sentence is thinking, hoping or feeling something about themselves.

Compare the following examples: in the sentences on the left side the two verbs have the same subect – I... I... and so on. These use **di** + infinitive. In the sentences on the right the two verbs have different subjects – I... they... and so on. These use **che** + subjunctive.

Infinitive construction	Subjunctive construction
Penso di <u>poter</u> venire.	**Penso che <u>possano</u> venire.**
I think I can come.	I think that <u>they</u> can come.
Credo di <u>aver sbagliato</u>.	**Credo che <u>abbiamo sbagliato</u>.**
I think I've made a mistake.	I think we've made a mistake.
È contenta di <u>essere stata promossa</u>.	**Sono contento che <u>sia stata promossa</u>.**
<u>She</u>'s glad <u>she</u> passed.	I'm glad <u>she</u> passed.
Vi dispiace <u>di partire</u>?	**Ti dispiace che loro <u>partano</u>?**
Are <u>you</u> sorry <u>you</u>'re leaving?	Are <u>you</u> sorry <u>they</u>'re leaving?

4 | Infinitive or subjunctive after volere?

➤ **volere** can be used with either the infinitive <u>or</u> the subjunctive.

➤ As in English, the <u>infinitive</u> is used in Italian to say what you want to do.

Voglio _essere_ felice.	I want <u>to be</u> happy.
Vogliamo _aiutarla_.	We want <u>to help</u> her.

➤ However, when you're saying what you want someone else to do, or how you want something to be, you use **che** followed by the <u>present subjunctive</u>.

Voglio _che_ tutto _sia_ pronto.	I want everything to be ready.
Vuole _che_ tu _faccia_ del tuo meglio.	He wants you to do your best.
Vogliamo _che_ loro _vadano_ via.	We want them to go away.

➤ When you're saying what you wanted someone else to do in the past, or how you wanted something to be, change the present subjunctive to the <u>imperfect subjunctive</u>.

Volevo _che_ tutto _fosse_ pronto.	I wanted everything to be ready.
Voleva _che_ loro _andassero_ via.	She wanted them to go away.

⇨ _For more information on the **Imperfect subjunctive**, see page 136._

Grammar Extra!

The subjunctive is used after certain conjunctions which include **che**:

- **prima che** before
  Vuoi parlargli _prima che parta_? Do you want to speak to him <u>before</u> he goes?

[_i_] Note that **prima di** and the <u>infinitive</u> is used if the two verbs have the same subject:

Mi ha parlato _prima di_ partire.	<u>He</u> spoke to me before <u>he</u> went.
Gli ho parlato _prima di_ partire.	<u>I</u> spoke to him before <u>I</u> went.

- **affinché** so that
  Ti do venti euro _affinché tu possa_ comprarlo. I'll give you twenty euros <u>so that</u> you can buy it.

- **a meno che** unless
  Lo prendo io, _a meno che_ tu lo _voglia_. I'll take it, <u>unless</u> you want it.

- **nel caso che** in case
  Ti do il mio numero di telefono _nel caso che_ tu _venga_ a Roma. I'll give you my phone number <u>in case</u> you come to Rome.

⇨ _For more information on **Conjunctions**, see page 187._

For further explanation of grammatical terms, please see pages viii–xii.

5 | How to make the perfect subjunctive

➤ To make the perfect subjunctive you simply use the subjunctive of **avere** (meaning *to have*) or **essere** (meaning *to be*) with the past participle.

➤ For example, **fare** (meaning *to make* or *to do*) makes its ordinary perfect tense and its perfect subjunctive with **avere**, while **essere** makes its ordinary perfect tense and its perfect subjunctive with **essere**.

➪ For more information on the **Perfect tense** and **Past participles**, see pages 108-109.

		ordinary perfect	perfect subjunctive
fare	io, tu, lui, lei, Lei	ho fatto, hai fatto, ha fatto	abbia fatto
to do/make	noi	abbiamo fatto	abbiamo fatto
	voi	avete fatto	abbiate fatto
	loro	hanno fatto	abbiano fatto
essere	io	sono stato, sono stata	sia stato, sia stata
to be	tu	sei stato, sei stata	sia stato, sia stata
	lui	è stato	sia stato
	lei	è stata	sia stata
	Lei	è stato, è stata	sia stato, sia stata
	noi	siamo stati, siamo state	siamo stati, siamo state
	voi	siete stati, siete state	siate stati, siate state
	loro	sono stati, sono state	siano stati, siano state

Non credo che l'abbiano fatto loro.   I don't think they did it.
È possibile che sia stato un errore.   It might have been a mistake.

6 | When to use the perfect subjunctive

➤ When you want to say what you think or hope about something in the past, use a verb such as **penso che** and **spero che**, followed by the perfect subjunctive.

Penso che sia stata una buona idea.   I think it was a good idea.
Spero che non si sia fatta male.   I hope she didn't hurt herself.
Spero che abbia detto la verità.   I hope you told the truth.
È possibile che abbiano cambiato idea.   It's possible they've changed their minds.

7 | Avoiding the perfect subjunctive

➤ Instead of using expressions such as **penso che** and **è possibile che** with the perfect subjunctive, you can use **secondo me** (meaning *in my opinion*) or **forse** (meaning *perhaps*) with the ordinary perfect tense to say what you think or believe.

Secondo me è stata una buona idea.   In my opinion it was a good idea.
Forse hanno cambiato idea.   Perhaps they've changed their minds.

➪ For more information on the **Perfect tense**, see page 108.

➤ You can also avoid using the perfect subjunctive by saying what you think first, and adding a verb such as **penso**, **credo** or **spero** to the end of the sentence.

Hai detto la verità, <u>spero</u>.	You told the truth, I hope.
Hanno fatto bene, <u>penso</u>.	They did the right thing, I think.

Key points

✔ When you express a wish, hope, or belief about something in the past, the verb following **che** should be in the perfect subjunctive.

✔ You can sometimes reword sentences to avoid using the perfect subjunctive.

---

8 How to make the imperfect subjunctive

➤ The imperfect subjunctive is made by adding endings to the verb <u>stem</u>.

➤ The endings for **–are** verbs are **–assi**, **–assi**, **–asse**, **–assimo**, **–aste**, and **–assero**; the endings for **–ere** verbs are **–essi**, **–essi**, **–esse**, **–essimo**, **–este**, and **–essero**; the endings for **–ire** verbs are **–issi**, **–issi**, **–isse**, **–issimo**, **–iste** and **–issero**.

➤ The following table shows the imperfect subjunctive of three regular verbs: **parlare** (meaning *to speak*), **credere** (meaning *to believe*) and **finire** (meaning *to finish*).

	parlare	credere	finire
(io)	parlassi	credessi	finissi
(tu)	parlassi	credessi	finissi
(lui/lei) (Lei)	parlasse	credesse	finisse
(noi)	parlassimo	credessimo	finissimo
(voi)	parlaste	credeste	finiste
(loro)	parlassero	credessero	finissero

Volevano che <u>parlassi</u> con l'inquilino.	They wanted me to speak to the tenant.
Anche se mi <u>credesse</u>, non farebbe niente.	Even if he believed me he wouldn't do anything.
Se solo <u>finisse</u> prima delle otto!	If only it finished before eight o'clock!

➤ The imperfect subjunctive of **essere** is as follows:

(io)	fossi
(tu)	fossi
(lui/lei)	fosse
(Lei)	fosse
(noi)	fossimo
(voi)	foste
(loro)	fossero

For further explanation of grammatical terms, please see pages viii–xii.

Se <u>fossi</u> in te non lo pagherei. If I were you I wouldn't pay it.

Se <u>fosse</u> più furba verrebbe. If she had more sense she'd come.

➤ The imperfect subjunctive of the other important irregular verbs – **bere** (meaning *to drink*), **dare** (meaning *to give*), **dire** (meaning *to say*), **fare** (meaning *to make* or *to do*) and **stare** (meaning *to be*) – is as follows:

	(io)	(tu)	(lui/lei/Lei)	(noi)	(voi)	(loro)
bere	bevessi	bevessi	bevesse	bevessimo	beveste	bevessero
dare	dessi	dessi	desse	dessimo	deste	dessero
dire	dicessi	dicessi	dicesse	dicessimo	diceste	dicessero
fare	facessi	facessi	facesse	facessimo	faceste	facessero
stare	stessi	stessi	stesse	stessimo	steste	stessero

Se solo <u>bevesse</u> meno! If only he drank less!

Voleva che gli <u>dessero</u> il permesso. He wanted them to give him permission.

9 When to use the imperfect subjunctive

➤ The imperfect subjunctive is used to talk about what you wanted someone to do in the past, or about how you wanted things to be.

Voleva che <u>fossimo</u> pronti alle otto. He wanted us to be ready at eight.

Volevano che tutto <u>fosse</u> in ordine. They wanted everything to be tidy.

Volevo che <u>andasse</u> più veloce. I wanted him to go faster.

➤ In English, when you are talking about what you would do in an imagined situation, the <u>past tense</u> is used to describe the situation, for example, *What would you do if you <u>won</u> the lottery?*

➤ In Italian the <u>imperfect subjunctive</u> is used for this kind of imagined situation, which is often introduced by **se** (meaning *if*).

Se ne <u>avessi</u> bisogno, te lo darei. If you needed it I'd give it to you.

Se lo <u>sapesse</u> sarebbe molto deluso. If he knew he'd be very disappointed.

Se solo <u>avessi</u> più denaro! If only I had more money!

Key points

✔ The imperfect subjunctive is used when talking about what you wanted someone to do, or how you wanted things to be.

✔ The imperfect subjunctive is used to talk about imagined situations.

The Infinitive

> **What is the infinitive?**
> In English the **infinitive** is the basic form of the verb, for example, *walk, see, hear.*
> It is used after other verbs such as *should, must* and *can.* The infinitive is often
> used with *to: to speak, to eat, to live.*

1 Using the infinitive

➤ In English the infinitive may be one word, for example, *speak*, or two words,
for example, *to speak*. In Italian the infinitive is always one word, and is the verb
form that ends in **−are**, **−ere**, or **−ire**, for example, **parlare** (meaning *to speak*),
credere (meaning *to believe*), **finire** (meaning *to finish*). The final **−e** of the infinitive
ending is sometimes dropped.

[i] Note that there are a few verbs with infinitives ending in **−urre**, for example,
tradurre (meaning *to translate*), **produrre** (meaning *to produce*) and **ridurre**
(meaning *to reduce*). **−urre** verbs follow the pattern of **produrre**, which you
can find in the verb tables in the middle section of the book.

➤ The infinitive is the form of the verb shown in dictionaries.

➤ In Italian the infinitive is used in the following ways:

- after adjectives and nouns that are followed by **di**

Sono <u>contento di veder</u>ti.	I'm glad to see you.
Sono <u>sorpreso di veder</u>ti qui.	I'm surprised to see you here.
Sono <u>stufo di studiare</u>.	I'm fed up of studying.
Ho <u>voglia di uscire</u>	I feel like going out.
Non c'è <u>bisogno di</u> prenotare.	There's no need to book.

- after another verb

Non <u>devi andar</u>ci se non vuoi.	You don't have to go if you don't want to.
<u>Posso entrare?</u>	Can I come in?
Cosa ti <u>piacerebbe fare?</u>	What would you like to do?
<u>Preferisce spendere</u> i suoi soldi in vestiti.	He prefers to spend his money on clothes.

- to give instructions and orders, particularly on signs, on forms, and in
  recipes and manuals

<u>Rallentare</u>.	Slow down.
<u>Spingere</u>.	Push.
<u>Scaldare</u> a fuoco lento per cinque minuti.	Heat gently for five minutes.

- to tell someone you call **tu** not to do something

Non fare sciocchezze!   Don't do anything silly!

Non toccarlo!   Don't touch it!

⇨ *For more information on the **Imperative**, see page 82.*

2   Infinitive or gerund?

➤ In English, prepositions such as *before, after* and *without*, are followed by the *-ing* form of the verb, for example, *before leaving, after eating.*

➤ In Italian prepositions are followed by the infinitive.

Prima di aprire il pacchetto,   Before opening the packet, read
leggi le istruzioni.   the instructions.

È andato via **senza dire** niente.   He went away without saying
     anything.

Dopo aver telefonato è uscita.   After making a phone call she went out.

➤ In English the *-ing* form of the verb can be used as a noun, for example, *They enjoy dancing.* In Italian the infinitive, not the gerund, is used as a noun.

Ascoltare la musica è rilassante.   Listening to music is relaxing.

Camminare fa bene.   Walking is good for you.

Tip

Remember to use the infinitive with **mi piace** when saying what activities you like:

Mi piace cavalcare.   I like riding.

Grammar Extra!

As well as the ordinary infinitive there is also the perfect infinitive. In English this is made with the infinitive *have* + the past participle, for example *He could have done better; He claims to have seen an eagle.* In Italian the perfect infinitive is made with **avere** or **essere** + the past participle.

Può **aver avuto** un incidente.   He may have had an accident.

Dev'**essere successo** ieri.   It must have happened yesterday.

Key point

✔ In Italian the infinitive is one word.

3 Linking verbs together

➤ In English both the infinitive and the –ing form can follow after another verb, for example, *Do you <u>want to come</u>?*; *They <u>stopped working</u>*.

➤ In Italian only the infinitive can follow another verb. Verbs are generally linked to the infinitive in one of these three ways:

- directly

  Volete <u>aspettare</u>?   Do you want to wait?

- with the preposition **a**

  Hanno cominciato <u>a ridere</u>.   They started to laugh.

- with the preposition **di**

  Quando sono entrato hanno   When I came in they stopped
  smesso <u>di parlare</u>.   talking.

⇨ *For more information on the **Prepositions a** and **di**, see pages 174 and 176.*

[i] Other linking prepositions are sometimes used, for example, **stare <u>per</u> far qualcosa** (meaning to *be about to do something*).

     Stavo <u>per uscire</u> quando ha   I was about to go out when the
     squillato il telefono.   phone rang.

4 Verbs that are not linked to the infinitive by a preposition

➤ A number of very common verbs are followed directly by the infinitive:

- **dovere** to have to, must

  È dovuto partire.   He had to leave.
  Dev'essere tardi.   It must be late.

- **potere** can, may

  Non <u>posso aiutar</u>ti.   I can't help you.
  <u>Potresti aprire</u> la finestra?   Could you open the window?
  <u>Potrebbe essere</u> vero.   It might be true.

- **sapere** to know how to, can

  <u>Sai farlo</u>?   Do you know how to do it?
  Non <u>sapeva nuotare</u>.   He couldn't swim.

- **volere** to want

  <u>Voglio comprare</u> una macchina nuova.   I want to buy a new car.

> *Tip*
>
> **voler dire** (literally *to want to say*) is the Italian for *to mean*.
>
>   **Non so che cosa vuol dire.**   I don't know what it means.

- verbs such as **piacere**, **dispiacere** and **convenire**

Mi <u>piace andare</u> in bici.	I like cycling.
Ci <u>dispiace andar</u> via.	We're sorry to be leaving.
Ti <u>conviene partire</u> presto.	You'd best set off early.

- **vedere** (meaning *to see*), **ascoltare** (meaning *to listen to*) and **sentire** (meaning *to hear*)

Ci <u>ha visto arrivare</u>.	He saw us arriving.
Ti <u>ho sentito cantare</u>.	I heard you singing.
L'<u>abbiamo ascoltato parlare</u>.	We listened to him talking.

- **fare** (meaning *to make*) and **lasciare** (meaning *to let*)

Non mi <u>far ridere</u>!	Don't make me laugh!
<u>Lascia fare</u> a me.	Let me do it.

[*i*] Note that **far fare qualcosa** and **farsi fare qualcosa** both mean *to have something done*:

<u>Ho fatto riparare</u> la macchina.	I had the car repaired.
Mi <u>sono fatta tagliare</u> i capelli.	I had my hair cut.

➤ The following common verbs are also followed directly by the infinitive:

bisognare	to be necessary
desiderare	to want
odiare	to hate
preferire	to prefer

<u>Odio alzarmi</u> presto al mattino.	I hate getting up early in the morning.
<u>Desiderava migliorare</u> il suo inglese.	He wanted to improve his English.
<u>Bisogna prenotare</u>.	You need to book.
<u>Preferisco</u> non <u>parlarne</u>.	I prefer not to talk about it.

---

5 | Verbs followed by a and the infinitive

➤ Some very common verbs can be followed by **a** and the infinitive:

andare a fare qualcosa	to go to do something
venire a fare qualcosa	to come to do something
imparare a fare qualcosa	to learn to do something
cominciare a fare qualcosa	to start doing or to do something
continuare a fare qualcosa	to go on doing something
abituarsi a fare qualcosa	to get used to doing something
riuscire a fare qualcosa	to manage to do something

Sono venuti <u>a trovarci</u>.	They came to see us.
Siamo riusciti <u>a convincerla</u>.	We managed to persuade her.
Dovrò abituarmi <u>ad alzarmi</u> presto.	I'll have to get used to getting up early.

➤ As in English, you can put an object between the verb and the infinitive:

aiutare <u>qualcuno</u> a fare qualcosa	to help <u>somebody</u> to do something
invitare <u>qualcuno</u> a fare qualcosa	to invite <u>somebody</u> to do something
insegnare <u>a qualcuno</u> a fare qualcosa	to teach <u>somebody</u> to do something

[*i*] Note that **insegnare** takes an indirect object.

<u>Hanno invitato Lucia a sedersi al loro tavolo.</u>	They invited Lucia to sit at their table.
<u>Ho aiutato mamma a lavare</u> i piatti.	I helped mum wash up.
<u>Ha insegnato a mio fratello a nuotare.</u>	He taught my brother to swim.

5 | Verbs followed by di and the infinitive

➤ The following are the most common verbs that can be followed by **di** and the infinitive:

cercare di fare qualcosa	to try to do something
decidere di fare qualcosa	to decide to do something
dimenticare di fare qualcosa	to forget to do something
smettere di fare qualcosa	to stop doing something
ricordarsi di aver fatto qualcosa	to remember having done something
negare di aver fatto qualcosa	to deny doing something

Cerca <u>di</u> smettere di fumare.	He's trying to stop smoking.
Ho deciso <u>di</u> non andarci.	I decided not to go.
Non mi ricordo <u>di</u> aver detto una cosa del genere.	I don't remember saying anything like that.
Ho dimenticato <u>di</u> prendere la chiave.	I forgot to take my key.

> *Tip*
>
> Learn the linking preposition that goes with important verbs.

Key points

✔ Italian verbs can be followed by the infinitive, with or without a linking preposition.

✔ Italian verbs are not followed by the gerund.

Prepositions after verbs

➤ English verbs are often followed by prepositions, for example, *I'm relying <u>on</u> you*, *They'll write <u>to</u> him*, *He was accused <u>of</u> murder*.

➤ The same is true of Italian verbs, which are often followed by prepositions.

- **entrare in** to go into
  Siamo entrati in aula.   We went into the classroom.

➤ As in English, Italian verbs can be followed by two prepositions.

  parlare <u>a</u> qualcuno <u>di</u> qualcosa   to talk <u>to</u> someone <u>about</u> something

➤ With some verbs the Italian preposition may not be the one you would expect. For example, *to* in English is not always **a** in Italian, **di** is not always translated by *of* and so forth. The most important ones of these are shown in the examples on the following pages.

⇨ For more information on **Verbs used with a preposition and the infinitive**, see page 141.

> ### *Tip*
>
> When you learn a new verb, check if there's a preposition that goes with it, and learn that too.

1 Verbs followed by a

➤ **a** is used with the indirect object of verbs such as **dire** (meaning *to say*) and **dare** (meaning *to give*).

dare qualcosa <u>a</u> qualcuno	to give something to someone
dire qualcosa <u>a</u> qualcuno	to say something to someone
mandare qualcosa <u>a</u> qualcuno	to send something to someone
scrivere qualcosa <u>a</u> qualcuno	to write something to someone
mostrare qualcosa <u>a</u> qualcuno	to show something to someone

⇨ For more information about **Indirect objects**, see page 46.

> ### *Tip*
> In English you can say *to give someone something*. In Italian you <u>cannot</u> leave out the preposition – you have to use **a** with the person who is the indirect object.

➤ Here are some verbs taking **a** in Italian when you might not expect it, since the English equivalent either does not have the preposition *to* or has no preposition at all:

arrivare **a** (una citt**à**)	to arrive at (*a town*)
avvicinarsi **a** qualcuno	to approach someone
chiedere qualcosa **a** qualcuno	to ask someone for something
far male **a** qualcuno	to hurt someone
giocare **a** qualcosa	to play something (*game/sport*)
insegnare qualcosa **a** qualcuno	to teach somebody something
partecipare **a** qualcosa	to take part in something
rispondere **a** qualcuno	to answer someone
rivolgersi **a** qualcuno	to ask someone
somigliare **a** qualcuno	to look like someone
permettere **a** qualcuno di fare qualcosa	to allow someone to do something
proibire **a** qualcuno di fare qualcosa	to forbid someone to do something
rubare qualcosa **a** qualcuno	to steal something from someone
ubbidire **a** qualcuno	to obey someone

Chiedi a Lidia come si chiama il suo cane.	Ask Lidia what her dog's called.
Quando arrivi a Londra?	When do you arrive in London?
Parteciperai alla gara?	Are you going to take part in the competition?
Non permette a Luca di uscire.	She doesn't allow Luca to go out.

⇨ *For verbs such as **piacere**, **mancare** and **rincrescere**, see **Verbal idioms** on page 146.*

> ## Tip
> Remember that you often have to use a preposition with an Italian verb when there is no preposition in English.

2 | Verbs followed by di

➤ Here are some verbs taking **di** in Italian when the English verb is not followed by *of*:

accorgersi **di** qualcosa	to realize something
aver bisogno **di** qualcosa	to need something
aver voglia **di** qualcosa	to want something
discutere **di** qualcosa	to discuss something
fidarsi **di** qualcosa/qualcuno	to trust something/someone
intendersi **di** qualcosa	to know about something
interessarsi **di** qualcosa	to be interested in something
lamentarsi **di** qualcosa	to complain about something
ricordarsi **di** qualcosa/qualcuno	to remember something/someone

ridere di qualcosa/qualcuno	to laugh at something/someone
stufarsi di qualcosa/qualcuno	to get fed up with something/someone
stupirsi di qualcosa	to be amazed by something
trattare di qualcosa	to be about something
vantarsi di qualcosa	to boast about something
Non mi fido di lui.	I don't trust him.
Ho bisogno di soldi.	I need money.
Discutono spesso di politica.	They often discuss politics.
Mi sono stufato di loro.	I got fed up with them.

3 Verbs followed by da

➤ Here are some verbs taking **da** in Italian when the English verb is not followed by *from*:

dipendere da qualcosa/qualcuno	to depend on something/someone
giudicare da qualcosa	to judge by something
scendere da qualcosa	to get off something (*bus, train, plane*)
sporgersi da qualcosa	to lean out of something
Dipende dal tempo.	It depends on the weather.

4 Verbs that are followed by a preposition in English but not in Italian

➤ Although the English verb is followed by a preposition, you <u>don't</u> use a preposition with the following Italian verbs:

guardare qualcosa/qualcuno	to look at something/someone
ascoltare qualcosa/qualcuno	to listen to something/someone
cercare qualcosa/qualcuno	to look for something/someone
chiedere qualcosa	to ask for something
aspettare qualcosa/qualcuno	to wait for something/someone
pagare qualcosa	to pay for something
Guarda la sua faccia.	Look at his face.
Mi stai ascoltando?	Are you listening to me?
Sto cercando la chiave.	I'm looking for my key.
Ha chiesto qualcosa da mangiare.	He asked for something to eat.
Aspettami!	Wait for me!
Ho già pagato il biglietto.	I've already paid for my ticket.

Key points

✔ Many Italian verbs are not followed by the preposition you would expect.

✔ There can be a preposition with a verb in Italian, but not in English, and vice versa.

Verbal Idioms

➤ Some important Italian verbs behave differently from their English equivalent, for example:

Mi piace l'Italia.	I like Italy.
Mi piacciono i cani.	I like dogs.

➤ Both English sentences have the same verb *like*, which agrees with the subject, *I*.

➤ The Italian sentences have different verbs, one singular (**piace**) and the other plural (**piacciono**). This is because the verb **piacere** literally means *to be pleasing*, and in one sentence what's pleasing is singular (**l'Italia**) and in the other it's plural (**i cani**).

➤ If you use this wording in English you also get two different verbs: Italy <u>is</u> pleasing to me; Dogs <u>are</u> pleasing to me.

Tip

Remember to turn the sentence around in this way when talking about what you like in Italian.

---

1 Present tense of piacere

➤ When talking about likes and dislikes in the present use **piace** if the subject of the verb is singular, and **piacciono** if it is plural.

➤ Use the appropriate indirect pronoun: **mi**, **ti**, **gli**, **le**, **ci**, or **vi**.

i Note that **gli** means both *to him*, and *to them*, so it is used to say what he likes, and what they like.

Questo colore non mi <u>piace</u>.	I don't like this colour. (*literally: this colour <u>is</u> not pleasing to me*)
Ti <u>piacciono</u> le mie scarpe?	Do you like my shoes? (*literally: <u>are</u> my shoes pleasing to you?*)
Non gli <u>piacciono</u> i dolci.	He doesn't like desserts. (*literally: desserts <u>are</u> not pleasing to him*)
Le <u>piace</u> l'Italia, signora?	Do you like Italy, madam? (*literally: <u>is</u> Italy pleasing to you?*)
Ci <u>piace</u> il mare.	We like the sea. (*literally: the sea <u>is</u> pleasing to us*)

For further explanation of grammatical terms, please see pages viii–xii.

Vi <u>piacciono</u> le montagne?	Do you like the mountains? (*literally: <u>are</u> the mountains pleasing to you?*)
Sono vecchi, non gli <u>piace</u> questa musica.	They're old, they don't like this music. (*literally: this music <u>isn't</u> pleasing to them*)

⇨ *For more information on **Indirect object pronouns**, see page 46.*

> ### Tip
>
> Use the infinitive, not the gerund, when talking about the activities you like:
>
> | | |
> |---|---|
> | **Mi piace cucinare.** | I like cooking. |
> | **Ci piace camminare.** | We like walking. |

➤ If it is not used with the pronouns **mi**, **ti**, **gli**, **le**, **ci**, or **vi**, **piacere** is followed by the preposition **a**.

Il giardinaggio piace <u>a</u> mia sorella.	My sister likes gardening. (*literally: gardening is pleasing to my sister*)
I suoi film non piacciono <u>a</u> tutti.	Not everyone likes his films. (*literally: his films are not pleasing to everyone*)
L'Italia piace <u>ai</u> tuoi?	Do your parents like Italy? (*literally: Is Italy pleasing to your parents?*)

2 Other tenses of piacere

➤ You can use **piacere** in any tense.

Credi che la casa <u>piacerà</u> a Sara?	Do you think Sara will like the house?
Questo libro ti <u>piacerebbe</u>.	You'd like this book.
Da giovane gli <u>piaceva</u> nuotare.	When he was young he liked swimming.
Il concerto <u>è piaciuto</u> a tutti.	Everyone liked the concert.
Non credo che il calcio <u>piaccia</u> al professore.	I don't think the teacher likes football.

> ### Tip
>
> **Mi dispiace** means *I'm sorry*. Change the pronoun to **gli**, **le**, **ci** and so on if you want to say *He's sorry*, *She's sorry* or *We're sorry*.

3 | Other verbs like piacere

➤ There are a number of other important verbs that are used with an indirect pronoun, or are followed by the preposition **a**.

➤ As with **piacere**, the person who is the subject of the verb in English is the indirect object in Italian.

- **convenire** (*literally*) to be advisable

Ti conviene partir presto.	You'd better set off early.
Non conviene a nessuno fare così.	Nobody should behave like that.

- **mancare** (*literally*) to be missing

Fammi sapere se ti manca qualcosa.	Let me know if you need anything.
Mi manchi.	I miss you.

- **interessare** to be of interest

Se ti interessa puoi venire.	If you're interested you can come.
Pensi che interesserebbe a Luigi?	Do you think Luigi would be interested?

- **importare** to be important

Non mi importa!	I don't care!
Non importa a mio marito.	My husband doesn't care.

- **rincrescere** (*literally*) to make sorry

Ci rincresce di non poterlo fare.	We're sorry we can't do it.
Se non ti rincresce vorrei pensarci su.	If you don't mind I'd like to think it over.

- **restare** to be left

Mi restano cinquanta euro.	I've got fifty euros left.
A Maria restano solo ricordi.	Maria only has memories left.

Key points

✔ Turn the sentence around when using verbs like **piacere**.

✔ Use the preposition **a**, or an indirect object pronoun.

Negatives

What is a negative?
A negative question or statement is one which contains a word such as *not*, *never* or *nothing*: *He's not here; I never eat meat; She's doing nothing about it.*

1 non

➤ The Italian word **non** (meaning *not*) is the one you need to make a statement or a question negative:

Non posso venire.	I can't come.
Non hai la chiave?	Haven't you got the key?
Giuliana **non** abita qui.	Giuliana doesn't live here.

➤ In English *not* or *n't* comes <u>after</u> verbs. In Italian **non** comes <u>in front of</u> verbs.

Non è qui.	It's not here.
Non è venuta.	She didn't come.
I miei **non hanno** la macchina.	My parents haven't got a car.
Lei **non è** molto alta.	She's not very tall.

➤ In English we sometimes make sentences negative by adding *don't, doesn't* or *didn't* before the main verb, but in Italian you always just add **non** to the verb.

Positive		**Negative**	
Lavorano.	They work.	**Non lavorano.**	They don't work.
Lo vuole.	He wants it.	**Non lo vuole.**	He doesn't want it.

> ### Típ
> NEVER use the verb **fare** to translate *don't, doesn't* or *didn't* in negatives.

➤ If there are words such as **mi**, **ti**, **lo**, **la**, **ci**, **vi**, **li** or **le** in front of the verb, **non** goes immediately <u>in front of</u> them.

Non l'ho visto.	I didn't see it.
Non mi piace il calcio.	I don't like football.

➤ If you have a phrase consisting of *not* with another word or phrase, such as *not now*, or *not yet*, use **non** before the other word.

non adesso	not now
non ancora	not yet
non sempre	not always
non dopo sabato	not after Saturday

➤ BUT, if you want to be more emphatic, or to make a contrast, use **no** instead of **non**, and put it <u>after</u> the other word.

> **Sempre no, qualche volta.**   Not ALWAYS, but sometimes.

➤ You use **no** instead of **non** in certain phrases:

● In the phrase **o no** (meaning *or not*)

> **Vieni <u>o no</u>?**   Are you coming or not?
> **che gli piaccia <u>o no</u>**   whether he likes it or not

● In the phrase **di no** after some verbs:

> **Credo <u>di no</u>.**   I don't think so.
> **Spero <u>di no</u>.**   I hope not.
> **Ha detto <u>di no</u>.**   He said not.

2 Other negative phrases

➤ In English you only use one negative word in a sentence: *I haven't ever seen him*. In Italian you use **non** followed by another negative word such as **niente** (meaning *nothing*), or **mai**, (meaning *never*).

> **<u>Non</u> succede <u>mai</u>.**   It never happens.
> **<u>Non</u> ha detto <u>niente</u>.**   She didn't say anything.

➤ The following are the most common phrases of this kind.

● **non ... mai**   never or not ever

> **<u>Non</u> la vedo <u>mai</u>.**   I never see her.

> *Tip*
>
> You put **mai** between the two parts of the perfect tense.
>
> > **Non l'<u>ho mai vista</u>.**   I've never seen her.
> > **Non ci <u>siamo mai stati</u>.**   We've never been there.

● **non ... niente**   nothing or not ...anything

> **<u>Non</u> hanno fatto <u>niente</u>.**   They didn't do anything.

● **non ... nessuno**   nobody or not ... anybody

> **<u>Non</u> ho visto <u>nessuno</u>.**   I didn't see anybody.

● **non ... da nessuna parte**   nowhere or not ... anywhere

> **<u>Non</u> riuscivo a trovarlo <u>da nessuna parte</u>.**   I couldn't find it anywhere.

For further explanation of grammatical terms, please see pages viii–xii.

- **non ... nessuno/nessuna** + *noun*   no *or* not ... any

  Non c'è <u>nessun</u> bisogno di andare.   There's no need to go. *or*
  There isn't any need to go.

- **non ... più**   no longer *or* not ... any more

  Non escono <u>più</u> insieme.   They're not going out together any more.

- **non ...né ... né ...**   neither ... nor

  Non verranno <u>né</u> Chiara <u>né</u> Donatella.   Neither Chiara nor Donatella are coming.

➤ If you <u>begin</u> a sentence with a negative word such as **nessuno** or **niente**, do not use **non** with the verb that comes after it.

    <u>Nessuno</u> è venuto.   Nobody came.
    <u>Niente</u> è cambiato.   Nothing has changed.
    BUT
    Non è venuto nessuno.
    Non è cambiato niente.

➤ In Italian you can have more than one negative word following a negative verb.

    Non fanno <u>mai niente</u>.   They never do anything.
    Non si confida <u>mai</u> con <u>nessuno</u>.   He never confides in anyone.

➤ As in English, negative words can be used on their own to answer a question.

    Cos'hai comprato? – <u>Niente</u>.   What did you buy? – Nothing.
    Chi ti accompagna? – <u>Nessuno</u>.   Who's going with you? – Nobody.

Key points

✔ To make a verb negative put **non** in front of it.
✔ Unlike English, in Italian it is good grammar to follow **non** with another negative word.

QUESTIONS

What is a question?
A **question** is a sentence which is used to ask someone about something and which often has the verb in front of the subject.

Different types of questions

➤ Some questions can be answered by <u>yes</u> or <u>no</u>. They are sometimes called <u>yes/no questions</u>. When you ask this type of question your voice goes up at the end of the sentence.

> Is it raining?
> Do you like olives?
> You're leaving tomorrow?

➤ Other questions begin with <u>question words</u> such as *why*, *where* and *when* and have to be answered with specific information.

> Why are you late?
> Where have you been?
> When did they leave?

1 How to ask yes/no questions in Italian

➤ If you are expecting the answer *yes* or *no*, make your voice go up at the end of the question.

> ### Tip
>
> In Italian you can turn an adjective or a verb into a question simply by making your voice go up on the last syllable.
>
> | | |
> |---|---|
> | **Basta?** | Is that enough? |
> | **Piove?** | Is it raining? |
> | **Chiaro?** | Is that clear? |
> | **Buono?** | Is it nice? |

➤ If you are asking about a person, place or thing using a noun, put the noun at the <u>end</u> of the question.

> **È partita <u>tua sorella</u>?**   Has your sister gone?
> **È bella <u>la Calabria</u>?**   Is Calabria beautiful?
> **Sono <u>buoni gli spaghetti</u>?**   Is the spaghetti nice?

➤ If the English question has a pronoun such as *you, they* or *he* in it, you:

- keep to normal word order
- don't translate the pronoun into Italian unless you want to stress it

> **Parlano italiano?**   Do they speak Italian?
> **Ha francobolli?**   Have you got stamps?
> **È caro?**   Is it expensive?
> **C'è tempo?**   Is there time?
> **Fa l'avvocato?**   Is he a lawyer?
> **Va bene?**   Is that okay?

➤ If you do want to stress *you, he, they* and so on, use a pronoun in Italian, and put it at the <u>end</u> of the sentence.

> **Parla italiano <u>Lei</u>?**   Do <u>you</u> speak Italian?
> **Viene anche <u>lui</u>?**   Is <u>he</u> coming too?
> **L'hanno fatto <u>loro</u>?**   Did <u>they</u> do it?

⇨ *For more information on **Pronouns**, see page 40.*

---

2   How to answer yes/no questions

➤ In English you can answer questions simply by saying *yes* or *no*. If this doesn't seem quite enough you add a short phrase, using the verb that starts the question.

> <u>Do</u> you speak Italian?   Yes, I <u>do</u>.
> <u>Can</u> he swim?   Yes, he <u>can</u>.
> <u>Have</u> you been to Rome?   No, I <u>haven't</u>.
> <u>Are</u> they leaving now?   No, they'<u>re</u> not.

➤ In Italian you can very often answer just with **sì** or **no**.

> **Stai bene? – <u>Sì</u>.**   Are you okay? – Yes.
> **Ti piace? – <u>No</u>.**   Do you like it? – No.

➤ If you don't want to answer this sort of question with a definite *yes* or *no* you can use phrases such as:

> **Penso di sì.**   I think so.
> **Spero di sì.**   I hope so.
> **Credo di no.**   I don't think so.
> **Spero di no.**   I hope not.

➤ If you want to answer more fully you have to repeat the verb that's in the Italian question.

<u>Sai</u> nuotare? – Sì, <u>so</u> nuotare.	Can you swim? – Yes, I can (swim).
<u>Piove</u>? – Sì, <u>piove</u>.	Is it raining? – Yes, it's raining OR Yes, it is.
<u>Capisci</u>? – No, non <u>capisco</u>.	Do you understand? – No, I don't (understand).

ℹ️ Note that there is no Italian equivalent for answers using short phrases such as *Yes, I do; No, I don't; No, they haven't.*

Key points

✔ Make your voice go up at the end of questions.

✔ Put nouns and stressed pronouns at the end of the question.

✔ If you want to answer more fully, repeat the verb that is used in the question.

Question words

1 How to ask questions using question words

➤ The following are common question words which never change their form:

- **dove?** where?

  Dove abiti?   Where do you live?

- **come?** how?

  Come si fa?   How do you do it?

ⓘ Note that **come** can be translated by *what?* when it is used to mean *pardon?*

  Scusi, come ha detto?   Sorry, what did you say?

- **quando?** when

  Quando parti?   When are you leaving?

- **perché?** why

  Perché non vieni?   Why don't you come?

ⓘ Note that **perché** also means *because*.

  Lo mangio perché ho fame.   I'm eating it because I'm hungry.

- **chi?** who?

  Chi è?   Who is it?
  Chi sono?   Who are they?

- **che?** what?

  Che giorno è oggi?   What day is it today?

- **cosa?** what?

  Cosa vuoi?   What do you want?

- **che cosa?** what?

  Che cosa fanno?   What are they doing?

➪ *For more information on **Conjunctions**, see page 187.*

> ## Tip
>
> Remember to shorten **che cosa** (meaning *what*) and **come** (meaning *how, what*) to **che cos'** and **com'** when they are followed by a vowel.
>
> **Che cos'è?**   What is it?
> **Com'è successo?**   How did it happen?

➤ Some question words do sometimes change their form.

➤ You can use **quale** to ask for precise information about people or things. It has a plural form **quali**, and a singular form **qual** which is used in front of a vowel:

- Use **quale** with a singular noun when you want to ask *which* or *what*.

Per <u>quale</u> motivo?	For what reason?
<u>Quale</u> stanza preferisci?	Which room do you prefer?

- Use the singular form **qual** when the next word starts with a vowel.

<u>Qual</u> è il tuo colore preferito?	What's your favourite colour?
<u>Qual</u> è la tua camera?	Which is your room?

- Use **quali** with plural nouns.

<u>Quali</u> programmi hai?	What plans have you got?
<u>Quali</u> sono i tuoi sport preferiti?	Which are your favourite sports?

- Use **quale** by itself when you want to ask *which one*.

<u>Quale</u> vuoi?	Which one would you like?

- Use **quali** by itself when you want to ask *which ones*.

<u>Quali</u> sono i migliori?	Which ones are the best?

➤ You can use **quanto** or the feminine form **quanta** to ask *how much*:

- Use **quanto** by itself to ask *how much?*

<u>Quanto</u> costa?	How much does it cost?
<u>Quanta</u> ne vuoi?	How much do you want?

- Use **quanto** as an adjective with masculine nouns and **quanta** with feminine nouns.

<u>Quanto</u> tempo hai?	How much time have you got?
<u>Quanta</u> stoffa ti serve?	How much material do you need?

➤ Use **quanti** to ask *how many*. Use **quanti** as an adjective with masculine nouns and **quante** with feminine nouns.

<u>Quanti</u> ne vuoi?	How many do you want?
<u>Quanti</u> giorni?	How many days?
<u>Quante</u> notti?	How many nights?

⇨ *For more information on **Adjectives**, see page 20.*

ℹ️ Note that some very common questions do not start with the Italian question word you might expect.

<u>Quanti</u> anni hai?	How old are you?
<u>Come</u> si chiama?	What's he called?
<u>Com'è</u>?	What's it like?

2 How to answer questions which use question words

➤ If someone asks you a question such as **Chi è?** or **Quanto costa?**, you answer using the same verb.

Chi è? – È Giulia.	Who's that? – That's Giulia.
Quanto costa? – Costa molto.	How much does it cost? – It costs a lot.

➤ When you don't know the answer you say **Non lo so**, or **Non so** followed by the original question.

Chi è? – Non lo so.	Who's that? – I don't know.
Non so chi è.	I don't know who it is.
Quanto costa? – Non lo so.	How much does it cost? – I don't know.
Non so quanto costa.	I don't know how much it costs.

Grammar Extra!

The question word *what* can be either a <u>pronoun</u> or an <u>adjective</u>. In the sentence *What do you want?* it's a <u>pronoun</u> and you can use **che**, **cosa**, or **che cosa** to translate it.

When *what* is an <u>adjective</u>, and is used with a noun, for example *What day is it today?* you translate it by **che**, and NOT by **cosa**, or **che cosa**.

Che giorno è?   What day is it?

ⓘ Note that when *what?* means *pardon?* it is translated by **come**?

⇨ For more information on **Adjectives** and **Pronouns**, see pages 20 and 40.

---

3 Where does the question word come in the sentence?

➤ In English, question words like *who*, *what*, *where* and *when* nearly always come at the beginning of the sentence.

<u>Who</u> are you?
<u>Who</u> does it belong to?
<u>Where</u> do you come from?
<u>What</u> do you think?

➤ Italian question words often come first in the sentence, but this is by no means always the case. Here are some exceptions:

● If you want to emphasize the person or thing you are asking about, you can put a noun or pronoun first.

Tu chi sei?	Who are <u>you</u>?
Lei cosa dice?	What do <u>you</u> think?
La mia borsa dov'è?	Where's <u>my bag</u>?

- If there is a preposition such as *with*, *for*, *from* or *to* at the end of the English question, you <u>MUST</u> put the Italian preposition at the start of the question.

<u>Di</u> dove sei?	Where do you come <u>from</u>?
<u>Con</u> chi parlavi?	Who were you talking <u>to</u>?
<u>A</u> che cosa serve?	What's it <u>for</u>?

i Note that when you ask someone what time they do something, the question starts with **a che ora**.

<u>A che ora</u> ti alzi?	What time do you get up?

⇨ *For more information on **Prepositions**, see page 172.*

- When you are asking about the colour, make, or type of something you must start the question with **di**.

<u>Di</u> che colore è?	What colour is it?
<u>Di</u> che marca è?	What make is it?

- When you are asking who owns something start the question in Italian with **di**.

<u>Di</u> chi è questa borsa?	Whose bag is this?
<u>Di</u> chi sono quelle scarpe rosse?	Who do those red shoes belong to?

Key points

✔ Most question words don't change their form.

✔ Question words do not always come first in Italian questions.

✔ If there is a preposition in the Italian question you MUST put it first.

---

4 | Questions which end with question phrases

➤ In English you add a question phrase (like <u>aren't you?</u>, <u>isn't it?</u>, <u>didn't I</u> and so on) to the end of a sentence to check that an idea you have is true. You expect the person you're speaking to will agree by saying *yes* (or *no*, if your idea is negative).

> This is the house, isn't it?
>
> You won't tell anyone, will you?

➤ In Italian, when you expect someone to say *yes* to your idea, you put either **no**, or **vero** at the end of the sentence and make your voice go up as you say the word.

Mi scriverai, <u>no</u>?	You'll write to me, won't you?
Vieni anche tu, <u>no</u>?	You're coming too, aren't you?
Hai finito, <u>no</u>?	You've finished, haven't you?

Questa è la tua macchina, <u>vero</u>?	This is your car, isn't it?
Ti piace la cioccolata, <u>vero</u>?	You like chocolate, don't you?

➤ When you expect someone to agree with you by saying *no*, use **vero** only.

Non sono partiti, <u>vero</u>?	They haven't gone, have they?
Non fa molto male, <u>vero</u>?	It doesn't hurt much, does it?

Grammar Extra!

Questions such as *Where are you going?* and *Why did he do that?* are <u>direct questions</u>.

Sometimes this type of question is phrased in a more roundabout way, for example:

Tell me where you are going.

Would you mind telling me where you are going?

Can you tell me why he did that?

I'd like to know why he did that.

I wonder why he did that.

This type of question is called an <u>indirect question</u>. It is very simple to ask indirect questions in Italian: you simply add a phrase to the beginning of the direct question, for example, you could add **Può dirmi** (meaning *Can you tell me*) to the question **Dove va?** (meaning *where are you going?*).

Può dirmi dove va?	Can you tell me where you're going?

The following are other phrases that introduce an indirect question:

Dimmi...	Tell me...
Vorrei sapere...	I'd like to know...
Mi domando...	I wonder...
Non capisco...	I don't understand...
<u>**Dimmi**</u> **perché l'hai fatto.**	Tell me why you did it.
<u>**Vorrei sapere**</u> **quanto costa.**	I'd like to know how much it costs.
<u>**Mi domando**</u> **cosa pensano.**	I wonder what they think.
<u>**Non capisco**</u> **che vuol dire.**	I don't understand what it means.

Adverbs

What is an adverb?
An **adverb** is a word used with verbs to give information on where, when or how an action takes place, for example, *here, today, quickly*. An adverb can also add information to adjectives and other adverbs, for example, *extremely quick, very quickly*.

How adverbs are used

➤ You use adverbs:
- with verbs: *He's never there; She smiled happily*.
- with adjectives: *She's rather ill; I feel a lot happier*.
- with other adverbs: *He drives really slowly; I'm very well*.

➤ Adverbs are also used at the start of a sentence to give an idea of what the speaker is thinking or feeling.

Luckily, nobody was hurt.
Surprisingly, he made no objection.

How to form adverbs

1 The basics

➤ In English you can make an adverb from the adjective *slow* by adding *–ly*. You can do a similar kind of thing in Italian.

➤ Here are some guidelines:
- if the adjective ends in **–o** in the masculine, take the feminine form, ending in **–a**, and add **–mente**

Masculine adjective	Feminine adjective	Adverb	Meaning
lento	lenta	lentamente	slowly
fortunato	fortunata	fortunatamente	luckily

Cammina molto lentamente.   He walks very slowly.
Fortunatamente non ha piovuto.   Luckily, it didn't rain.

For further explanation of grammatical terms, please see pages viii–xii.

- if the adjective ends in **-e** for both masculine and feminine, just add **-mente**

Adjective	Adverb	Meaning
veloce	velocemente	quickly, fast
corrente	correntemente	fluently

Parla corrent<u>emente</u> l'italiano.   She speaks Italian fluently.

- if the adjective ends in **-le**, or **-re**, you drop the final **e** before adding **-mente**

Adjective	Adverb	Meaning
facile	facilmente	easily
particolare	particolarmente	particularly

Puoi farlo <u>facilmente</u>.   You can easily do it.
Non è <u>particolarmente</u> buono.   It's not particularly nice.

> *Tip*
>
> Don't try to make adverbs agree with anything – they always keep the same form.

2 Irregular adverbs

➤ In Italian there are two kinds of adverbs which do not behave in the way just described. They are:

- adverbs which are completely different from the adjective
- adverbs which are exactly the same as the masculine adjective

➤ The adverb related to **buono** (meaning *good*) is **bene** (meaning *well*). The adverb related to **cattivo** (meaning *bad*) is **male** (meaning *badly*).

Parlano <u>bene</u> l'italiano.   They speak Italian well.
Ho giocato <u>male</u>.   I played badly.

➤ Words such as *fast* and *hard* can be both adjectives and adverbs:

a <u>fast</u> car
You're driving too <u>fast</u>.
a <u>hard</u> question
He works very <u>hard</u>.

➤ The same kind of thing happens in Italian: some adverbs are the same as the masculine adjective. The following are the most common ones:

- **chiaro** (adjective: *clear*; adverb: *clearly*)

Il significato è <u>chiaro</u>.   The meaning is clear.
Giulia parla <u>chiaro</u>.   Giulia speaks clearly.

- **giusto** (adjective: *right*, *correct*; adverb: *correctly*, *right*)

il momento <u>giusto</u>.	the right moment.
Marco ha risposto <u>giusto</u>.	Marco answered correctly.

- **vicino** (adjective: *near*, *close*; adverb: *nearby*, *near here*)

È molto <u>vicino</u>.	He's very close.
I miei amici abitano <u>vicino</u>.	My friends live nearby.
C'è una piscina <u>vicino</u>?	Is there a swimming pool near here?

- **diritto** (adjective: *straight*; adverb: *straight on*)

Il bordo non è <u>diritto</u>.	The edge is not straight.
Siamo andati sempre <u>diritto</u>.	We kept straight on.

- **certo** (adjective: *sure*, *certain*; adverb: *of course*)

Non ne sono <u>certo</u>.	I'm not sure.
Vieni stasera? – <u>Certo</u>!	Are you coming this evening? – Of course!

- **solo** (adjective: *alone*, *lonely*; adverb: *only*)

Si sente <u>solo</u>.	He feels lonely.
L'ho incontrata <u>solo</u> due volte.	I've only met her twice.

- **forte** (adjective: *strong*, *hard*; adverb: *fast*, *hard*)

È più <u>forte</u> di me.	He's stronger than me.
Correva <u>forte</u>.	He was running fast.

- **molto** (adjective: *a lot of*; adverb: *a lot*, *very*, *very much*)

Non hanno <u>molto</u> denaro.	They haven't got a lot of money.
Quel quadro mi piace <u>molto</u>.	I like that picture a lot.

- **poco** (adjective: *little*, *not very much*; adverb *not very much*, *not very*)

Hai mangiato poco riso.	You haven't eaten very much rice.
Viene in ufficio <u>poco</u> spesso.	She doesn't come to the office very often.

> 📋 Note that although these adverbs look like adjectives, they NEVER change their form.

Key points

✔ You generally make adverbs by adding **–mente** to adjectives.

✔ Adverbs never agree with anything.

✔ Some adverbs have the same form as the masculine adjective.

Making comparisons using adverbs

➤ In English, there are two major ways of comparing things using an adverb.

- To express the idea of 'more' or 'less' you either put **–er** on the end of the adverb, or *more* or *less* in front of it: *earlier, sooner, more/less* often. This way of comparing things is called the comparative.

- To express the idea of 'the most' or 'the least' you either put **–est** on the end, or *most* or *least* in front of it: *earliest, soonest, most/least* often. This way of comparing things is called the superlative.

1 | Comparatives and superlatives of adverbs

➤ In Italian you make comparisons expressing the idea of 'more' or 'less' by putting **più** (meaning *more*) and **meno** (meaning *less*) in front of the adverb.

più spesso	more often
più lentamente	more slowly
meno velocemente	less quickly

➤ You use **di** to say *than*.

Correva più forte di me.	He was running faster than me.
Viene meno spesso di lui.	She comes less often than he does.
Luca parla più correttamente l'inglese di me.	Luca speaks English more correctly than I do.
Ha agito più prudentemente di me.	She's acted more sensibly than I have.
Loro lavorano più sodo di prima.	They work harder than before.

➤ In Italian you can make comparisons expressing the idea of 'the most' or 'the least' by putting **più** (meaning *more*) or **meno** (meaning *less*) in front of the adverb and by putting **di tutti** (meaning *of all*) after it.

Cammina più piano di tutti.	She walks the slowest (of all).
L'ha fatto meno volentieri di tutti.	He did it the least willingly.
Mia madre ci veniva più spesso di tutti.	My mother came most often.

⤷ For more information on **Adjectives** see page 20.

2 | Irregular comparatives and superlatives of adverbs

➤ Some very common Italian adverbs have irregular comparatives and superlatives. Here are the commonest ones.

Adverb	Meaning	Comparative	Meaning	Superlative	Meaning
bene	well	**meglio**	better	**meglio di tutti**	best (of all)
male	badly	**peggio**	worse	**peggio di tutti**	worst (of all)
molto	a lot	**più**	more	**più di tutti**	most (of all)
poco	not much	**meno**	less	**meno di tutti**	least (of all)

Loro hanno giocato meglio di noi.	They played better than us.
Si sono comportati peggio del solito.	They behaved worse than usual.
Ho speso più di dieci sterline.	I spent more than ten pounds.
Andrea ha giocato meglio di tutti.	Andrea played best of all.

3 | più di..., meno di...: di più, di meno

➤ These are very common phrases, meaning *more* and *less*, which are used in rather different ways.

- You use **più di** and **meno di** to say *more than* and *less than* when comparing things where you would use *than* in English.

Paolo le piace più di Marco.	She likes Paolo more than Marco.
Leggo meno di te.	I read less than you.
Non guadagna più di me.	He doesn't earn more than I do.
Pesa meno di Luca.	He weighs less than Luca.

- If there is no *than* in the sentence in English use **di più** and **di meno**.

Costa di più.	It costs more.
Quello mi piace di meno.	I like that one less.
Ho speso di meno.	I spent less.

- **di più** and **di meno** are also used to mean *most* and *least*.

la cosa che temeva di più	the thing she feared most
quello che mi piace di meno	the one I like least
Sono quelli che guadagnano di meno.	They're the ones who earn least.

Grammar Extra!

To say that something is getting *better and better, worse and worse, slower and slower*, and so on, use **sempre** with the comparative adverb.

Le cose vanno sempre meglio.	Things are going better and better.
Mio nonno sta sempre peggio.	My grandfather's getting worse and worse.
Cammina sempre più lento.	He's walking slower and slower.

Key points

✔ To express the idea of 'more' and 'most' with adverbs use **più**.

✔ To express the idea of 'less' and 'least' use **meno**.

✔ Use **di** to mean 'than'.

Some common adverbs

1 Adverbs to use in everyday conversation

➤ Just as in English, you can often answer a question simply by using an adverb.

Vieni alla festa? – <u>Forse</u>.	Are you coming to the party? – <u>Maybe</u>.
Deve proprio partire? –	Do you really have to go? –
Sì, <u>purtroppo</u>.	Yes, <u>unfortunately</u>.

➤ The following are particularly useful adverbs:

- **ecco** here

<u>Ecco</u> l'*autobus*!	Here's the bus!
<u>Ecco</u> la sua birra!	Here's your beer!

i Note that you can say **ecco** (meaning *here you are*) when you hand somebody something. **Ecco** combines with the pronouns **lo**, **la**, **li** and **le** to mean *Here she is*, *Here they are* and so forth:

Dov'è Carla? – <u>Eccola</u>!	Where's Carla? – Here she is!
Non vedo i libri – Ah, <u>eccoli</u>!	I can't see the books – Oh, here they are!
<u>Eccolo</u>!	Here he is!

- **anche** too

È venuta <u>anche</u> mia sorella.	My sister came too.

- **certo** certainly, of course

<u>Certo</u> che puoi.	Of course you can.
<u>Certo</u> che sì.	Certainly.

- **così** so, like this, like that

È <u>così</u> simp*a*tica!	She's so nice!
Si apre <u>così</u>.	It opens like this.
Non si fa <u>così</u>.	You don't do it like that.

- **davvero** really

È successo <u>davvero</u>.	It really happened.

- **forse** perhaps, maybe

<u>Forse</u> hanno ragione.	Maybe they're right.

- **proprio** really

Sono <u>proprio</u> stanca.	I'm really tired.

- **purtroppo** unfortunately

<u>Purtroppo</u> non posso venire.	Unfortunately I can't come.

For further explanation of grammatical terms, please see pages viii–xii.

> **Tip**
> These adverbs are such common words that it's a good idea to learn as many as possible.

2 | Adverbs that tell you HOW MUCH

➤ **molto**, **poco**, **troppo** and **tanto** are used with adjectives, verbs and other adverbs;

- Use **molto** to mean *very* or *very much*.

Sono <u>molto</u> stanca.	I'm very tired.
Ti piace? – Sì, <u>molto</u>.	Do you like it? – Yes, very much.
Ora mi sento <u>molto</u> meglio.	I feel much better now.

- Use **poco** to mean *not very* or *not very much*.

Questa mela è <u>poco</u> buona.	This apple isn't very nice.
Mi piacciono <u>poco</u>.	I don't like them very much.
Ci vado <u>poco</u> spesso.	I don't go there very often.

- Use **tanto** to mean *so* or *so much*.

Questo libro è <u>tanto</u> noioso.	This book is so boring.
Tu mi manchi <u>tanto</u>.	I miss you so much.
Mi sento <u>tanto</u> meglio.	I feel so much better.

- Use **troppo** to mean *too* or *too much*.

È <u>troppo</u> caro.	It's too expensive.
Parlano <u>troppo</u>.	They talk too much.
Le sei? È <u>troppo</u> presto.	Six o'clock? That's too early.

> Note that **molto**, **poco**, **troppo** and **tanto** can also be used as adjectives. When you use them as adverbs they do NOT agree with anything.

3 | Adverbs that tell you TO WHAT EXTENT

- **abbastanza** quite, enough

È <u>abbastanza</u> alta.	She's quite tall.
Non studia <u>abbastanza</u>.	He doesn't study enough.

- **appena** just, only just

L'ho <u>appena</u> fatto.	I've just done it.
L'indirizzo ere <u>appena</u> leggibile.	The address was only just legible.

- **piuttosto** quite, rather
  Fa <u>piuttosto</u> caldo oggi.   It's quite warm today.
  È <u>piuttosto</u> lontano.   It's rather a long way.

- **quasi** nearly
  Sono <u>quasi</u> pronta.   I'm nearly ready.
  Hanno <u>quasi</u> finito.   They've nearly finished.

4   Adverbs that tell you WHEN

- **adesso** now
  Non posso farlo <u>adesso</u>.   I can't do it now.

- **ancora** still, yet
  Sei <u>ancora</u> a letto?   Are you still in bed?
  Silvia non è <u>ancora</u> arrivata.   Silvia's not here yet.

- **domani** tomorrow
  Ci vediamo <u>domani</u>.   See you tomorrow.

- **dopo** after, later
  Ci vediamo <u>dopo</u>.   See you later.

- **già** already
  Te l'ho <u>già</u> detto.   I've already told you.

- **ieri** yesterday
  <u>Ieri</u> ha piovuto molto.   It rained a lot yesterday.

- **mai** never, ever
  Non sono <u>mai</u> stato in America.   I've never been to America.
  Sei <u>mai</u> stato in America?   Have you ever been to America?

- **oggi** today
  <u>Oggi</u> andiamo al mare.   We're going to the seaside today.

- **ora** now
  <u>Ora</u> cosa facciamo?   What are we going to do now?

- **poi** then
  E <u>poi</u> che cos'è successo?   And then what happened?

- **presto** soon, early
  Arriverà <u>presto</u>.   He'll be here soon.
  Mi alzo sempre <u>presto</u>.   I always get up early.

- **prima** before
  <u>Prima</u> non lo sapevo. — I didn't know that before.

- **spesso** often
  Vanno <u>spesso</u> in centro. — They often go into town.

- **subito** at once
  Fallo <u>subito</u>! — Do it at once.

- **tardi** late
  Oggi mi sono alzata <u>tardi</u>. — I got up late today.

5 Adverbs that tell you WHERE

- **là** there
  Vieni via di <u>là</u>. — Come away from there.

- **laggiù** down there, over there
  È <u>laggiù</u> da qualche parte. — It's down there somewhere.
  È apparso <u>laggiù</u> in lontananza. — It appeared over there in the distance.

- **lassù** up there
  un paesino <u>lassù</u> in montagna — a little village up there in the mountains

- **lì** there
  Mettilo <u>lì</u>. — Put it there.

- **qua** here
  Eccomi <u>qua</u>! — I'm here!

- **qui** here
  Vieni <u>qui</u>. — Come here.

[i] Note that **lì** has an accent to distinguish it from the pronoun **li** (meaning *them*) and **là** has an accent to distinguish it from **la** (meaning *the, her* or *it*).

⇨ *For more information on* **Articles** *and* **Pronouns**, *see pages 10 and 40.*

- **ci** there
  <u>Ci</u> sei mai stato? — Have you ever been there?

- **dappertutto** everywhere
  Ho cercato <u>dappertutto</u>. — I looked everywhere.

- **lontano** a long way away
  Abita <u>lontano</u>. — He lives a long way away.

- **sotto** underneath, downstairs
  Porta una giacca con una maglietta <u>sotto</u>. — He's wearing a jacket with a t-shirt underneath.
  Il bagno è <u>sotto</u>. — The bathroom is downstairs.

- **sopra** up, on top

qui <u>sopra</u>	up here
Il dizionario è <u>sopra</u> quella pila di libri.	The dictionary is on top of that pile of books.

- **fuori** outside

Ti aspetto <u>fuori</u>.	I'll wait for you outside.

- **dentro** inside

Vai <u>dentro</u>.	Go inside.

- **indietro** back

Torniamo <u>indietro</u>.	Let's turn back.

- **davanti** at the front

Voglio sedermi <u>davanti</u>.	I want to sit at the front.

6 | Adverbs consisting of more than one word

➤ In English you sometimes use a phrase instead of a single word to give information about time, place and so on, and the same is true in Italian.

- **una volta** once

<u>una volta</u> la settimana	once a week

- **due volte** twice

Ho provato <u>due volte</u>.	I tried twice.

- **molte volte** many times

L'ho fatto <u>molte volte</u>.	I've done it many times.

- **da qualche parte** somewhere

Ho lasciato le chiavi <u>da qualche parte</u>.	I've left my keys somewhere.

- **qualche volta** sometimes

<u>Qualche volta</u> arriva in ritardo.	She sometimes arrives late.

- **di solito** usually

<u>Di solito</u> arrivo prima.	I usually get here earlier.

Where to put adverbs

1 Adverbs with verbs

➤ You normally put adverbs immediately after the verb.

Non posso farlo <u>adesso</u>.	I can't do it now.
Parli <u>bene</u> l'italiano.	You speak Italian well.
Non torno <u>più</u>.	I'm not coming back.

➤ If you want to emphasize the adverb you can put it at the beginning of the sentence.

<u>Ora</u> non posso.	I can't do it just now.
<u>Prima</u> non lo sapevo.	I didn't know that before.

> ### Tip
> In English adverbs can come between the subject and the verb:
> It <u>often</u> changes. Adverbs can NEVER come in this position in Italian.
>
> | | |
> |---|---|
> | **Marco viene sempre.** | Marco always comes. |
> | **Di solito vince Jessica.** | Jessica usually wins. |

➤ When you are using adverbs such as **mai** (meaning *never*), **sempre** (meaning *always*), **già** (meaning *already*), **più** (meaning *again*) and **appena** (meaning *just*) with verbs in the perfect tense, you put the adverb between the two parts of the verb:

Non sono <u>mai</u> stata a Milano.	I've never been to Milan.
È <u>sempre</u> venuto con me.	He always came with me.
L'ho <u>già</u> letto.	I've already read it.

⇨ *For more information on the **Perfect tense**, see page 108.*

2 Adverbs with adjectives and adverbs

➤ Put the adverb in front of the adjective or other adverb, as you do in English.

Fa <u>troppo</u> freddo.	It's too cold.
Vai <u>più</u> piano.	Go more slowly.

Key points

✔ Some adverbs are very common in Italian, and it's a good idea to learn as many as possible.

✔ You usually put adverbs after the verb.

✔ If you want to emphasize the adverb, you put it at the beginning of the sentence.

✔ Adverbs go before adjectives or other adverbs.

Prepositions

> **What is a preposition?**
> **A preposition** is one word such as *at*, *for*, *with*, *into* or *from*, or words such as *in front of* or *near to*, which are usually followed by a noun or a pronoun.
>
> Prepositions show how people and things relate to the rest of the sentence, for example, *She's at home; It's for you; You'll get into trouble; It's in front of you.*

Using prepositions

1 Where they go

➤ Prepositions are used in front of nouns and pronouns to show the relationship between the noun or pronoun and the rest of the sentence.

Andiamo a Roma.	We're going to Rome.
Vieni con me.	Come with me.

➤ In English you can separate a preposition from its noun or pronoun and put it at the end of a question, or at the end of part of a sentence, for example, *Who were you talking to?; the people I came with.*

➤ In Italian prepositions <u>always</u> go in front of another word and <u>never</u> at the end of a question or part of a sentence:

Con chi sei venuto?	Who did you come with?
la ragazza alla quale ho dato la chiave	the girl I gave the key to

2 Which preposition to use

➤ In English certain adjectives and verbs are always followed by particular prepositions, for example, *happy with, afraid of, talk to, smile at*. The same is true in Italian.

Sono deluso del voto che ho preso.	I'm disappointed with the mark I got.
Andiamo in Italia.	We're going to Italy.

i Note that when a preposition is used in front of the *-ing* form in English, a preposition is used in front of the <u>infinitive</u> (the **-re** form of the verb) in Italian.

È andato via senza salutarci.	He went away without saying goodbye to us.
Sono stufo di studiare.	I'm fed up of studying.

For further explanation of grammatical terms, please see pages viii–xii.

➤ The prepositions used in Italian may not be what you expect, for example, the Italian preposition **in** is used for both the following:

I miei sono <u>in</u> Italia.	My parents are <u>in</u> Italy.
I miei vanno <u>in</u> Italia.	My parents are going <u>to</u> Italy.

➤ You sometimes need to use a preposition in Italian when there is no preposition in English.

Hai bisogno <u>di</u> qualcosa?	Do you need anything?
Chiedi <u>a</u> Lidia cosa vuole.	Ask Lidia what she wants.

⇨ *For more information on **Prepositions after verbs**, see page 143.*

> ## Tip
>
> When you look up a verb in the dictionary, take note of any preposition that is shown with the translation.
>
> | | |
> |---|---|
> | **congratularsi <u>con</u>** | to congratulate |
> | **dire qualcosa <u>a</u> qualcuno** | to tell someone something |

---

3 | Prepositions that combine with the definite article

➤ When the prepositions **a**, **di**, **da**, **in** and **su** are followed by the <u>definite article</u> – **il**, **la**, **i**, **le** and so on, they combine with it to make one word.

	+ il	+ lo	+ la	+ l'	+ i	+ gli	+ le
a	al	allo	alla	all'	ai	agli	alle
di	del	dello	della	dell'	dei	degli	delle
da	dal	dallo	dalla	dall'	dai	dagli	dalle
in	nel	nello	nella	nell'	nei	negli	nelle
su	sul	sullo	sulla	sull'	sui	sugli	sulle

⇨ *For more information on **Articles**, see page 10.*

Si guardava <u>allo</u> specchio.	He was looking at himself <u>in the</u> mirror.
la cima <u>del</u> monte	the top <u>of the</u> mountain
Sto <u>dai</u> miei.	I live <u>with</u> my parents.
Cos'hai <u>nella</u> tasca?	What have you got <u>in</u> your pocket?
I soldi sono <u>sul</u> tavolo.	The money's <u>on the</u> table.

Key points

✔ Italian prepositions are always used in front of another word.

✔ The preposition used in Italian may not be what you expect.

✔ Italian prepositions combine with the definite article to make one word.

a, di, da, in, su and per

1 a

➤ **a** is used with nouns to tell you <u>where</u>.

<u>alla</u> porta	<u>at</u> the door
<u>al</u> sole	<u>in</u> the sun
<u>all'</u>ombra	<u>in</u> the shade
Vivo <u>al</u> terzo piano.	I live <u>on</u> the third floor.
È <u>a</u> letto.	He's <u>in</u> bed.
<u>alla</u> radio	<u>on</u> the radio
<u>alla</u> tivù	<u>on</u> TV

➤ Use **a** to mean *to* when you're talking about <u>going to a place</u>.

Andiamo <u>al</u> cinema?	Shall we go <u>to</u> the cinema?
Sei mai stato <u>a</u> New York?	Have you ever been <u>to</u> New York?

(i) Note that if the place is a country, use **in** in Italian.

Andrò **in** Germania quest'estate.	I'm going <u>to</u> Germany this summer.

➤ Use **a** to mean *at* when you're talking about <u>being at a place</u>.

Devo essere <u>all'</u>aeroporto alle dieci.	I've got to be <u>at</u> the airport at ten.
Scendo <u>alla</u> prossima fermata.	I'm getting off <u>at</u> the next stop.
Luigi è <u>a</u> casa.	Luigi is <u>at</u> home.

➤ Use **a** to mean *in* when you're talking about being <u>in a town</u>.

Abitano <u>a</u> Bologna.	They live <u>in</u> Bologna.

(i) Note that if the place is a country, use **in** in Italian.

Vivo **in** Scozia.	I live <u>in</u> Scotland.
Vive **in** Canada.	He lives <u>in</u> Canada.

➤ Use **a** to mean *away* when you're talking about distances.

<u>a</u> tre chilometri da qui	three kilometres <u>away</u> from here
<u>a</u> due ore di distanza in macchina	two hours <u>away</u> by car

(i) Note that *away* can be left out of this kind of phrase, but **a** has to be used in Italian.

L'albergo è <u>ad</u> un chilometro dalla spiaggia.	The hotel is a kilometre from the beach.

➤ **a** is used with nouns to tell you <u>when</u>.

<u>a</u> volte	<u>at</u> times
<u>a</u> tempo	<u>on</u> time
<u>alla</u> fine	<u>in</u> the end

For further explanation of grammatical terms, please see pages viii–xii.

➤ Use **a** to mean *at* with <u>times and festivals</u>.

<u>alle</u> cinque	<u>at</u> five o'clock
<u>a</u> mezzogiorno	<u>at</u> midday
<u>al</u> fine settimana	<u>at</u> the weekend
<u>a</u> Pasqua	<u>at</u> Easter
<u>a</u> Natale	<u>at</u> Christmas

Tip

Remember that questions beginning *What time ...* must start with the preposition **a** in Italian.

<u>A</u> che ora parti? What time are you leaving?

• Use **a** with <u>months</u> to mean *in*.

Sono nata <u>a</u> maggio. I was born <u>in</u> May.

➤ **a** is used with nouns to tell you <u>how</u>.

<u>a</u> piedi	<u>on</u> foot
<u>a</u> mano	<u>by</u> hand
<u>a</u> poco <u>a</u> poco	little <u>by</u> little

• Use **a** with <u>flavours</u>.

un gelato <u>alla</u> fragola	a strawberry ice cream
una torta <u>al</u> cioccolato	a chocolate cake
gli spaghetti <u>al</u> pomodoro	spaghetti with tomato sauce

➤ **a** is used with <u>nouns and pronouns</u> after some verbs.

L'ho dato <u>a</u> Selene.	I gave it to Selene.
Piace <u>a</u> me, ma <u>a</u> mia sorella no.	I like it, but my sister doesn't.
<u>A</u> che cosa stai pensando?	What are you thinking about?

➭ *For more information on **Prepositions after verbs**, see page 143.*

📖 Note that the unstressed pronouns **mi**, **ti**, **gli**, **le**, **ci** and **vi** come in front of the verb and are not used with **a**.

Ti ha parlato?	Did she speak to you?
Gliel'ho dato.	I gave it to her.
Mi piace.	I like it.

➭ *For more information on **Indirect pronouns**, see page 46.*

➤ **a** is used with the <u>infinitive</u> (the **–re** form of the verb) to say what your purpose is.

Sono uscita <u>a</u> fare due passi.	I went out for a little walk.
Sono andati <u>a</u> fare il bagno.	They've gone to have a swim.

2 di

➤ **di** is used to talk about who or what something belongs to.

il nome <u>del</u> ristorante	the name of the restaurant
il capitano <u>della</u> squadra	the captain of the team
È <u>di</u> Marco.	It belongs to Marco.
<u>Di</u> chi è?	Whose is it?

➤ Use **di** to refer to the person who made something.

un quadro <u>di</u> Picasso	a picture <u>by</u> Picasso
una commedia <u>di</u> Shakespeare	a play <u>by</u> Shakespeare
un film <u>di</u> Fellini	a Fellini film

➤ In English, ownership can be shown by using a noun with '*s*, or *s'* added to it, for example the *child's name, the boys' teacher*. In Italian you change the word order and use **di** to translate this sort of phrase.

la macchina <u>di</u> mia madre	my mother's car
	(*literally: the car of my mother*)
la casa <u>dei</u> miei amici	my friends' house
l'Otello di Verdi	Verdi's Othello

➪ *For more information on **Possessive adjectives** and **Possessive pronouns**, see pages 34 and 52.*

➤ In English, when there is a connection between two things, one noun can be used in front of another, for example the *car* keys, the *bathroom* window. In Italian you change the word order and use **di** to translate this sort of phrase.

il tavolo <u>della</u> cucina	the kitchen table
il periodo <u>delle</u> vacanze	the holiday season
il professore <u>di</u> inglese	the English teacher
il campione <u>del</u> mondo	the world champion

➤ When a noun such as *cotton, silver, paper* is used as an adjective, use **di** in Italian.

una maglietta <u>di</u> cotone	a cotton T-shirt
una collana <u>d'</u>argento	a silver necklace
dei tovaglioli <u>di</u> carta	paper napkins

➤ **di** sometimes means *from*.

È <u>di</u> Firenze.	He's <u>from</u> Florence.
<u>Di</u> dove sei?	Where are you <u>from</u>?

➤ **di** is used to say what something contains or what it is made of.

un gruppo <u>di</u> studenti	a group <u>of</u> students
un bicchiere <u>di</u> vino	a glass <u>of</u> wine
È fatto <u>di</u> plastica.	It's made <u>of</u> plastic.

➤ **di** is used after **milione** (meaning *million*), and words for approximate numbers, such as **un migliaio** (meaning *about a thousand*) and **una ventina** (meaning *about twenty*).

un milione **di** dollari	a million dollars
un migliaio **di** persone	about a thousand people
una ventina **di** macchine	about twenty cars

➤ **di** is used after certain verbs and adjectives.

Ti ricordi **di** Laura?	Do you remember Laura?
Sto tentando **di** concentrarmi.	I'm trying to concentrate.
Le arance sono ricche **di** vitamina C.	Oranges are rich in vitamin C.
Era pieno **di** gente.	It was full of people.

➰ *For more information on **Prepositions after verbs** and **Adjectives**, see pages 143 and 20.*

Tip

Remember that some verbs are single words in English, but in Italian they are phrases ending with **di**, for example, **aver bisogno di** (meaning *to need*) and **aver voglia di** (meaning *to want*).

Non <u>ho bisogno di</u> niente.	I don't <u>need</u> anything.
Non <u>ho voglia di</u> andare a letto.	I don't <u>want</u> to go to bed.

➤ **di** is used with nouns to say <u>when</u>.

di domenica	<u>on</u> Sundays
di notte	<u>at</u> night
di giorno	<u>during</u> the day

➤ Use **di** to mean *in* with seasons and parts of the day.

d'estate	<u>in</u> summer
d'inverno	<u>in</u> winter

ⓘ Note that **in** can also be used with seasons, for example, **in estate** (meaning *in summer*).

di mattina	<u>in</u> the morning
di sera	<u>in</u> the evening

➤ **di** is used in comparisons to mean *than*.

È più alto **di** me.	He's taller <u>than</u> me.
È più brava **di** lui.	She's better <u>than</u> him.

➤ Use **di** to mean *in* after a superlative.

il più grande **del** mondo	the biggest <u>in</u> the world
la più brava **della** classe	the best <u>in</u> the class
il migliore **d'**Italia	the best <u>in</u> Italy

➰ *For more information on **Superlatives**, see page 27.*

> **Tip**
>
> **È più bravo di tutti** and **è più brava di tutti** are ways of saying
> *He's the best* and *She's the best*.

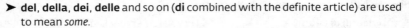

➤ **del**, **della**, **dei**, **delle** and so on (**di** combined with the definite article) are used
to mean *some*.

C'era <u>della</u> gente che aspettava.	There were <u>some</u> people waiting.
Vuoi <u>dei</u> biscotti?	Would you like <u>some</u> biscuits?

➤ **di** is used with the <u>infinitive</u> (the **–re** form of the verb) when it is used as a noun.

Ho paura <u>di</u> volare.	I'm afraid of flying.
Non ho voglia <u>di</u> mangiare.	I don't feel like eating.

3 | <u>da</u>

➤ **da** is used with places to mean *from*.

a tre chilometri <u>da</u> qui	three kilometres <u>from</u> here.
Viene <u>da</u> Roma.	He comes <u>from</u> Rome.

➤ Use **da** to talk about getting, jumping or falling <u>off</u> something, or getting or falling
<u>out of</u> something.

Chiara è scesa <u>dal</u> treno.	Chiara got <u>off</u> the train.
Il vaso è cascato <u>dal</u> terrazzo.	The plant pot fell <u>off</u> the balcony.
Il gatto è saltato <u>dal</u> muro.	The cat jumped <u>off</u> the wall.
È scesa <u>dalla</u> macchina.	She got <u>out of</u> the car.
Sono cascato <u>dal</u> letto.	I fell <u>out of</u> bed.

ℹ Note that **da ... a...** means *from ... to...*

<u>da</u> cima <u>a</u> fondo	<u>from</u> top <u>to</u> bottom
<u>dalle</u> otto <u>alle</u> dieci	<u>from</u> eight <u>to</u> ten

➤ Use **da** with **andare** to say you're going <u>to</u> a shop, or <u>to</u> someone's house or
workplace.

<u>Vado dal</u> giornalaio.	I'm going <u>to</u> the paper shop.
È <u>andato dal</u> dentista.	He's gone <u>to</u> the dentist's.
<u>Andiamo da</u> Gabriele?	Shall we go <u>to</u> Gabriele's house?

➤ Use **da** with *essere* to say you're <u>at</u> a shop, or <u>at</u> someone's house or workplace.

Laura è <u>dal</u> parucchiere.	Laura's <u>at</u> the hairdresser's.
Sono <u>da</u> Anna.	I'm <u>at</u> Anna's house.

For further explanation of grammatical terms, please see pages viii–xii.

➤ **da** is used to talk about <u>how long</u> something has been happening.

- Use **da** with periods of time to mean *for*.

  Vivo qui <u>da</u> un anno.　　　　　I've been living here <u>for</u> a year.

- Use **da** with points in time to mean *since*.

  <u>da</u> allora　　　　　<u>since</u> then
  Ti aspetto <u>dalle</u> tre.　　　　　I've been waiting for you <u>since</u> three o'clock.

> [i] Note that the present tense is used in Italian to talk about what has been happening for a period, or since a certain time.
>
>　　**È a Londra <u>da</u> martedì.**　　　　　He's been in London <u>since</u> Tuesday.

⇨ *For more information on the **Present tense**, see page 69.*

➤ **da** is used with passive verbs to mean *by*.

　　dipinto <u>da</u> un grande artista　　　painted <u>by</u> a great artist
　　I ladri sono stati catturati <u>dalla</u> polizia.　　The thieves were caught <u>by</u> the police.

⇨ *For more information on the **Passive**, see page 119.*

➤ **da** is used with the <u>infinitive</u> (the **–re** form of the verb) when you're talking about things to do.

　　C'è molto <u>da</u> fare.　　　　　There's lots to do.
　　È un film <u>da</u> vedere.　　　　　It's a film that you've got to see.
　　Non c'è niente <u>da</u> mangiare.　　There's nothing to eat.
　　E <u>da</u> bere?　　　　　And what would you like to drink?

➤ In English you can say what something is used for by putting one noun in front of another, for example a <u>racing</u> car, an <u>evening</u> dress. In Italian change the word order and use **da**.

　　un nuovo paio di scarpe <u>da</u> corsa　　a new pair of running shoes
　　Paolo non ha il costume <u>da</u> bagno.　　Paolo hasn't got his swimming trunks.

➤ **da** is used when describing someone or something.

　　una ragazza <u>dagli</u> occhi azzurri　　a girl with blue eyes
　　un vestito <u>da</u> cento euro　　a dress costing a hundred euros

➤ **da** is used with nouns to mean *as*.

　　<u>Da</u> bambino avevo paura del buio.　　<u>As</u> a child I was afraid of the dark.

4 | in

➤ Use **in** with **essere** to mean *in* when you are talking about where someone or something is – except in the case of towns.

Vive in Canada.	He lives in Canada.
È nel cassetto.	It's in the drawer.

i Note that in the case of towns you use **a** in Italian.

Abitano a Bologna.	They live in Bologna.

> ### Tip
> You don't use **in** with adverbs such as **qui** (meaning *here*) and **lì** (meaning *there*).
>
> | qui dentro | in here |
> |---|---|
> | lì dentro | in there |

➤ Use **in** with **andare** to mean *to* when you're talking about where someone or something is going *to*, except in the case of towns.

Andrò in Germania quest'estate.	I'm going to Germany this summer.
È andato in ufficio.	He's gone to the office.

i Note that in the case of towns you use **a** in Italian.

Sei mai stato a New York?	Have you ever been to New York?

> ### Tip
> **essere in vacanza** means *to be on holiday*, **andare in vacanza** means *to go on holiday*.

➤ Use **in** to mean *into* when you're talking about getting into something, or putting something into something.

Su, sali in macchina.	Come on, get into the car.
Come sono penetrati in banca?	How did they get into the bank?
L'ha gettato in acqua.	He threw it into the water.

i Note that **in** is also used with verbs such as **dividere** (meaning *to divide*) and **tagliare** (meaning *to cut*).

L'ha tagliato in due.	She cut it into two.

➪ *For more information on **Prepositions after verbs**, see page 143.*

➤ Use **in** to mean *in* with years, seasons and months.

nel duemilasedici	in two thousand and sixteen
in estate	in summer
in ottobre	in October

For further explanation of grammatical terms, please see pages viii–xii.

ⓘ Note that you can also use **di** with seasons (**d'estate**) and **a** with months (**ad ottobre**).

➤ **in** is used with periods of time to mean *in*.

L'ha fatto <u>in</u> sei mesi.	He did it <u>in</u> six months.
Puoi finirlo <u>in</u> trenta minuti.	You can finish it <u>in</u> thirty minutes.

➤ **in** is used with modes of transport to mean *by*.

Siamo andati <u>in</u> treno.	We went <u>by</u> train.
È meglio andare <u>in</u> bici.	It's better to go <u>by</u> bike.

➤ **in** is used to say <u>how</u> something is done.

Camminavano <u>in</u> silenzio.	They walked in silence.
È scritto <u>in</u> tedesco.	It's written in German.

5 | <u>su</u>

➤ Use **su** to mean *on*.

Il tuo telefonino è <u>sul</u> pavimento.	Your mobile phone is <u>on</u> the floor.
Mettilo <u>sulla</u> sedia.	Put it <u>on</u> the chair.
È <u>sulla</u> sinistra.	It's <u>on</u> the left.

ⓘ Note that **sul giornale** means *in the newspaper*.

L'ho letto <u>sul</u> giornale.	I read it in the newspaper.

> ## *Tip*
>
> **qui su** and **qua su** mean *up here*. **là** combines with **su** to make one word with a double s: **lassù** (meaning *up there*).
>
> | | |
> |---|---|
> | **Siamo <u>qui su</u>.** | We're <u>up here</u>. |
> | **Eccoli <u>lassù</u>.** | They're <u>up there</u>. |

➤ **su** is used with topics to mean *about*.

un libro <u>sugli</u> animali	a book <u>about</u> animals

➤ **su** is used with numbers:

- to talk about ratios

in tre casi <u>su</u> dieci	in three cases <u>out of</u> ten
due giorni <u>su</u> tre	two days <u>out of</u> three

- with an article and a number to indicate an approximate amount

È costato <u>sui</u> cinquecento euro.	It cost <u>around</u> five hundred euros.
È <u>sulla</u> trentina.	She's <u>about</u> thirty.

6 | per

➤ **per** often means *for*.

Questo è per te.	This is <u>for</u> you.
È troppo difficile per lui.	It's too difficult <u>for</u> him.
L'ho comprato per trenta euro.	I bought it <u>for</u> thirty euros.
Ho guidato per trecento chilometri.	I drove <u>for</u> three hundred kilometres.

[i] Note that when you are talking about how long you <u>have been doing</u> something you use **da**.

Aspetto da un pezzo.	I've been waiting for a while.

➤ **per** is used with destinations.

il volo per Londra	the flight <u>to</u> London
il treno per Roma	the train <u>to</u> Rome

➤ **per** is used with verbs of movement to mean *through*.

I ladri sono entrati per la finestra.	The burglars got in <u>through</u> the window.
Siamo passati per Birmingham.	We went <u>through</u> Birmingham.

➤ **per** is used to indicate how something is transported or communicated.

per posta	<u>by</u> post
per via aerea	<u>by</u> airmail
per email	<u>by</u> email
per ferrovia	<u>by</u> rail
per telefono	<u>by</u> *or* <u>on</u> the phone

[i] Note that **per** is NOT used when referring to means of transport for people, **in** is used instead.

<u>in</u> **macchina**	<u>by</u> car

➤ **per** is used to explain the reason for something.

L'ho fatto per aiutarti.	I did it to help you.
L'abbiamo fatto per ridere.	We did it for a laugh.
Ci sono andato per abitudine.	I went out of habit.
Non l'ho fatto per pigrizia.	I didn't do it out of laziness.
È successo per errore.	It happened by mistake.

➤ **per** is used in some very common phrases.

uno per uno	one by one
giorno per giorno	day by day
una per volta	one at a time
due per tre	two times three

Some other common prepositions

1 One- word and two-word prepositions

➤ As in English, Italian prepositions can be one word or consist of more than one word, for example **vicino a** (meaning *near*) and **prima di** (meaning *before*).

The following are some of the commonest prepositions in Italian:

- **prima di** before, until

prima di me	before me
prima delle sette	before seven o'clock
Non sarà pronto prima delle otto.	It won't be ready until eight o'clock.

> **Tip**
>
> When a preposition includes **a** or **di** remember to combine these words with definite articles such as **il**, **la** and **le**.

i Note that **prima di**, like many other Italian prepositions, can be used in front of an infinitive (the **–re** form of the verb).

Dobbiamo informarci prima di cominciare.	We need to find out before starting *or* before we start.

- **dopo** after

Ci vediamo dopo le vacanze.	See you after the holidays.
Dopo aver mandato messaggino ha spento il telefonino.	After sending *or* after she'd sent the text she switched off the phone.

i Note that **dopo di** is used with pronouns.

Loro sono arrivati dopo di noi.	They arrived after us.

➪ *For more information on **Pronouns**, see page 40.*

- **fino a** until, as far as

Resto fino a venerdì.	I'm staying until Friday.
Vengo con te fino alla posta.	I'll come with you as far as the post office.

i Note that **Fino a quando?** (meaning literally *until when*) is used to ask *How long?*

Fino a quando puoi rimanere?	How long can you stay?

> **Tip**
>
> When a preposition includes **a** or **di** remember to combine these words with definite articles such as **il**, **la** and **le**.

- **fra** in, between, among

Torno <u>fra</u> un'ora.	I'll be back <u>in</u> an hour.
Era seduto <u>fra</u> il padre e lo zio.	He was sitting <u>between</u> his father and his uncle.
<u>Fra</u> i sopravvissuti c'era anche il pilota.	The pilot was <u>among</u> the survivors.

[i] Note that **fra di** is used with pronouns.

<u>Fra di noi</u> ci sono alcuni mancini.	There are some left-handers <u>among us</u>.

⇨ *For more information on **Pronouns**, see page 40.*

> ### Tip
>
> **fra poco** means *in a short time*, or *soon*.
>
> | | |
> |---|---|
> | Lo sapremo <u>fra poco</u>. | We'll <u>soon</u> know. |

- **tra** is an alternative form of **fra**, and can be used in exactly the same way

<u>tra</u> un'ora	<u>in</u> an hour
<u>tra</u> poco	soon
<u>tra</u> il padre e lo zio	<u>between</u> his father and his uncle
<u>tra</u> i feriti	<u>among</u> the injured

- **durante** during

<u>durante</u> la notte	<u>during</u> the night

- **con** with, to

Ci andrò <u>con</u> lei.	I'll go <u>with</u> her.
Hai parlato <u>con</u> lui?	Have you spoken <u>to</u> him?

- **senza** without

Esci <u>senza</u> cappotto?	Are you going out <u>without</u> a coat?

[i] Note that **senza di** is used with pronouns.

Non posso vivere <u>senza di lui</u>.	I can't live <u>without him</u>.

⇨ *For more information on **Pronouns**, see page 40.*

- **contro** against

Sono <u>contro</u> la caccia.	I'm <u>against</u> hunting.

[i] Note that **contro di** is used with pronouns.

Non ho niente <u>contro di lui</u>.	I've got nothing <u>against him</u>.

- **davanti a** in front of, opposite

  Era seduta <u>davanti a</u> me nell'aereo. She was sitting <u>in front of</u> me in the plane.

  la casa <u>davanti alla</u> mia the house <u>opposite</u> mine

> ### Tip
> When a preposition includes **a** or **di** remember to combine these words with definite articles such as **il**, **la** and **le**.

- **dietro** behind

  <u>dietro</u> la porta <u>behind</u> the door

[i] Note that **dietro di** is used with pronouns.

  Sono seduti <u>dietro di</u> me. They're sitting <u>behind me.</u>

⇨ *For more information on **Pronouns**, see page 40.*

- **sotto** under, below

  Il gatto si è nascosto <u>sotto</u> il letto. The cat hid <u>under</u> the bed.
  cinque gradi <u>sotto</u> zero five degrees <u>below</u> zero

- **sopra** over, above, on top of

  le donne <u>sopra</u> i sessant'anni women <u>over</u> sixty
  cento metri <u>sopra</u> il livello del mare a hundred metres <u>above</u> sea level
  <u>sopra</u> l'armadio <u>on top of</u> the cupboard

- **accanto a** next to

  Siediti <u>accanto a</u> me. Sit <u>next to</u> me.

> ### Tip
> When a preposition includes **a** or **di** remember to combine these words with definite articles such as **il**, **la** and **le**.

- **verso** towards, around

  Correva <u>verso</u> l'uscita. He was running <u>towards</u> the exit.
  Arriverò <u>verso</u> le sette. I'll arrive <u>around</u> seven.

[i] Note that **verso di** is used with pronouns.

  Correvano <u>verso di</u> lui. They were running <u>towards him.</u>

⇨ *For more information on **Pronouns**, see page 40.*

- **a causa di** because of

  L'aeroporto è chiuso <u>a causa della</u> nebbia. The airport is closed <u>because of</u> fog.

- **malgrado** in spite of

  Malgrado tutto siamo ancora amici.

  We're still friends <u>in spite of</u> everything.

2 Preposition or adverb?

➤ In English some words can be used both as <u>adverbs</u>, which describe verbs, and as <u>prepositions</u>, which go in front of nouns and pronouns.

➤ The word *before* is an <u>adverb</u> in the sentence *We've met before* and a <u>preposition</u> in the phrase *before dinner*.

⇨ *For more information on **Adverbs**, see page 160.*

➤ In Italian you <u>don't</u> usually use exactly the same word as both an adverb and a preposition:

- **prima** and **davanti** are <u>adverbs</u>

  Perché non me l'hai detto <u>prima</u>?

  Why didn't you tell me <u>before</u>?

  la casa <u>davanti</u>

  the house <u>opposite</u>.

- **prima di** and **davanti a** are <u>prepositions</u>

  Ne ho bisogno <u>prima di</u> giovedì.

  I need it <u>before</u> Thursday.

  Ero seduto <u>davanti a</u> lui a cena.

  I was sitting <u>opposite</u> him at dinner.

Key points

✔ **dopo**, **senza**, **fra**, **dietro**, **contro**, **verso** are used without **di**, except when followed by a pronoun.

✔ Italian prepositions often have **di** or **a** as their second element; Italian adverbs are not followed by **di** or **a**.

Conjunctions

> **What is a conjunction?**
> A **conjunction** is a word such as *and, but, or, so, if* and *because*, that links two words or phrases, or two parts of a sentence, for example, *Diane <u>and</u> I have been friends for years; I left <u>because</u> I was bored.*

e, ma, anche, o, perché, che and se

➤ These common Italian conjunctions correspond to common English conjunctions, such as *and* and *but*. However they are sometimes used differently from their English counterparts, for example, **Ma no!** (literally, *But no!*) means *No!*, or *Of course not!*

➤ Shown below are the common Italian conjunctions **e**, **anche**, **o**, **ma**, **perché**, **che** and **se** and how they are used:

- **e** and, but, what about

io <u>e</u> Giovanni	Giovanni <u>and</u> I
tu <u>ed</u> io	you <u>and</u> me
Lo credevo simpatico <u>e</u> non lo è.	I thought he was nice, <u>but</u> he isn't.
Io non ci vado, <u>e</u> tu?	I'm not going, <u>what about</u> you?

[*i*] Note that you use **di** or **a**, not the conjunction **e**, to translate *try <u>and</u>, go <u>and</u>* and so on.

Cerca <u>di</u> capire!	Try and understand!
Vado <u>a</u> vedere.	I'll go and see.

⇨ *For more information on **di** and **a**, see page 174.*

- **ma** but

strano <u>ma</u> vero	strange <u>but</u> true
Dice così, <u>ma</u> non ci credo.	That's what he says, <u>but</u> I don't believe it.

[*i*] Note that **ma** is used for emphasis with **sì** and **no**.

Ti dispiace? – <u>Ma</u> no!	Do you mind? – <u>Of course</u> not.
Non ti piace? – <u>Ma</u> sì!	Don't you like it? – Yes <u>of course</u> I do.

- **anche** also, too, even

Parla tedesco e <u>anche</u> francese.	She speaks German and <u>also</u> French.
Ho fame. – <u>Anch'</u>io!	I'm hungry. – Me <u>too</u>!
Lo saprebbe fare <u>anche</u> un bambino.	<u>Even</u> a child could do it.

- **o** or

due <u>o</u> tre volte	two <u>or</u> three times

> ## Tip
>
> **oppure** is another word for *or*. It is used to join two parts of a sentence when you're talking about alternatives.
>
> **Possiamo guardare la TV oppure ascoltare musica.**   We can watch TV or listen to music.

- **perché** because
  Non posso uscire perché ho molto da fare.   I can't go out because I've got a lot to do.

[i] Note that **perché** also means *why*.

  Perché vai via? – Perché è tardi.   Why are you going? – Because it's late.

- **che** that
  Ha detto che farà tardi.   He said that he'll be late.
  Penso che sia il migliore.   I think that it's the best.

⇨ *For more information on* **che** *followed by the* **Subjunctive**, *see page 130.*

> ## Tip
>
> In English you can say either *He says he loves me* or *He says that he loves me*. In Italian **che** is NOT optional in this way.
>
> **So che le piace la cioccolata.**   I know (that) she likes chocolate.

- **se** if, whether
  Fammi sapere se c'è qualche problema.   Let me know if there are any problems.
  Se fosse più furbo verrebbe.   If he had more sense he'd come.
  Non so se dirglielo o no.   I don't know whether to tell him or not.

⇨ *For more information on* **se** *followed by the* **Subjunctive**, *see page 130.*

Some other common conjunctions

➤ The following conjunctions are used a lot in colloquial Italian:

- **allora** so, right then

Allora, cosa pensi?	<u>So</u>, what do you think?
Allora, cosa facciamo stasera?	<u>Right then</u>, what shall we do this evening?

- **dunque** so, well

Ha sbagliato lui, <u>dunque</u> è giusto che paghi.	It was his mistake, <u>so</u> it's right he should pay.
<u>Dunque</u>, come dicevo...	<u>Well</u>, as I was saying...

- **quindi** so

L'ho già visto, <u>quindi</u> non vado.	I've already seen it, <u>so</u> I'm not going.

- **però** but, however, though

Mi piace, <u>però</u> è troppo caro.	I like it – <u>but</u> it's too expensive.
Non è l'ideale, <u>però</u> può andare.	It's not ideal, <u>however</u> it'll do.
Sì, lo so – strano <u>però</u>.	Yes, I know – it's odd <u>though</u>.

- **invece** actually

Ero un po' pessimista, ma <u>invece</u> è andato tutto bene.	I wasn't too hopeful, but <u>actually</u> it all went fine.

> ## Tip
>
> **invece** is often used for emphasis in Italian – it isn't always translated in English.
>
> | | |
> |---|---|
> | Ho pensato che fosse lui, ma <u>invece</u> no. | I thought it was him but it wasn't. |

- **anzi** in fact

Non mi dispiace, <u>anzi</u> sono contento.	I don't mind, <u>in fact</u> I'm glad.

- **quando** when

Giocano fuori <u>quando</u> fa bel tempo.	They play outside <u>when</u> the weather's nice.

[i] Note that in sentences referring to the future, the future tense is used after **quando**.

Lo farò <u>quando</u> <u>avrò</u> tempo.	I'll do it <u>when</u> I <u>have</u> time.

➪ *For more information on the **Future tense**, see page* 93.

- **mentre** while

È successo <u>mentre</u> eri fuori.	It happened <u>while</u> you were out.

- **come** as

Ho fatto <u>come</u> hai detto tu.	I did <u>as</u> you told me.

[i] Note that **quando** and **mentre** tell you <u>WHEN</u> something happens; **come** tells you <u>HOW</u> something happens.

Split conjunctions

➤ English split conjunctions such as *either ... or* and *both ... and* are translated by split conjunctions in Italian.

- **o ... o** either ... or

  o oggi o domani — either today or tomorrow

  Ti accompagneranno o Carlo o Marco. — Either Carlo or Marco will go with you.

- **né ... né** neither ... nor, either ... or

  Non mi hanno chiamato né Claudio né Luca. — Neither Claudio nor Luca has phoned me.

  Non avevo né guanti né scarponi. — I didn't have either gloves or boots.

- **sia ... che** both ... and

  Verrano sia Luigi che suo fratello. — Both Luigi and his brother are coming.

📝 Note that in English a <u>singular</u> verb is used in sentences that have split conjunctions. In Italian a <u>plural</u> verb is used in sentences with split conjunctions if the two people or things involved are both the subject of the verb.

Non vengono né lui né sua moglie. — Neither he nor his wife is coming.

Spelling

1 How to spell words that have a hard k or g sound

➤ In Italian the [k] sound you have in the English words *kite* and *car* is spelled in two different ways, depending on the following vowel:

- **c** before **a**, **o** and **u**
- **ch** before **e** and **i**

➤ This means that the Italian word for *singer* is spelled **cantante** (pronounced [*kan-tan-tay*]; the word for *necklace* is spelled **collana** (pronounced [*kol-la-na*]), and the word for *cure* is spelled **cura** (pronounced [*koo-ra*]).

➤ However, the Italian word for *that* is spelled **che** (pronounced [*kay*]) and the word for *chemistry* is spelled **chimica** (pronounced [*kee-mee-ka*].

> ### Tip
> Remember that the Italian words for *kilo* and *kilometre* are spelled with **ch**:
>
> | **due chili** | two kilos |
> | **cento chilometri** | a hundred kilometres |

➤ In the same way, the hard [g] sound that you have in the English word *gas* is also spelled two ways in Italian:

- **g** before **a**, **o** and **u**
- **gh** before **e** and **i**

➤ This means that the Italian word for *cat* is spelled **gatto** (pronounced [*ga-toe*]; the word for *elbow* is spelled **gomito** (pronounced [*go-mee-toe*]), and the word for *taste* is spelled **gusto** (pronounced [*goos-toe*]).

➤ However, the Italian word for *leagues* is spelled **leghe** (pronounced [*lay-gay*]) and the word for *lakes* is spelled **laghi** (pronounced [*lah-ghee*].

2 How to pronounce c + a vowel

➤ As we have seen, the Italian letter **c** is pronounced like a [k] when it's followed by **a**, **o**, or **u**.

➤ When **c** is followed by **e** or **i** it is pronounced like the [ch] in *children*. This means that **centro** (meaning *centre*) is pronounced [*chen-tro*] and **città** (meaning *city*) is pronounced [*chee-tah*].

3 How to pronounce g + a vowel

➤ The Italian letter **g** is pronounced like the [g] in *gas* when it's followed by **a**, **o**, or **u**. When an Italian **g** is followed by **e** or **i**, however, it's pronounced like the [j] in *jet*. This means that **gente** (meaning *people*) is pronounced [*jen-tay*] and **giorno** (meaning *day*) is pronounced [*jor-no*].

4 How to spell verb endings which have c or g + vowel

➤ When an Italian verb has a hard [k] or [g] sound before the infinitive ending, for example **cercare** (meaning *to look for*) and **pagare** (meaning *to pay*), you have to change the spelling to **ch** and **gh** in forms of the verb that have endings starting with **e** or **i**.

➤ Here are the present and future tenses of **cercare** and **pagare**, showing how the spelling changes.

Vowel that follows c/g	Present of cercare	Meaning	Present of pagare	Meaning
o	cerco	I look for	pago	I pay
i	cerchi	you look for	paghi	you pay
a	cerca	he/she looks for	paga	he/she pays
i	cerchiamo	we look for	paghiamo	we pay
a	cercate	you look for	pagate	you pay
a	cercano	they look for	pagano	they pay

Vowel that follows c/g	Future of cercare	Meaning	Future of pagare	Meaning
e	cercherò	I'll look for	pagherò	I'll pay
e	cercherai	you'll look for	pagherai	you'll pay
e	cercherà	he/she will look for	pagherà	he/she will pay
e	cercheremo	we'll look for	pagheremo	we'll pay
e	cercherete	you'll look for	pagherete	you'll pay
e	cercheranno	they'll look for	pagheranno	they'll pay

Cosa cerchi? – Cerco le chiavi. What are you looking for?
– I'm looking for my keys.

Pago io. – No, paghiamo noi. I'll pay. – No, we'll pay.

➤ When an Italian verb has a [sh] or [j] sound before the infinitive ending, for example **la<u>sci</u>are** (meaning *to leave*) and **man<u>gi</u>are** (meaning *to eat*), you drop the **i** of the stem before endings starting with **e** or **i**.

➤ This means that you spell the **tu** form of the present tense of these verbs **la<u>sci</u>** and **man<u>gi</u>**.

La<u>sci</u> la finestra aperta?	Are you leaving the window open?
Cosa man<u>gi</u>?	What are you eating?

➤ The futures of the two verbs are spelled **lascerò, lascerai, lascerà, lasceremo, lascerete, lasceranno** and **mangerò, mangerai, mangerà, mangeremo, mangerete, mangeranno**.

Fa caldo, la<u>sce</u>rò a casa il maglione.	It's hot, I'll leave my jumper at home.
Domani man<u>ge</u>remo meno.	We'll eat less tomorrow.

> ## *Tip*
> Although the spelling of some verb endings changes, the pronunciation stays the same.

---

5 | How to spell plurals of nouns and adjectives ending in –ca or –ga

➤ When a feminine noun or adjective has a hard [k] or [g] sound before the singular ending **–a**, you add an **h** to the plural ending.

Singular	Meaning	Plural	Meaning
amica	friend	**amiche**	friends
riga	line	**righe**	lines
ricca	rich	**ricche**	rich
lunga	long	**lunghe**	long

una sua amica ricca	a rich friend of hers
le sue ami<u>che</u> ri<u>cche</u>	her rich friends
una riga sotto le parole	a line under the words
Ne ho letto solo po<u>che</u> ri<u>ghe</u>.	I just read a few lines of it.

> ## *Tip*
> Feminine nouns and adjectives always keep their hard [k] and [g] sounds in the plural.

6 | How to spell plurals of nouns and adjectives ending in –co or –go

➤ There is not a fixed rule for the sound of the consonants **c** and **g** in the plural of masculine nouns and adjectives ending in **–co** and **–go**.

➤ Some words keep the hard sound of their **c** or **g** in the plural, and add an **h** to the spelling.

Singular	Meaning	Plural	Meaning
fuoco	fire	**fuochi**	fires
albergo	hotel	**alberghi**	hotels
ricco	rich	**ricchi**	rich
lungo	long	**lunghi**	long

È un albergo per ricchi.   It's a hotel for rich people.
Ho i capelli lunghi.   I've got long hair.

➤ The plurals of many other words, however, change from the hard [k] sound to the [ch] sound, or from the hard [g] to [j]. This means their plurals are not spelled with an added **h**.

Singular	Meaning	Plural	Meaning
amico	friend	**amici**	friends
astrologo	astrologer	**astrologi**	astrologers
greco	Greek	**greci**	Greek
psicologico	psychological	**psicologici**	psychological

un astrologo greco   a Greek astrologer
i miei amici e i loro problemi   my friends and their psychological
psicologici   problems

7 | How to spell plurals of nouns ending in –io

➤ When the **i** of the **–io** ending is stressed, as it is in **zio** (meaning *uncle*) and **invio** (meaning *dispatch*), the plural is spelled with double **i**: **zii**, **invii**.

Ho sei zii e sette zie.   I've got six uncles and seven aunts.

➤ If the **i** of the **–io** ending is not stressed you spell the plural ending with only one **i**, for example **figlio** → **figli**; **occhio** → **occhi**.

Ha gli occhi azzurri.   He's got blue eyes.

8 | How to spell plurals of nouns ending in –cia and –gia

➤ The spelling of the plurals of these words also depends on whether the **i** of the ending is stressed.

➤ In some words, such words as **farmacia** (meaning *chemist's*) and **bugia** (meaning *lie*), the stress is on the **i**, and the plurals keep the **i**: **farmacie**; **bugie**.

> **Non dire bugie.**   Don't tell lies.

➤ In others, such as **faccia** (meaning *face*) and **spiaggia** (meaning *beach*) the **i** of the singular ending is not stressed, and the plural is not spelled with **i**: **facce**; **spiagge**.

> **le nostre spiagge preferite**   our favourite beaches

9 | How to use accents

➤ Accents have two main uses: one is to show that a word is stressed on the last syllable, which is not normal in Italian, for example **città** (meaning *city*), **università** (meaning *university*), **perché** (meaning *why/because*), **cercherò** (meaning *I will look for*).

⇨ *For more information on **Stress**, see page 196.*

➤ The second use of accents is to distinguish between words that have identical pronunciations and spellings.

Without an accent		With an accent	
da	from	dà	he/she/it gives
e	and	è	is
la	the/it	là	there
li	them	lì	there
ne	of it/them	né	neither
se	if	sé	himself
si	himself/herself/one	sì	yes
te	you	tè	tea

> **Mettila là.**   Put it there.
> **Non so se l'ha fatto da sé.**   I don't know if he made it himself.

Tip

The words **può**, **già**, **ciò**, **più** and **giù** are spelled with an accent.

Key points

✔ Spelling changes are sometimes necessary to keep the consonants **c** and **g** hard.

✔ Accents show that the last syllable of a word is stressed.

Stress

Which syllable to stress

➤ Most Italian words have two or more <u>syllables</u>, (units containing a vowel sound). In this section syllables are shown divided by | and the stressed vowel is in italic.

➤ Most words are stressed on the next to the last syllable, for example, **fi|ne|stra**.

➤ Some words are stressed on the last vowel, and this is always shown by an accent, for example, **u|ni|ver|si|tà**.

➤ Some words have their stress on an unexpected vowel, but are not spelled with an accent, for example, **mac|chi|na** (meaning *car*).

➤ If a word has the stress on a vowel you wouldn't expect, the stressed vowel is in italics, for example, **vogliono** (meaning *they want*), **vendere** (meaning *to sell*), **quindici** (meaning *fifteen*), **medico** (meaning *doctor*).

➤ This book also marks the stress in words in which **i** before another vowel is pronounced like **y**, for example **Lidia**.

1 Words that are stressed on the next to last syllable

➤ Two-syllable words <u>always</u> stress the first vowel, unless the final vowel has an accent:

ca|sa	house	**gior|no**	day
bel|la	beautiful	**du|e**	two
so|no	I am	**spes|so**	often
lu|i	he	**og|gi**	today

➤ Words with three or more syllables <u>generally</u> have the stress on the next to the last vowel:

in|gle|se	English	**par|la|vo**	I was speaking
gen|ti|le	nice	**an|dreb|be**	he'd go
set|ti|ma|na	week	**par|le|re|mo**	we'll speak
sta|zio|ne	station	**su|per|mer|ca|to**	supermarket
stra|or|di|na|ria|men|te	extraordinarily		

2 Words that stress the last syllable

➤ There are a number of nouns in Italian that have the stress on the final syllable and are spelled with an accent. They sometimes correspond to English nouns that end with *ty*, such as *university* and *faculty*.

For further explanation of grammatical terms, please see pages viii–xii.

re|al|tà	reality	u|ni|ver|si|tà	university
fe|li|ci|tà	happiness, felicity	fe|del|tà	fidelity
cu|rio|si|tà	curiosity	fa|col|tà	faculty
bon|tà	goodness	cit|tà	city
cru|del|tà	cruelty	e|tà	age
ti|vù	TV	me|tà	half

➤ There are some common adverbs and conjunctions that have the stress on the final syllable and are spelled with an accent, for example, **per\|ché**, **co\|sì**, and **pe\|rò**.

⇨ *For more information about **Spelling**, see page 191.*

3 | Words that stress an unexpected syllable

➤ Some words have the stress on a syllable which is neither the last, nor the next to the last.

u|ti|le	useful	por|*ta*|ti|le	portable
dif|*fi*|ci|le	difficult	*su*|bi|to	suddenly
nu|me|ro	number	*pen*|to|la	saucepan
ca|me|ra	bedroom	com|*pi*|to	homework
mo|du|lo	form		

ℹ Note that <u>past participles</u> such as **fi\|*ni*\|to** (meaning *finished*) and **par\|*ti*\|to** (meaning *left*) <u>always</u> have the stress on the next to last syllable, but there are similar-looking words, such as **su\|bi\|to** (meaning *immediately*) and **com\|pi\|to** (meaning *homework*), that are not past participles, and that have the stress on a syllable you wouldn't expect.

> ## Tip
> When learning new vocabulary, check in the dictionary where the stress goes.

4 | Stress in verb forms

➤ In the present tense, the **loro** form <u>always</u> has the stress on the same vowel as the **io** form:

io form		loro form	
par|lo	I speak	*par*|la|no	they speak
con|*si*|de|ro	I consider	con|*si*|de|ra|no	they consider
mi al|*le*|no	I'm training	si al|*le*|na|no	they're training

➤ In the future tense of all verbs the stress is on the last syllable of the **io** form and the **lui/lei** form. These two verb forms are spelled with an accent on the stressed vowel.

> **Future**
> **sa|rò**   I will be
> **la|vo|re|rò**   I will work
> **fi|ni|rà**   it will finish
> **as|pet|te|rà**   she'll wait

➤ The infinitive of **–are** verbs <u>always</u> has the stress on the **a** of the ending, for example **in|vi|ta|re** (meaning to invite) and **cam|mi|na|re** (meaning to walk). The infinitive of **–ire** verbs always has the stress on the **i** of the ending, for example **par|ti|re** (meaning to leave) and **fi|ni|re** (meaning to finish).

➤ The infinitive of **–ere** verbs <u>sometimes</u> has the stress on the first **e** of the ending, for example, **ve|de|re** (meaning to see) and **av|e|re** (meaning to have). However, these verbs <u>often</u> stress a syllable before the **–ere** ending, for example **ven|de|re** (meaning to sell), **di|vi|de|re** (meaning to divide) and **es|se|re** (meaning to be).

Tip

Remember that **–ere** verbs do not always stress the **e** of the ending, and take note of the stress when learning a new verb.

---

5 | **Different stress for different meanings**

➤ In a few cases one word has two pronunciations, depending on its meaning. The following are some examples:

Normal stress	Meaning	Unusual stress	Meaning
an|co|ra	again	*an*|co|ra	anchor
ca|pi|ta|no	captain	*ca*|pi|ta|no	they happen
me|tro	meter	me|trò	metro

Key points

✔ Two-syllable words are stesssed on the first syllable, unless there's an accent.

✔ Longer words are usually stressed on the next to the last syllable.

✔ If the stress is on an unexpected vowel you need to learn it.

For further explanation of grammatical terms, please see pages viii–xii.

Numbers

1	uno (un, una)	31	trentuno
2	due	40	quaranta
3	tre	41	quarantuno
4	quattro	50	cinquanta
5	cinque	58	cinquantotto
6	sei	60	sessanta
7	sette	63	sessantatré
8	otto	70	settanta
9	nove	75	settantacinque
10	dieci	80	ottanta
11	undici	81	ottantuno
12	dodici	90	novanta
13	tredici	99	novantanove
14	quattordici	100	cento
15	quindici	101	centouno
16	sedici	200	duecento
17	diciassette	203	duecentotré
18	diciotto	300	trecento
19	diciannove	400	quattrocento
20	venti	500	cinquecento
21	ventuno	600	seicento
22	ventidue	700	settecento
23	ventitré	800	ottocento
24	ventiquattro	900	novecento
25	venticinque	1000	mille
26	ventisei	1001	milleuno
27	ventisette	2000	duemila
28	ventotto	2500	duemilacinquecento
29	ventinove	1.000.000	un milione
30	trenta		(*in English* 1,000,000)

a pagina diciannove	on page nineteen
nel capitolo sette	in chapter seven
dieci per cento	ten per cent
seicento euro	six hundred euros
tremila persone	three thousand people

ⓘ Note that in the numbers 21, 31, 41 and so on, the final vowel of **venti**, **trenta** and **quaranta** is lost: **ventuno**, **trentuno**, **quarantuno**. The same thing happens with the numbers 28, 38, 48 and so on: **ventotto**, **trentotto**, **quarantotto**. When **tre** is combined with another number it takes an accent: **trentatré** (33), **centotré** (103), **milletré** (1003).

1 | uno, un or una?

➤ In Italian the same word – **uno** – is used for the number *one* and the indefinite article *a*.

➤ When using **uno** as a number in front of a noun, follow the same rules as for the indefinite article.

un uomo	one man
uno scienzato	one scientist
una ragazza	one girl
un'anatra	one duck

⇨ *For more information on the **Indefinite article**, see page 17.*

➤ When replying to a question, use **uno** if what's referred to is masculine, and **una** if it's feminine.

Quanti giorni? – Uno.	How many days? – One.
Quante notti? – Una.	How many nights? – One.

➤ Use **uno** when counting, unless referring to something or someone feminine.

➤ Do NOT use **un** to translate *one hundred*, or *one thousand*.

cento metri	one hundred metres
mille euro	one thousand euros

➤ You do use **un** with **milione** (meaning *million*) and **miliardo** (meaning *thousand million*).

Quante persone? – Un milione.	How many people? – One million.
un milione di dollari	one million dollars
un miliardo di euro	one thousand million euros

ⓘ Note that when **un milione** and **un miliardo** are followed by a noun, **di** is added.

2 | Which numbers have plurals?

➤ The only numbers which have plurals are **mille**, **milione**, and **miliardo**. **Due**, **tre**, **quattro** and so on are added to **mila** to make **duemila** (meaning *two thousand*), **tremila** (meaning *three thousand*) and **quattromila** (meaning *four thousand*).

mille euro	one thousand euros
diecimila euro	ten thousand euros
un milione di dollari	one million dollars
venti milioni di dollari	twenty million dollars
un miliardo di sterline	one thousand million pounds
due miliardi di sterline	two thousand million pounds

3 | Full stop or comma?

➤ Use a full stop, not a comma, to separate thousands and millions in figures.

700.000 (settecentomila)	700,000 (seven hundred thousand)
5.000.000 (cinque milioni)	5,000,000 (five million)

➤ Use a comma instead of a decimal point to show decimals in Italian.

0,5 (zero virgola cinque)	0.5 (nought point five)
3,4 (tre virgola quattro)	3.4 (three point four)

1st	**primo (1°)**
2nd	**secondo (2°)**
3rd	**terzo (3°)**
4th	**quarto (4°)**
5th	**quinto (5°)**
6th	**sesto (6°)**
7th	**settimo (7°)**
8th	**ottavo (8°)**
9th	**nono (9°)**
10th	**decimo (10°)**
11th	**undicesimo (11°)**
18th	**diciottesimo (18°)**
21st	**ventunesimo (21°)**
33rd	**trentatreesimo (33°)**
100th	**centesimo (100°)**
101st	**centunesimo (101°)**
1000th	**millesimo (1000°)**

Tip

Learn the first ten of these numbers.

➤ To make the others, take numbers such as **venti** and **trentotto**, drop the final vowel and add **–esimo**. If the number ends in **tre**, DON'T drop the final **e** before adding **–esimo**.

la ventesima settimana	the twentieth week
il trentottesimo anno	the thirty-eighth year
il loro trentatreesimo anniversario di matrimonio	their thirty-third anniversary

➤ These numbers are adjectives and can be made masculine or feminine, singular or plural.

il quindicesimo piano	the fifteenth floor
la terza lezione	the third lesson
i primi piatti	the first courses
le loro seconde scelte	their second choices

[i] Note that when writing these numbers in figures you should use a little °, or ª, depending on whether what's referred to is masculine or feminine.

il 15° piano	the 15th floor
la 24ª giornata	the 24th day

➤ Roman numerals are often used for centuries, popes and monarchs.

il XIV secolo	the 14th century
Paolo VI	Paul VI
Enrico III	Henry III

⇨ *For more information on **Numbers used in dates**, see page 204.*

Time and Date

L'ORA	THE TIME
Che ora è? *or* **Che ore sono?**	**What time is it?**
È l'una meno venti.	It's twenty to one.
È l'una meno un quarto.	It's a quarter to one.
È l'una.	It's one o'clock.
È l'una e dieci.	It's ten past one.
È l'una e un quarto.	It's a quarter past one.
È l'una e mezza.	It's half past one.
Sono le due meno venticinque.	It's twenty-five to two.
Sono le due meno un quarto.	It's a quarter to two.
Sono le due.	It's two o'clock.
Sono le due e dieci.	It's ten past two.
Sono le due e un quarto.	It's a quarter past two.
Sono le due e mezza.	It's half past two.
Sono le tre.	It's three o'clock.

> ### *Tip*
> Use **sono le** for all times not involving **una** (meaning *one*).

A che ora?	(At) what time?
Arrivano oggi. – A che ora?	They're arriving today. – What time?

[i] Note that *at* is optional in English when asking what time something happens, but **a** must always be used in Italian.

a mezzanotte	at midnight
a mezzogiorno	at midday
all'una (del pomeriggio)	at one o'clock (in the afternoon)
alle otto (di sera)	at eight o'clock (in the evening)
alle 9:25 *or* alle nove e venticinque	at twenty-five past nine
alle 16:50 *or* alle sedici e cinquanta	at 16:50 *or* sixteen fifty

[i] Note that the twenty-four hour clock is often used in Italy.

LA DATA	THE DATE
I giorni della settimana	**The days of the week**
lunedì	Monday
martedì	Tuesday
mercoledì	Wednesday
giovedì	Thursday
venerdì	Friday
sabato	Saturday
domenica	Sunday

Quando?	**When?**
lunedì	on Monday
di lunedì	on Mondays
tutti i lunedì	every Monday
martedì scorso	last Tuesday
venerdì prossimo	next Friday
sabato della settimana prossima	a week on Saturday
sabato tra due settimane	two weeks on Saturday

i Note that days of the week <u>DON'T</u> have a capital letter in Italian.

I mesi dell'anno	**The months of the year**
gennaio	January
febbraio	February
marzo	March
aprile	April
maggio	May
giugno	June
luglio	July
agosto	August
settembre	September
ottobre	October
novembre	November
dicembre	December

Quando?	**When?**
in *or* a febbraio	in February
il primo dicembre	on December 1st
il due dicembre	on December 2nd
nel 1969 (millenovecento-sessantanove)	in 1969 (in nineteen sixty-nine)
il primo dicembre 2016	on December 1st 2016
nel duemilasei	in two thousand and six

i Note that months of the year <u>DON'T</u> have a capital letter in Italian.

For further explanation of grammatical terms, please see pages viii–xii.

Tip

In Italian you use **il primo** for the first day of the month. For all the other days you use the equivalent of *two*, *three*, *four* and so on.

il tre maggio   the third of May

FRASI UTILI	USEFUL PHRASES
Quando?	**When?**
oggi	today
stamattina	this morning
stasera	this evening
Ogni quanto?	**How often?**
ogni giorno	every day
ogni due giorni	every other day
una volta alla settimana	once a week
due volte alla settimana	twice a week
una volta al mese	once a month
Quando è successo?	**When did it happen?**
di mattina	in the morning
di sera	in the evening
ieri	yesterday
ieri mattina	yesterday morning
ieri sera	yesterday evening/last night
ieri notte	last night
l'altro ieri	the day before yesterday
una settimana fa	a week ago
due settimane fa	two weeks ago
la settimana scorsa	last week
l'anno scorso	last year
Quando succederà?	**When is it going to happen?**
domani	tomorrow
domani mattina	tomorrow morning
domani sera	tomorrow evening/night
dopodomani	the day after tomorrow
fra *or* tra due giorni	in two days' time
fra *or* tra una settimana	in a week's time
fra *or* tra quindici giorni	in two weeks' time
il mese prossimo	next month
l'anno prossimo	next year

Main Index

VERB TABLES

Introduction

The **Verb Tables** in the following section contain 90 tables of Italian verbs (some regular and some irregular) in alphabetical order. Each table shows you the following forms: **Present**, **Perfect**, **Imperfect**, **Future**, **Conditional**, **Present Subjunctive**, **Imperative** and the **Past Participle** and **Gerund**. For more information on these tenses, how they are formed, when they are used and so on, you should look at the section on **Verbs** in the main text on pages 66–148.

In order to help you use the verbs shown in the **Verb Tables** correctly, there are also a number of example phrases at the bottom of each page to show the verb as it is used in context.

In Italian there are **regular** verbs (their forms follow the regular patterns of **-are**, **-ere** or **-ire** verbs), and **irregular** verbs (their forms do not follow the normal rules). Examples of regular verbs in these tables are:

> **parlare** (regular **-are** verb, Verb Table 50)
> **credere** (regular **-ere** verb, Verb Table 20)
> **capire** (regular **-ire** verb, Verb Table 13)

Some irregular verbs are irregular in most of their forms, while others may only have a couple of irregular forms.

The **Verb Index** at the end of this section contains over 1000 verbs, each of which is cross-referred to one of the verbs given in the Verb Tables. The table shows the patterns that the verb listed in the index follows.

accorgersi (to realize)

PRESENT

(io)	**mi accorgo**
(tu)	**ti accorgi**
(lui/lei) (lei/Lei)	**si accorge**
(noi)	**ci accorgiamo**
(voi)	**vi accorgete**
(loro)	**si accorgono**

PERFECT

(io)	**mi sono accorto/a**
(tu)	**ti sei accorto/a**
(lui/lei) (lei/Lei)	**si è accorto/a**
(noi)	**ci siamo accorti/e**
(voi)	**vi siete accorti/e**
(loro)	**si sono accorti/e**

IMPERFECT

(io)	**mi accorgevo**
(tu)	**ti accorgevi**
(lui/lei) (lei/Lei)	**si accorgeva**
(noi)	**ci accorgevamo**
(voi)	**vi accorgevate**
(loro)	**si accorgevano**

IMPERATIVE

accorgiti
accorgiamoci
accorgetevi

FUTURE

(io)	**mi accorgerò**
(tu)	**ti accorgerai**
(lui/lei) (lei/Lei)	**si accorgerà**
(noi)	**ci accorgeremo**
(voi)	**vi accorgerete**
(loro)	**si accorgeranno**

CONDITIONAL

(io)	**mi accorgerei**
(tu)	**ti accorgeresti**
(lui/lei) (lei/Lei)	**si accorgerebbe**
(noi)	**ci accorgeremmo**
(voi)	**vi accorgereste**
(loro)	**si accorgerebbero**

PRESENT SUBJUNCTIVE

(io)	**mi accorga**
(tu)	**ti accorga**
(lui/lei) (lei/Lei)	**si accorga**
(noi)	**ci accorgiamo**
(voi)	**vi accorgiate**
(loro)	**si accorgano**

PAST PARTICIPLE

accorto

GERUND

accorgendosi

EXAMPLE PHRASES

Si è **accorto** del furto solo il giorno dopo. *He only noticed it had been stolen the next day.*

Mi **sono accorto** subito che qualcosa non andava. *I immediately realized something was wrong.*

Avvisami se non mi **accorgo** che è tardi. *Warn me if I don't notice it's getting late.*

Remember that subject pronouns are not used very often in Italian.

addormentarsi (to go to sleep)

PRESENT

(io)	mi addormento
(tu)	ti addormenti
(lui/lei) (lei/Lei)	si addormenta
(noi)	ci addormentiamo
(voi)	vi addormentate
(loro)	si addormentano

PERFECT

(io)	mi sono addormentato/a
(tu)	ti sei addormentato/a
(lui/lei) (lei/Lei)	si è addormentato/a
(noi)	ci siamo addormentati/e
(voi)	vi siete addormentati/e
(loro)	si sono addormentati/e

IMPERFECT

(io)	mi addormentavo
(tu)	ti addormentavi
(lui/lei) (lei/Lei)	si addormentava
(noi)	ci addormentavamo
(voi)	vi addormentavate
(loro)	si addormentavano

IMPERATIVE

addormentati
addormentiamoci
addormentatevi

FUTURE

(io)	mi addormenterò
(tu)	ti addormenterai
(lui/lei) (lei/Lei)	si addormenterà
(noi)	ci addormenteremo
(voi)	vi addormenterete
(loro)	si addormenteranno

CONDITIONAL

(io)	mi addormenterei
(tu)	ti addormenteresti
(lui/lei) (lei/Lei)	si addormenterebbe
(noi)	ci addormenteremmo
(voi)	vi addormentereste
(loro)	si addormenterebbero

PRESENT SUBJUNCTIVE

(io)	mi addormenti
(tu)	ti addormenti
(lui/lei) (lei/Lei)	si addormenti
(noi)	ci addormentiamo
(voi)	vi addormentiate
(loro)	si addormentino

PAST PARTICIPLE

addormentato

GERUND

addormentando

EXAMPLE PHRASES

Non voleva **addormentarsi**. *He didn't want to go to sleep.*
Mi si **è addormentato** un piede. *My foot has gone to sleep.*
Sono stanco: stasera **mi addormenterò** subito. *I'm tired: I'll go to sleep immediately tonight.*

Italic letters in Italian words show where stress does not follow the usual rules.

andare (to go)

PRESENT

(io)	**vado**
(tu)	**vai**
(lui/lei) (lei/Lei)	**va**
(noi)	**andiamo**
(voi)	**andate**
(loro)	**vanno**

FUTURE

(io)	**andrò**
(tu)	**andrai**
(lui/lei) (lei/Lei)	**andrà**
(noi)	**andremo**
(voi)	**andrete**
(loro)	**andranno**

PERFECT

(io)	**sono andato/a**
(tu)	**sei andato/a**
(lui/lei) (lei/Lei)	**è andato/a**
(noi)	**siamo andati/e**
(voi)	**siete andati/e**
(loro)	**sono andati/e**

CONDITIONAL

(io)	**andrei**
(tu)	**andresti**
(lui/lei) (lei/Lei)	**andrebbe**
(noi)	**andremmo**
(voi)	**andreste**
(loro)	**andrebbero**

IMPERFECT

(io)	**andavo**
(tu)	**andavi**
(lui/lei) (lei/Lei)	**andava**
(noi)	**andavamo**
(voi)	**andavate**
(loro)	**andavano**

PRESENT SUBJUNCTIVE

(io)	**vada**
(tu)	**vada**
(lui/lei) (lei/Lei)	**vada**
(noi)	**andiamo**
(voi)	**andiate**
(loro)	**vadano**

IMPERATIVE

vai
andiamo
andate

PAST PARTICIPLE

andato

GERUND

andando

EXAMPLE PHRASES

Andremo in Grecia quest'estate. *We're going to Greece this summer.*
Su, **andiamo**! *Come on, let's go!*
Com'**è andata**? *How did it go?*
Come **va**? — Bene, grazie! *How are you? — Fine, thanks!*
Stasera **andrei** volentieri al ristorante. *I'd like to go to a restaurant this evening.*

Remember that subject pronouns are not used very often in Italian.

apparire (to appear)

PRESENT

(io)	**appaio**
(tu)	**appari**
(lui/lei) (lei/Lei)	**appare**
(noi)	**appariamo**
(voi)	**apparite**
(loro)	**app*a*iono**

PERFECT

(io)	**sono apparso/a**
(tu)	**sei apparso/a**
(lui/lei) (lei/Lei)	**è apparso/a**
(noi)	**siamo apparsi/e**
(voi)	**siete apparsi/e**
(loro)	**sono apparsi/e**

IMPERFECT

(io)	**apparivo**
(tu)	**apparivi**
(lui/lei) (lei/Lei)	**appariva**
(noi)	**apparivamo**
(voi)	**apparivate**
(loro)	**appar*i*vano**

IMPERATIVE

appari
appariamo
apparite

FUTURE

(io)	**apparirò**
(tu)	**apparirai**
(lui/lei) (lei/Lei)	**apparir*à***
(noi)	**appariremo**
(voi)	**apparirete**
(loro)	**appariranno**

CONDITIONAL

(io)	**apparirei**
(tu)	**appariresti**
(lui/lei) (lei/Lei)	**apparirebbe**
(noi)	**appariremmo**
(voi)	**apparireste**
(loro)	**apparirebbero**

PRESENT SUBJUNCTIVE

(io)	**appaia**
(tu)	**appaia**
(lui/lei) (lei/Lei)	**appaia**
(noi)	**appaiamo**
(voi)	**appaiate**
(loro)	**app*a*iano**

PAST PARTICIPLE

apparso

GERUND

apparendo

EXAMPLE PHRASES

Oggi Mario **appare** turbato. *Mario seems upset today.*

Il fantasma **appariva** ogni sera a mezzanotte. *The ghost appeared at midnight every night.*

Tra poco il sole **apparir*à*** in cielo. *The sun will soon appear in the sky.*

Italic letters in Italian words show where stress does not follow the usual rules.

aprire (to open)

PRESENT

(io)	apro
(tu)	apri
(lui/lei) (lei/Lei)	apre
(noi)	apriamo
(voi)	aprite
(loro)	*aprono*

FUTURE

(io)	aprirò
(tu)	aprirai
(lui/lei) (lei/Lei)	*aprirà*
(noi)	apriremo
(voi)	aprirete
(loro)	apriranno

PERFECT

(io)	ho aperto
(tu)	hai aperto
(lui/lei) (lei/Lei)	ha aperto
(noi)	abbiamo aperto
(voi)	avete aperto
(loro)	hanno aperto

CONDITIONAL

(io)	aprirei
(tu)	apriresti
(lui/lei) (lei/Lei)	aprirebbe
(noi)	apriremmo
(voi)	aprireste
(loro)	aprirebbero

IMPERFECT

(io)	aprivo
(tu)	aprivi
(lui/lei) (lei/Lei)	apriva
(noi)	aprivamo
(voi)	aprivate
(loro)	aprivano

PRESENT SUBJUNCTIVE

(io)	apra
(tu)	apra
(lui/lei) (lei/Lei)	apra
(noi)	apriamo
(voi)	apriate
(loro)	*aprano*

IMPERATIVE

apri
apriamo
aprite

PAST PARTICIPLE

aperto

GERUND

aprendo

EXAMPLE PHRASES

Posso **aprire** la finestra? *Can I open the window?*
Dai, non **apri** il pacco? *Come on, aren't you going to open the package?*
Non **ha aperto** bocca. *She didn't say a word.*

arrivare (to arrive)

PRESENT

(io)	**arrivo**
(tu)	**arrivi**
(lui/lei) (lei/Lei)	**arriva**
(noi)	**arriviamo**
(voi)	**arrivate**
(loro)	**arrivano**

PERFECT

(io)	**sono arrivato/a**
(tu)	**sei arrivato/a**
(lui/lei) (lei/Lei)	**è arrivato/a**
(noi)	**siamo arrivati/e**
(voi)	**siete arrivati/e**
(loro)	**sono arrivati/e**

IMPERFECT

(io)	**arrivavo**
(tu)	**arrivavi**
(lui/lei) (lei/Lei)	**arrivava**
(noi)	**arrivavamo**
(voi)	**arrivavate**
(loro)	**arriv*a*vano**

IMPERATIVE

arriva
arriviamo
arrivate

FUTURE

(io)	**arriverò**
(tu)	**arriverai**
(lui/lei) (lei/Lei)	**arriver*à***
(noi)	**arriveremo**
(voi)	**arriverete**
(loro)	**arriveranno**

CONDITIONAL

(io)	**arriverei**
(tu)	**arriveresti**
(lui/lei) (lei/Lei)	**arriverebbe**
(noi)	**arriveremmo**
(voi)	**arrivereste**
(loro)	**arriver*e*bbero**

PRESENT SUBJUNCTIVE

(io)	**arrivi**
(tu)	**arrivi**
(lui/lei) (lei/Lei)	**arrivi**
(noi)	**arriviamo**
(voi)	**arriviate**
(loro)	**arriv*i*no**

PAST PARTICIPLE

arrivato

GERUND

arrivando

EXAMPLE PHRASES

A che ora **arrivi** a scuola? *What time do you arrive at school?*
Sono arrivato a Londra alle sette. *I arrived in London at seven.*
Non **arrivava** mai in orario. *He never arrived on time.*
Aspettami, **sto arrivando**! *Wait for me, I'm coming!*
È troppo in alto, non ci **arrivo**. *It's too high, I can't reach it.*

Italic letters in Italian words show where stress does not follow the usual rules.

assumere (to take on; to employ)

PRESENT

(io)	assumo
(tu)	assumi
(lui/lei) (lei/Lei)	assume
(noi)	assumiamo
(voi)	assumete
(loro)	assumono

FUTURE

(io)	assumerò
(tu)	assumerai
(lui/lei) (lei/Lei)	assumerà
(noi)	assumeremo
(voi)	assumerete
(loro)	assumeranno

PERFECT

(io)	ho assunto
(tu)	hai assunto
(lui/lei) (lei/Lei)	ha assunto
(noi)	abbiamo assunto
(voi)	avete assunto
(loro)	hanno assunto

CONDITIONAL

(io)	assumerei
(tu)	assumeresti
(lui/lei) (lei/Lei)	assumerebbe
(noi)	assumeremmo
(voi)	assumereste
(loro)	assumerebbero

IMPERFECT

(io)	assumevo
(tu)	assumevi
(lui/lei) (lei/Lei)	assumeva
(noi)	assumevamo
(voi)	assumevate
(loro)	assumevano

PRESENT SUBJUNCTIVE

(io)	assuma
(tu)	assuma
(lui/lei) (lei/Lei)	assuma
(noi)	assumiamo
(voi)	assumiate
(loro)	assumano

IMPERATIVE

assumi
assumiamo
assumete

PAST PARTICIPLE

assunto

GERUND

assumendo

EXAMPLE PHRASES

L'azienda **assumerà** due operai. *The company is going to take on two workers.*

È **stata assunta** come programmatrice. *She's got a job as a programmer.*

Sei bravo: ti **assumerei** come assistente. *You're good: I'd give you a job as an assistant.*

Remember that subject pronouns are not used very often in Italian.

avere (to have)

PRESENT

(io)	**ho**
(tu)	**hai**
(lui/lei) (lei/Lei)	**ha**
(noi)	**abbiamo**
(voi)	**avete**
(loro)	**hanno**

PERFECT

(io)	**ho avuto**
(tu)	**hai avuto**
(lui/lei) (lei/Lei)	**ha avuto**
(noi)	**abbiamo avuto**
(voi)	**avete avuto**
(loro)	**hanno avuto**

IMPERFECT

(io)	**avevo**
(tu)	**avevi**
(lui/lei) (lei/Lei)	**aveva**
(noi)	**avevamo**
(voi)	**avevate**
(loro)	**avevano**

IMPERATIVE

abbi
abbiamo
abbiate

FUTURE

(io)	**avrò**
(tu)	**avrai**
(lui/lei) (lei/Lei)	**avrà**
(noi)	**avremo**
(voi)	**avrete**
(loro)	**avranno**

CONDITIONAL

(io)	**avrei**
(tu)	**avresti**
(lui/lei) (lei/Lei)	**avrebbe**
(noi)	**avremmo**
(voi)	**avreste**
(loro)	**avrebbero**

PRESENT SUBJUNCTIVE

(io)	*abbia*
(tu)	*abbia*
(lui/lei) (lei/Lei)	*abbia*
(noi)	**abbiamo**
(voi)	**abbiate**
(loro)	*abbiano*

PAST PARTICIPLE

avuto

GERUND

avendo

EXAMPLE PHRASES

All'inizio **ha avuto** un sacco di problemi. *He had a lot of problems at first.*
Ho già **mangiato**. *I've already eaten.*
Ora **ha** uno smartphone. *Now she's got a smartphone.*
Aveva la mia età. *He was the same age as me.*
Quanti ne **abbiamo** oggi? *What's the date today?*

Italic letters in Italian words show where stress does not follow the usual rules.

bere (to drink)

PRESENT

(io)	bevo
(tu)	bevi
(lui/lei) (lei/Lei)	beve
(noi)	beviamo
(voi)	bevete
(loro)	bevono

FUTURE

(io)	berrò
(tu)	berrai
(lui/lei) (lei/Lei)	berrà
(noi)	berremo
(voi)	berrete
(loro)	berranno

PERFECT

(io)	ho bevuto
(tu)	hai bevuto
(lui/lei) (lei/Lei)	ha bevuto
(noi)	abbiamo bevuto
(voi)	avete bevuto
(loro)	hanno bevuto

CONDITIONAL

(io)	berrei
(tu)	berresti
(lui/lei) (lei/Lei)	berrebbe
(noi)	berremmo
(voi)	berreste
(loro)	berrebbero

IMPERFECT

(io)	bevevo
(tu)	bevevi
(lui/lei) (lei/Lei)	beveva
(noi)	bevevamo
(voi)	bevevate
(loro)	bevevano

PRESENT SUBJUNCTIVE

(io)	beva
(tu)	beva
(lui/lei) (lei/Lei)	beva
(noi)	beviamo
(voi)	beviate
(loro)	bevano

IMPERATIVE

bevi
beviamo
bevete

PAST PARTICIPLE

bevuto

GERUND

bevendo

EXAMPLE PHRASES

Vuoi **bere** qualcosa? *Would you like something to drink?*
Berrei volentieri un bicchiere di vino bianco. *I'd love a glass of white wine.*
Beveva sei caffè al giorno, ma ora ha smesso. *He used to drink six cups of coffee a day, but he's stopped now.*

Remember that subject pronouns are not used very often in Italian.

cadere (to fall)

PRESENT

(io)	cado
(tu)	cadi
(lui/lei) (lei/Lei)	cade
(noi)	cadiamo
(voi)	cadete
(loro)	cadono

PERFECT

(io)	sono caduto/a
(tu)	sei caduto/a
(lui/lei) (lei/Lei)	è caduto/a
(noi)	siamo caduti/e
(voi)	siete caduti/e
(loro)	sono caduti/e

IMPERFECT

(io)	cadevo
(tu)	cadevi
(lui/lei) (lei/Lei)	cadeva
(noi)	cadevamo
(voi)	cadevate
(loro)	cadevano

IMPERATIVE

cadi
cadiamo
cadete

FUTURE

(io)	cadrò
(tu)	cadrai
(lui/lei) (lei/Lei)	cadrà
(noi)	cadremo
(voi)	cadrete
(loro)	cadranno

CONDITIONAL

(io)	cadrei
(tu)	cadresti
(lui/lei) (lei/Lei)	cadrebbe
(noi)	cadremmo
(voi)	cadreste
(loro)	cadrebbero

PRESENT SUBJUNCTIVE

(io)	cada
(tu)	cada
(lui/lei) (lei/Lei)	cada
(noi)	cadiamo
(voi)	cadiate
(loro)	cadano

PAST PARTICIPLE

caduto

GERUND

cadendo

EXAMPLE PHRASES

Ho inciampato e **sono caduta**. *I tripped and fell.*
Il mio compleanno **cade** di lunedì. *My birthday is on a Monday.*
Ti **è caduta** la sciarpa. *You've dropped your scarf.*
Attento che fai **cadere** il bicchiere. *Mind you don't knock over your glass.*

Italic letters in Italian words show where stress does not follow the usual rules.

cambiare (to change)

PRESENT

(io)	**cambio**
(tu)	**cambi**
(lui/lei) (lei/Lei)	**cambia**
(noi)	**cambiamo**
(voi)	**cambiate**
(loro)	**cambiano**

PERFECT

(io)	**ho cambiato**
(tu)	**hai cambiato**
(lui/lei) (lei/Lei)	**ha cambiato**
(noi)	**abbiamo cambiato**
(voi)	**avete cambiato**
(loro)	**hanno cambiato**

IMPERFECT

(io)	**cambiavo**
(tu)	**cambiavi**
(lui/lei) (lei/Lei)	**cambiava**
(noi)	**cambiavamo**
(voi)	**cambiavate**
(loro)	**cambiavano**

IMPERATIVE

cambia
cambiamo
cambiate

FUTURE

(io)	**cambierò**
(tu)	**cambierai**
(lui/lei) (lei/Lei)	**cambierà**
(noi)	**cambieremo**
(voi)	**cambierete**
(loro)	**cambieranno**

CONDITIONAL

(io)	**cambierei**
(tu)	**cambieresti**
(lui/lei) (lei/Lei)	**cambierebbe**
(noi)	**cambieremmo**
(voi)	**cambiereste**
(loro)	**cambierebbero**

PRESENT SUBJUNCTIVE

(io)	**cambi**
(tu)	**cambi**
(lui/lei) (lei/Lei)	**cambi**
(noi)	**cambiamo**
(voi)	**cambiate**
(loro)	**cambino**

PAST PARTICIPLE

cambiato

GERUND

cambiando

EXAMPLE PHRASES

Ultimamente è molto **cambiato**. *He's changed a lot recently.*
Cambiamo argomento. *Let's change the subject.*
Vorrei **cambiare** questi euro in sterline. *I'd like to change these euros into pounds.*

Remember that subject pronouns are not used very often in Italian.

capire (to understand)

PRESENT

(io)	**capisco**
(tu)	**capisci**
(lui/lei) (lei/Lei)	**capisce**
(noi)	**capiamo**
(voi)	**capite**
(loro)	**capiscono**

FUTURE

(io)	**capirò**
(tu)	**capirai**
(lui/lei) (lei/Lei)	**capirà**
(noi)	**capiremo**
(voi)	**capirete**
(loro)	**capiranno**

PERFECT

(io)	**ho capito**
(tu)	**hai capito**
(lui/lei) (lei/Lei)	**ha capito**
(noi)	**abbiamo capito**
(voi)	**avete capito**
(loro)	**hanno capito**

CONDITIONAL

(io)	**capirei**
(tu)	**capiresti**
(lui/lei) (lei/Lei)	**capirebbe**
(noi)	**capiremmo**
(voi)	**capireste**
(loro)	**capirebbero**

IMPERFECT

(io)	**capivo**
(tu)	**capivi**
(lui/lei) (lei/Lei)	**capiva**
(noi)	**capivamo**
(voi)	**capivate**
(loro)	**capivano**

PRESENT SUBJUNCTIVE

(io)	**capisca**
(tu)	**capisca**
(lui/lei) (lei/Lei)	**capisca**
(noi)	**capiamo**
(voi)	**capiate**
(loro)	**capiscano**

IMPERATIVE

capisci
capiamo
capite

PAST PARTICIPLE

capito

GERUND

capendo

EXAMPLE PHRASES

Va bene, **capisco**. *OK, I understand.*
Non **ho capito** una parola. *I didn't understand a word.*
Fammi **capire**... *Let me get this straight...*
Non ti **capirò** mai. *I'll never understand you.*

Italic letters in Italian words show where stress does not follow the usual rules.

cercare (to look for)

PRESENT

(io)	cerco
(tu)	cerchi
(lui/lei) (lei/Lei)	cerca
(noi)	cerchiamo
(voi)	cercate
(loro)	cercano

PERFECT

(io)	ho cercato
(tu)	hai cercato
(lui/lei) (lei/Lei)	ha cercato
(noi)	abbiamo cercato
(voi)	avete cercato
(loro)	hanno cercato

IMPERFECT

(io)	cercavo
(tu)	cercavi
(lui/lei) (lei/Lei)	cercava
(noi)	cercavamo
(voi)	cercavate
(loro)	cercavano

IMPERATIVE

cerca
cerchiamo
cercate

FUTURE

(io)	cercherò
(tu)	cercherai
(lui/lei) (lei/Lei)	cercherà
(noi)	cercheremo
(voi)	cercherete
(loro)	cercheranno

CONDITIONAL

(io)	cercherei
(tu)	cercheresti
(lui/lei) (lei/Lei)	cercherebbe
(noi)	cercheremmo
(voi)	cerchereste
(loro)	cercherebbero

PRESENT SUBJUNCTIVE

(io)	cerchi
(tu)	cerchi
(lui/lei) (lei/Lei)	cerchi
(noi)	cerchiamo
(voi)	cerchiate
(loro)	cerchino

PAST PARTICIPLE

cercato

GERUND

cercando

EXAMPLE PHRASES

Le **ho cercate** dappertutto. *I've looked for them everywhere.*
Stai cercando lavoro? *Are you looking for a job?*
Cerca di non fare tardi. *Try not to be late.*

Remember that subject pronouns are not used very often in Italian.

chiudere (to close)

PRESENT

(io)	chiudo
(tu)	chiudi
(lui/lei) (lei/Lei)	chiude
(noi)	chiudiamo
(voi)	chiudete
(loro)	chiudono

PERFECT

(io)	ho chiuso
(tu)	hai chiuso
(lui/lei) (lei/Lei)	ha chiuso
(noi)	abbiamo chiuso
(voi)	avete chiuso
(loro)	hanno chiuso

IMPERFECT

(io)	chiudevo
(tu)	chiudevi
(lui/lei) (lei/Lei)	chiudeva
(noi)	chiudevamo
(voi)	chiudevate
(loro)	chiudevano

IMPERATIVE

chiudi
chiudiamo
chiudete

FUTURE

(io)	chiuderò
(tu)	chiuderai
(lui/lei) (lei/Lei)	chiuderà
(noi)	chiuderemo
(voi)	chiuderete
(loro)	chiuderanno

CONDITIONAL

(io)	chiuderei
(tu)	chiuderesti
(lui/lei) (lei/Lei)	chiuderebbe
(noi)	chiuderemmo
(voi)	chiudereste
(loro)	chiuderebbero

PRESENT SUBJUNCTIVE

(io)	chiuda
(tu)	chiuda
(lui/lei) (lei/Lei)	chiuda
(noi)	chiudiamo
(voi)	chiudiate
(loro)	chiudano

PAST PARTICIPLE

chiuso

GERUND

chiudendo

EXAMPLE PHRASES

La fabbrica **ha chiuso** due anni fa. *The factory closed two years ago.*
Con lui **ho chiuso**. *I've finished with him.*
Chiudi bene il rubinetto. *Turn the tap off properly.*

Italic letters in Italian words show where stress does not follow the usual rules.

cominciare (to start)

PRESENT

(io)	comincio
(tu)	cominci
(lui/lei) (lei/Lei)	comincia
(noi)	cominciamo
(voi)	cominciate
(loro)	cominciano

FUTURE

(io)	comincerò
(tu)	comincerai
(lui/lei) (lei/Lei)	comincerà
(noi)	cominceremo
(voi)	comincerete
(loro)	cominceranno

PERFECT

(io)	ho cominciato
(tu)	hai cominciato
(lui/lei) (lei/Lei)	ha cominciato
(noi)	abbiamo cominciato
(voi)	avete cominciato
(loro)	hanno cominciato

CONDITIONAL

(io)	comincerei
(tu)	cominceresti
(lui/lei) (lei/Lei)	comincerebbe
(noi)	cominceremmo
(voi)	comincereste
(loro)	comincerebbero

IMPERFECT

(io)	cominciavo
(tu)	cominciavi
(lui/lei) (lei/Lei)	cominciava
(noi)	cominciavamo
(voi)	cominciavate
(loro)	cominciavano

PRESENT SUBJUNCTIVE

(io)	cominci
(tu)	cominci
(lui/lei) (lei/Lei)	cominci
(noi)	cominciamo
(voi)	cominciate
(loro)	comincino

IMPERATIVE

comincia
cominciamo
cominciate

PAST PARTICIPLE

cominciato

GERUND

cominciando

EXAMPLE PHRASES

Il film **comincia** con un'esplosione. *The film starts with an explosion.*
Hai cominciato il libro che ti ho prestato? *Have you started the book I lent you?*
Cominciamo bene! *This is a fine start!*

Remember that subject pronouns are not used very often in Italian.

compiere (to complete)

PRESENT

(io)	compio
(tu)	compi
(lui/lei) (lei/Lei)	compie
(noi)	compiamo
(voi)	compite
(loro)	compiono

PERFECT

(io)	ho compiuto
(tu)	hai compiuto
(lui/lei) (lei/Lei)	ha compiuto
(noi)	abbiamo compiuto
(voi)	avete compiuto
(loro)	hanno compiuto

IMPERFECT

(io)	compivo
(tu)	compivi
(lui/lei) (lei/Lei)	compiva
(noi)	compivamo
(voi)	compivate
(loro)	compivano

IMPERATIVE

compi
compiamo
compite

FUTURE

(io)	compirò
(tu)	compirai
(lui/lei) (lei/Lei)	compirà
(noi)	compiremo
(voi)	compirete
(loro)	compiranno

CONDITIONAL

(io)	compirei
(tu)	compiresti
(lui/lei) (lei/Lei)	compirebbe
(noi)	compiremmo
(voi)	compireste
(loro)	compirebbero

PRESENT SUBJUNCTIVE

(io)	compia
(tu)	compia
(lui/lei) (lei/Lei)	compia
(noi)	compiamo
(voi)	compiate
(loro)	compiano

PAST PARTICIPLE

compiuto

GERUND

compiendo

EXAMPLE PHRASES

Quanti anni **compi**? *How old will you be?*
Ho compiuto sedici anni il mese scorso. *I was sixteen last month.*
Quando **compirai** gli anni? *When's your birthday?*

Italic letters in Italian words show where stress does not follow the usual rules.

confondere (to mix up)

PRESENT

(io)	**confondo**
(tu)	**confondi**
(lui/lei) (lei/Lei)	**confonde**
(noi)	**confondiamo**
(voi)	**confondete**
(loro)	**confondono**

FUTURE

(io)	**confonderò**
(tu)	**confonderai**
(lui/lei) (lei/Lei)	**confonderà**
(noi)	**confonderemo**
(voi)	**confonderete**
(loro)	**confonderanno**

PERFECT

(io)	**ho confuso**
(tu)	**hai confuso**
(lui/lei) (lei/Lei)	**ha confuso**
(noi)	**abbiamo confuso**
(voi)	**avete confuso**
(loro)	**hanno confuso**

CONDITIONAL

(io)	**confonderei**
(tu)	**confonderesti**
(lui/lei) (lei/Lei)	**confonderebbe**
(noi)	**confonderemmo**
(voi)	**confondereste**
(loro)	**confonderebbero**

IMPERFECT

(io)	**confondevo**
(tu)	**confondevi**
(lui/lei) (lei/Lei)	**confondeva**
(noi)	**confondevamo**
(voi)	**confondevate**
(loro)	**confondevano**

PRESENT SUBJUNCTIVE

(io)	**confonda**
(tu)	**confonda**
(lui/lei) (lei/Lei)	**confonda**
(noi)	**confondiamo**
(voi)	**confondiate**
(loro)	**confondano**

IMPERATIVE

confondi
confondiamo
confondete

PAST PARTICIPLE

confuso

GERUND

confondendo

EXAMPLE PHRASES

Ho confuso le date. *I mixed up the dates.*
Non **starai confondendo** i nomi? *You're not mixing up the names, are you?*
No, scusa, mi **sono confuso**: era ieri. *No, sorry, I've got mixed up: it was yesterday.*
Tutti questi discorsi **mi confondono** le idee. *All this talk is getting me confused.*

Remember that subject pronouns are not used very often in Italian.

correre (to run)

PRESENT

(io)	**corro**
(tu)	**corri**
(lui/lei) (lei/Lei)	**corre**
(noi)	**corriamo**
(voi)	**correte**
(loro)	**corrono**

FUTURE

(io)	**correrò**
(tu)	**correrai**
(lui/lei) (lei/Lei)	**correrà**
(noi)	**correremo**
(voi)	**correrete**
(loro)	**correranno**

PERFECT

(io)	**ho corso**
(tu)	**hai corso**
(lui/lei) (lei/Lei)	**ha corso**
(noi)	**abbiamo corso**
(voi)	**avete corso**
(loro)	**hanno corso**

CONDITIONAL

(io)	**correrei**
(tu)	**correresti**
(lui/lei) (lei/Lei)	**correrebbe**
(noi)	**correremmo**
(voi)	**correreste**
(loro)	**correrebbero**

IMPERFECT

(io)	**correvo**
(tu)	**correvi**
(lui/lei) (lei/Lei)	**correva**
(noi)	**correvamo**
(voi)	**correvate**
(loro)	**correvano**

PRESENT SUBJUNCTIVE

(io)	**corra**
(tu)	**corra**
(lui/lei) (lei/Lei)	**corra**
(noi)	**corriamo**
(voi)	**corriate**
(loro)	**corrano**

IMPERATIVE

corri
corriamo
correte

PAST PARTICIPLE

corso

GERUND

correndo

EXAMPLE PHRASES

Abbiamo corso come pazzi per non perdere il treno. *We ran like mad to catch the train.*
Sono corso subito fuori. *I immediately rushed outside.*
Corre troppo in macchina. *He drives too fast.*

Italic letters in Italian words show where stress does not follow the usual rules.

credere (to believe)

PRESENT

(io)	credo
(tu)	credi
(lui/lei) (lei/Lei)	crede
(noi)	crediamo
(voi)	credete
(loro)	credono

PERFECT

(io)	ho creduto
(tu)	hai creduto
(lui/lei) (lei/Lei)	ha creduto
(noi)	abbiamo creduto
(voi)	avete creduto
(loro)	hanno creduto

IMPERFECT

(io)	credevo
(tu)	credevi
(lui/lei) (lei/Lei)	credeva
(noi)	credevamo
(voi)	credevate
(loro)	credevano

IMPERATIVE

credi
crediamo
credete

FUTURE

(io)	crederò
(tu)	crederai
(lui/lei) (lei/Lei)	crederà
(noi)	crederemo
(voi)	crederete
(loro)	crederanno

CONDITIONAL

(io)	crederei
(tu)	crederesti
(lui/lei) (lei/Lei)	crederebbe
(noi)	crederemmo
(voi)	credereste
(loro)	crederebbero

PRESENT SUBJUNCTIVE

(io)	creda
(tu)	creda
(lui/lei) (lei/Lei)	creda
(noi)	crediamo
(voi)	crediate
(loro)	credano

PAST PARTICIPLE

creduto

GERUND

credendo

EXAMPLE PHRASES

Non dirmi che **credi** ai fantasmi! *Don't tell me you believe in ghosts!*
Non **credeva** ai suoi occhi. *She couldn't believe her eyes.*
Non ti **crederò** mai. *I'll never believe you.*

Remember that subject pronouns are not used very often in Italian.

crescere (to grow)

PRESENT

(io)	**cresco**
(tu)	**cresci**
(lui/lei) (lei/Lei)	**cresce**
(noi)	**cresciamo**
(voi)	**crescete**
(loro)	**crescono**

PERFECT

(io)	**sono cresciuto/a**
(tu)	**sei cresciuto/a**
(lui/lei) (lei/Lei)	**è cresciuto/a**
(noi)	**siamo cresciuti/e**
(voi)	**siete cresciuti/e**
(loro)	**sono cresciuti/e**

IMPERFECT

(io)	**crescevo**
(tu)	**crescevi**
(lui/lei) (lei/Lei)	**cresceva**
(noi)	**crescevamo**
(voi)	**crescevate**
(loro)	**crescevano**

IMPERATIVE

cresci
cresciamo
crescete

FUTURE

(io)	**crescerò**
(tu)	**crescerai**
(lui/lei) (lei/Lei)	**crescerà**
(noi)	**cresceremo**
(voi)	**crescerete**
(loro)	**cresceranno**

CONDITIONAL

(io)	**crescerei**
(tu)	**cresceresti**
(lui/lei) (lei/Lei)	**crescerebbe**
(noi)	**cresceremmo**
(voi)	**crescereste**
(loro)	**crescerebbero**

PRESENT SUBJUNCTIVE

(io)	**cresca**
(tu)	**cresca**
(lui/lei) (lei/Lei)	**cresca**
(noi)	**cresciamo**
(voi)	**cresciate**
(loro)	**crescano**

PAST PARTICIPLE

cresciuto

GERUND

crescendo

EXAMPLE PHRASES

Com'è **cresciuto** tuo fratello! *Hasn't your brother grown!*
Si **sta facendo crescere** i capelli. *She's growing her hair.*
I prezzi **cresceranno** durante le feste. *Prices will go up during the holiday season.*

Italic letters in Italian words show where stress does not follow the usual rules.

cucire (to sew)

PRESENT

(io)	**cucio**
(tu)	**cuci**
(lui/lei) (lei/Lei)	**cuce**
(noi)	**cuciamo**
(voi)	**cucite**
(loro)	**cuciono**

FUTURE

(io)	**cucirò**
(tu)	**cucirai**
(lui/lei) (lei/Lei)	**cucirà**
(noi)	**cuciremo**
(voi)	**cucirete**
(loro)	**cuciranno**

PERFECT

(io)	**ho cucito**
(tu)	**hai cucito**
(lui/lei) (lei/Lei)	**ha cucito**
(noi)	**abbiamo cucito**
(voi)	**avete cucito**
(loro)	**hanno cucito**

CONDITIONAL

(io)	**cucirei**
(tu)	**cuciresti**
(lui/lei) (lei/Lei)	**cucirebbe**
(noi)	**cuciremmo**
(voi)	**cucireste**
(loro)	**cucirebbero**

IMPERFECT

(io)	**cucivo**
(tu)	**cucivi**
(lui/lei) (lei/Lei)	**cuciva**
(noi)	**cucivamo**
(voi)	**cucivate**
(loro)	**cucivano**

PRESENT SUBJUNCTIVE

(io)	**cucia**
(tu)	**cucia**
(lui/lei) (lei/Lei)	**cucia**
(noi)	**cuciamo**
(voi)	**cuciate**
(loro)	**cuciano**

IMPERATIVE

cuci
cuciamo
cucite

PAST PARTICIPLE

cucito

GERUND

cucendo

EXAMPLE PHRASES

Non so **cucire**. *I can't sew.*
Sta cucendo uno strappo sul vestito. *She's mending a tear in her dress.*
Mi piacciono le toppe che **hai cucito** sulla giacca. *I like the patches you've sewn on your jacket.*

Remember that subject pronouns are not used very often in Italian.

cuocere (to cook)

PRESENT

(io)	**cuocio**
(tu)	**cuoci**
(lui/lei) (lei/Lei)	**cuoce**
(noi)	**cuociamo**
(voi)	**cuocete**
(loro)	**cuociono**

FUTURE

(io)	**cuocerò**
(tu)	**cuocerai**
(lui/lei) (lei/Lei)	**cuocerà**
(noi)	**cuoceremo**
(voi)	**cuocerete**
(loro)	**cuoceranno**

PERFECT

(io)	**ho cotto**
(tu)	**hai cotto**
(lui/lei) (lei/Lei)	**ha cotto**
(noi)	**abbiamo cotto**
(voi)	**avete cotto**
(loro)	**hanno cotto**

CONDITIONAL

(io)	**cuocerei**
(tu)	**cuoceresti**
(lui/lei) (lei/Lei)	**cuocerebbe**
(noi)	**cuoceremmo**
(voi)	**cuocereste**
(loro)	**cuocerebbero**

IMPERFECT

(io)	**cuocevo**
(tu)	**cuocevi**
(lui/lei) (lei/Lei)	**cuoceva**
(noi)	**cuocevamo**
(voi)	**cuocevate**
(loro)	**cuocevano**

PRESENT SUBJUNCTIVE

(io)	**cuocia**
(tu)	**cuocia**
(lui/lei) (lei/Lei)	**cuocia**
(noi)	**cuociamo**
(voi)	**cuociate**
(loro)	**cuociano**

IMPERATIVE

cuoci
cuociamo
cuocete

PAST PARTICIPLE

cotto

GERUND

cuocendo

EXAMPLE PHRASES

Cuocilo per mezz'ora. *Cook it for half an hour.*
La carne **cuoceva** sulla brace. *The meat was cooking on the barbecue.*
Stasera, il pesce, lo **cuocerò** alla griglia. *This evening I'll grill the fish.*

Italic letters in Italian words show where stress does not follow the usual rules.

dare (to give)

PRESENT

(io)	**do**
(tu)	**dai**
(lui/lei) (lei/Lei)	**dà**
(noi)	**diamo**
(voi)	**date**
(loro)	**danno**

FUTURE

(io)	**darò**
(tu)	**darai**
(lui/lei) (lei/Lei)	**darà**
(noi)	**daremo**
(voi)	**darete**
(loro)	**daranno**

PERFECT

(io)	**ho dato**
(tu)	**hai dato**
(lui/lei) (lei/Lei)	**ha dato**
(noi)	**abbiamo dato**
(voi)	**avete dato**
(loro)	**hanno dato**

CONDITIONAL

(io)	**darei**
(tu)	**daresti**
(lui/lei) (lei/Lei)	**darebbe**
(noi)	**daremmo**
(voi)	**dareste**
(loro)	**darebbero**

IMPERFECT

(io)	**davo**
(tu)	**davi**
(lui/lei) (lei/Lei)	**dava**
(noi)	**davamo**
(voi)	**davate**
(loro)	**davano**

PRESENT SUBJUNCTIVE

(io)	**dia**
(tu)	**dia**
(lui/lei) (lei/Lei)	**dia**
(noi)	**diamo**
(voi)	**diate**
(loro)	**diano**

IMPERATIVE

dai
diamo
date

PAST PARTICIPLE

dato

GERUND

dando

EXAMPLE PHRASES

Gli **ho dato** un libro. *I gave him a book.*
Dammelo. *Give it to me.*
La mia finestra **dà** sul giardino. *My window looks onto the garden.*
Domani sera **daranno** un bel film in TV. *There's a good film on TV tomorrow evening.*
Dandoti da fare, potresti ottenere molto di più. *If you exerted yourself you could achieve a lot more.*

Remember that subject pronouns are not used very often in Italian.

dire (to say)

PRESENT

(io)	dico
(tu)	dici
(lui/lei) (lei/Lei)	dice
(noi)	diciamo
(voi)	dite
(loro)	dicono

PERFECT

(io)	ho detto
(tu)	hai detto
(lui/lei) (lei/Lei)	ha detto
(noi)	abbiamo detto
(voi)	avete detto
(loro)	hanno detto

IMPERFECT

(io)	dicevo
(tu)	dicevi
(lui/lei) (lei/Lei)	diceva
(noi)	dicevamo
(voi)	dicevate
(loro)	dicevano

IMPERATIVE

di'
diciamo
dite

FUTURE

(io)	dirò
(tu)	dirai
(lui/lei) (lei/Lei)	dirà
(noi)	diremo
(voi)	direte
(loro)	diranno

CONDITIONAL

(io)	direi
(tu)	diresti
(lui/lei) (lei/Lei)	direbbe
(noi)	diremmo
(voi)	direste
(loro)	direbbero

PRESENT SUBJUNCTIVE

(io)	dica
(tu)	dica
(lui/lei) (lei/Lei)	dica
(noi)	diciamo
(voi)	diciate
(loro)	dicano

PAST PARTICIPLE

detto

GERUND

dicendo

EXAMPLE PHRASES

Ha detto che verrà. *He said he'll come.*
Come si **dice** "quadro" in inglese? *How do you say "quadro" in English?*
Che ne **diresti** di farci un selfie? *Shall we take a selfie?*
Ti **dirò** un segreto. *I'll tell you a secret.*
Dimmi dov'è. *Tell me where it is.*

Italic letters in Italian words show where stress does not follow the usual rules.

dirigere (to direct)

PRESENT

(io)	dirigo
(tu)	dirigi
(lui/lei)(lei/Lei)	dirige
(noi)	dirigiamo
(voi)	dirigete
(loro)	dirigono

FUTURE

(io)	dirigerò
(tu)	dirigerai
(lui/lei)(lei/Lei)	dirigerà
(noi)	dirigeremo
(voi)	dirigerete
(loro)	dirigeranno

PERFECT

(io)	ho diretto
(tu)	hai diretto
(lui/lei)(lei/Lei)	ha diretto
(noi)	abbiamo diretto
(voi)	avete diretto
(loro)	hanno diretto

CONDITIONAL

(io)	dirigerei
(tu)	dirigeresti
(lui/lei)(lei/Lei)	dirigerebbe
(noi)	dirigeremmo
(voi)	dirigereste
(loro)	dirigerebbero

IMPERFECT

(io)	dirigevo
(tu)	dirigevi
(lui/lei)(lei/Lei)	dirigeva
(noi)	dirigevamo
(voi)	dirigevate
(loro)	dirigevano

PRESENT SUBJUNCTIVE

(io)	diriga
(tu)	diriga
(lui/lei)(lei/Lei)	diriga
(noi)	dirigiamo
(voi)	dirigiate
(loro)	dirigano

IMPERATIVE

dirigi
dirigiamo
dirigete

PAST PARTICIPLE

diretto

GERUND

dirigendo

EXAMPLE PHRASES

I vigili **dirigono** il traffico. *The police are directing the traffic.*
Ha diretto l'orchestra con grande abilità. *He conducted the orchestra with great skill.*
Si **è diretto** verso la porta. *He made for the door.*

Remember that subject pronouns are not used very often in Italian.

discutere (to discuss)

PRESENT

(io)	**discuto**
(tu)	**discuti**
(lui/lei) (lei/Lei)	**discute**
(noi)	**discutiamo**
(voi)	**discutete**
(loro)	**discutono**

FUTURE

(io)	**discuterò**
(tu)	**discuterai**
(lui/lei) (lei/Lei)	**discuterà**
(noi)	**discuteremo**
(voi)	**discuterete**
(loro)	**discuteranno**

PERFECT

(io)	**ho discusso**
(tu)	**hai discusso**
(lui/lei) (lei/Lei)	**ha discusso**
(noi)	**abbiamo discusso**
(voi)	**avete discusso**
(loro)	**hanno discusso**

CONDITIONAL

(io)	**discuterei**
(tu)	**discuteresti**
(lui/lei) (lei/Lei)	**discuterebbe**
(noi)	**discuteremmo**
(voi)	**discutereste**
(loro)	**discuterebbero**

IMPERFECT

(io)	**discutevo**
(tu)	**discutevi**
(lui/lei) (lei/Lei)	**discuteva**
(noi)	**discutevamo**
(voi)	**discutevate**
(loro)	**discutevano**

PRESENT SUBJUNCTIVE

(io)	**discuta**
(tu)	**discuta**
(lui/lei) (lei/Lei)	**discuta**
(noi)	**discutiamo**
(voi)	**discutiate**
(loro)	**discutano**

IMPERATIVE

discuti
discutiamo
discutete

PAST PARTICIPLE

discusso

GERUND

discutendo

EXAMPLE PHRASES

Discutono spesso di politica. *They often discuss politics.*
Ho discusso a lungo con lui. *I had a long discussion with him.*
Mi ha ubbidito senza **discutere**. *He obeyed me without question.*

Italic letters in Italian words show where stress does not follow the usual rules.

distinguere (to see)

PRESENT

(io)	**distinguo**
(tu)	**distingui**
(lui/lei) (lei/Lei)	**distingue**
(noi)	**distinguiamo**
(voi)	**distinguete**
(loro)	**distinguono**

PERFECT

(io)	**ho distinto**
(tu)	**hai distinto**
(lui/lei) (lei/Lei)	**ha distinto**
(noi)	**abbiamo distinto**
(voi)	**avete distinto**
(loro)	**hanno distinto**

IMPERFECT

(io)	**distinguevo**
(tu)	**distinguevi**
(lui/lei) (lei/Lei)	**distingueva**
(noi)	**distinguevamo**
(voi)	**distinguevate**
(loro)	**distinguevano**

IMPERATIVE

distingui
distinguiamo
distinguete

FUTURE

(io)	**distinguerò**
(tu)	**distinguerai**
(lui/lei) (lei/Lei)	**distinguerà**
(noi)	**distingueremo**
(voi)	**distinguerete**
(loro)	**distingueranno**

CONDITIONAL

(io)	**distinguerei**
(tu)	**distingueresti**
(lui/lei) (lei/Lei)	**distinguerebbe**
(noi)	**distingueremmo**
(voi)	**distinguereste**
(loro)	**distinguerebbero**

PRESENT SUBJUNCTIVE

(io)	**distingua**
(tu)	**distingua**
(lui/lei) (lei/Lei)	**distingua**
(noi)	**distinguiamo**
(voi)	**distinguiate**
(loro)	**distinguano**

PAST PARTICIPLE

distinto

GERUND

distinguendo

EXAMPLE PHRASES

Non **distinguevo** il numero dell'autobus. *I couldn't see the number of the bus.*
Non li **distinguo** tra loro. *I can't tell the difference between them.*
Si è **distinto** per efficienza. *He's exceptionally efficient.*

dormire (to sleep)

PRESENT

(io)	dormo
(tu)	dormi
(lui/lei) (lei/Lei)	dorme
(noi)	dormiamo
(voi)	dormite
(loro)	dormono

PERFECT

(io)	ho dormito
(tu)	hai dormito
(lui/lei) (lei/Lei)	ha dormito
(noi)	abbiamo dormito
(voi)	avete dormito
(loro)	hanno dormito

IMPERFECT

(io)	dormivo
(tu)	dormivi
(lui/lei) (lei/Lei)	dormiva
(noi)	dormivamo
(voi)	dormivate
(loro)	dormivano

IMPERATIVE

dormi
dormiamo
dormite

FUTURE

(io)	dormirò
(tu)	dormirai
(lui/lei) (lei/Lei)	dormirà
(noi)	dormiremo
(voi)	dormirete
(loro)	dormiranno

CONDITIONAL

(io)	dormirei
(tu)	dormiresti
(lui/lei) (lei/Lei)	dormirebbe
(noi)	dormiremmo
(voi)	dormireste
(loro)	dormirebbero

PRESENT SUBJUNCTIVE

(io)	dorma
(tu)	dorma
(lui/lei) (lei/Lei)	dorma
(noi)	dormiamo
(voi)	dormiate
(loro)	dormano

PAST PARTICIPLE

dormito

GERUND

dormendo

EXAMPLE PHRASES

Sta dormendo. *She's sleeping.*
Vado a **dormire**. *I'm going to bed.*
Stanotte **dormirò** come un ghiro. *I'll sleep like a log tonight.*

Italic letters in Italian words show where stress does not follow the usual rules.

dovere (to have to)

PRESENT

(io)	**devo**
(tu)	**devi**
(lui/lei) (lei/Lei)	**deve**
(noi)	**dobbiamo**
(voi)	**dovete**
(loro)	**devono**

PERFECT

(io)	**ho dovuto**
(tu)	**hai dovuto**
(lui/lei) (lei/Lei)	**ha dovuto**
(noi)	**abbiamo dovuto**
(voi)	**avete dovuto**
(loro)	**hanno dovuto**

IMPERFECT

(io)	**dovevo**
(tu)	**dovevi**
(lui/lei) (lei/Lei)	**doveva**
(noi)	**dovevamo**
(voi)	**dovevate**
(loro)	**dovevano**

IMPERATIVE

–

FUTURE

(io)	**dovrò**
(tu)	**dovrai**
(lui/lei) (lei/Lei)	**dovrà**
(noi)	**dovremo**
(voi)	**dovrete**
(loro)	**dovranno**

CONDITIONAL

(io)	**dovrei**
(tu)	**dovresti**
(lui/lei) (lei/Lei)	**dovrebbe**
(noi)	**dovremmo**
(voi)	**dovreste**
(loro)	**dovrebbero**

PRESENT SUBJUNCTIVE

(io)	**debba**
(tu)	**debba**
(lui/lei) (lei/Lei)	**debba**
(noi)	**dobbiamo**
(voi)	**dobbiate**
(loro)	**debbano**

PAST PARTICIPLE

dovuto

GERUND

dovendo

EXAMPLE PHRASES

È **dovuto** partire. *He had to leave.*
Devi finire i compiti prima di uscire. *You must finish your homework before you go out.*
Dev'essere tardi. *It must be late.*
Dovrebbe arrivare alle dieci. *He should arrive at ten.*
Gli **dovevo** 30 euro e così l'ho invitato a cena. *I owed him 30 euros so I took him out to dinner.*

Remember that subject pronouns are not used very often in Italian.

esigere (to require)

PRESENT

(io)	**esigo**
(tu)	**esigi**
(lui/lei) (lei/Lei)	**esige**
(noi)	**esigiamo**
(voi)	**esigete**
(loro)	**esigono**

PERFECT

(io)	–
(tu)	
(lui/lei) (lei/Lei)	
(noi)	
(voi)	
(loro)	

IMPERFECT

(io)	**esigevo**
(tu)	**esigevi**
(lui/lei) (lei/Lei)	**esigeva**
(noi)	**esigevamo**
(voi)	**esigevate**
(loro)	**esigevano**

IMPERATIVE

esigi
esigiamo
esigete

FUTURE

(io)	**esigerò**
(tu)	**esigerai**
(lui/lei) (lei/Lei)	**esigerà**
(noi)	**esigeremo**
(voi)	**esigerete**
(loro)	**esigeranno**

CONDITIONAL

(io)	**esigerei**
(tu)	**esigeresti**
(lui/lei) (lei/Lei)	**esigerebbe**
(noi)	**esigeremmo**
(voi)	**esigereste**
(loro)	**esigerebbero**

PRESENT SUBJUNCTIVE

(io)	**esiga**
(tu)	**esiga**
(lui/lei) (lei/Lei)	**esiga**
(noi)	**esigiamo**
(voi)	**esigiate**
(loro)	**esigano**

PAST PARTICIPLE

–

GERUND

esigendo

EXAMPLE PHRASES

Il proprietario **esige** il pagamento immediato. *The owner is demanding immediate payment.*

È un lavoro che **esige** molta concentrazione. *It's a job which demands a lot of concentration.*

Il capufficio **esigeva** sempre la perfezione. *The office manager always demanded perfection.*

Italic letters in Italian words show where stress does not follow the usual rules.

esistere (to exist)

PRESENT

(io)	**esisto**
(tu)	**esisti**
(lui/lei) (lei/Lei)	**esiste**
(noi)	**esistiamo**
(voi)	**esistete**
(loro)	**esistono**

PERFECT

(io)	**sono esistito/a**
(tu)	**sei esistito/a**
(lui/lei) (lei/Lei)	**è esistito/a**
(noi)	**siamo esistiti/e**
(voi)	**siete esistiti/e**
(loro)	**sono esistiti/e**

IMPERFECT

(io)	**esistevo**
(tu)	**esistevi**
(lui/lei) (lei/Lei)	**esisteva**
(noi)	**esistevamo**
(voi)	**esistevate**
(loro)	**esistevano**

IMPERATIVE

esisti
esistiamo
esistite

FUTURE

(io)	**esisterò**
(tu)	**esisterai**
(lui/lei) (lei/Lei)	**esisterà**
(noi)	**esisteremo**
(voi)	**esisterete**
(loro)	**esisteranno**

CONDITIONAL

(io)	**esisterei**
(tu)	**esisteresti**
(lui/lei) (lei/Lei)	**esisterebbe**
(noi)	**esisteremmo**
(voi)	**esistereste**
(loro)	**esisterebbero**

PRESENT SUBJUNCTIVE

(io)	**esista**
(tu)	**esista**
(lui/lei) (lei/Lei)	**esista**
(noi)	**esistiamo**
(voi)	**esistiate**
(loro)	**esistano**

PAST PARTICIPLE

esistito

GERUND

esistendo

EXAMPLE PHRASES

Babbo Natale non **esiste**. *Father Christmas doesn't exist.*
Non **esiste**! *No way!*
Il 221b di Baker Street non **è** mai **esistito**. *There never really was a 221b Baker Street.*

Remember that subject pronouns are not used very often in Italian.

espellere (to expel)

PRESENT

(io)	espello
(tu)	espelli
(lui/lei) (lei/Lei)	espelle
(noi)	espelliamo
(voi)	espellete
(loro)	espellono

PERFECT

(io)	ho espulso
(tu)	hai espulso
(lui/lei) (lei/Lei)	ha espulso
(noi)	abbiamo espulso
(voi)	avete espulso
(loro)	hanno espulso

IMPERFECT

(io)	espellevo
(tu)	espellevi
(lui/lei) (lei/Lei)	espelleva
(noi)	espellevamo
(voi)	espellevate
(loro)	espellevano

IMPERATIVE

espelli
espelliamo
espellete

FUTURE

(io)	espellerò
(tu)	espellerai
(lui/lei) (lei/Lei)	espellerà
(noi)	espelleremo
(voi)	espellerete
(loro)	espelleranno

CONDITIONAL

(io)	espellerei
(tu)	espelleresti
(lui/lei) (lei/Lei)	espellerebbe
(noi)	espelleremmo
(voi)	espellereste
(loro)	espellerebbero

PRESENT SUBJUNCTIVE

(io)	espella
(tu)	espella
(lui/lei) (lei/Lei)	espella
(noi)	espelliamo
(voi)	espelliate
(loro)	espellano

PAST PARTICIPLE

espulso

GERUND

espellendo

EXAMPLE PHRASES

Tutt'e due i calciatori **sono stati espulsi**. *Both players were sent off.*
Se farai un altro fallo ti **espelleranno**. *If you commit another foul you'll be sent off.*
Non va a scuola perché l'**hanno espulso**. *He doesn't go to school because he's been expelled.*

Italic letters in Italian words show where stress does not follow the usual rules.

esprimere (to express)

PRESENT

(io)	**esprimo**
(tu)	**esprimi**
(lui/lei) (lei/Lei)	**esprime**
(noi)	**esprimiamo**
(voi)	**esprimete**
(loro)	**esprimono**

PERFECT

(io)	**ho espresso**
(tu)	**hai espresso**
(lui/lei) (lei/Lei)	**ha espresso**
(noi)	**abbiamo espresso**
(voi)	**avete espresso**
(loro)	**hanno espresso**

IMPERFECT

(io)	**esprimevo**
(tu)	**esprimevi**
(lui/lei) (lei/Lei)	**esprimeva**
(noi)	**esprimevamo**
(voi)	**esprimevate**
(loro)	**esprimevano**

IMPERATIVE

esprimi
esprimiamo
esprimete

FUTURE

(io)	**esprimerò**
(tu)	**esprimerai**
(lui/lei) (lei/Lei)	**esprimerà**
(noi)	**esprimeremo**
(voi)	**esprimerete**
(loro)	**esprimeranno**

CONDITIONAL

(io)	**esprimerei**
(tu)	**esprimeresti**
(lui/lei) (lei/Lei)	**esprimerebbe**
(noi)	**esprimeremmo**
(voi)	**esprimereste**
(loro)	**esprimerebbero**

PRESENT SUBJUNCTIVE

(io)	**esprima**
(tu)	**esprima**
(lui/lei) (lei/Lei)	**esprima**
(noi)	**esprimiamo**
(voi)	**esprimiate**
(loro)	**esprimano**

PAST PARTICIPLE

espresso

GERUND

esprimendo

EXAMPLE PHRASES

Dai, **esprimi** un desiderio! *Go on, make a wish!*
Non **esprime** mai la sua opinione. *He never expresses his own opinion.*
Abbiamo espresso i nostri dubbi nei social network. *We expressed our doubts via social media.*

essere (to be)

PRESENT

(io)	**sono**
(tu)	**sei**
(lui/lei) (lei/Lei)	**è**
(noi)	**siamo**
(voi)	**siete**
(loro)	**sono**

PERFECT

(io)	**sono stato/a**
(tu)	**sei stato/a**
(lui/lei) (lei/Lei)	**è stato/a**
(noi)	**siamo stati/e**
(voi)	**siete stati/e**
(loro)	**sono stati/e**

IMPERFECT

(io)	**ero**
(tu)	**eri**
(lui/lei) (lei/Lei)	**era**
(noi)	**eravamo**
(voi)	**eravate**
(loro)	**erano**

IMPERATIVE

sii
siamo
siate

FUTURE

(io)	**sarò**
(tu)	**sarai**
(lui/lei) (lei/Lei)	**sarà**
(noi)	**saremo**
(voi)	**sarete**
(loro)	**saranno**

CONDITIONAL

(io)	**sarei**
(tu)	**saresti**
(lui/lei) (lei/Lei)	**sarebbe**
(noi)	**saremmo**
(voi)	**sareste**
(loro)	**sarebbero**

PRESENT SUBJUNCTIVE

(io)	**sia**
(tu)	**sia**
(lui/lei) (lei/Lei)	**sia**
(noi)	**siamo**
(voi)	**siate**
(loro)	**siano**

PAST PARTICIPLE

stato

GERUND

essendo

EXAMPLE PHRASES

Sono italiana. *I'm Italian.*

Mario **è** appena partito. *Mario has just left.*

Siete mai **stati** in Africa? *Have you ever been to Africa?*

Quando **è** arrivato erano le quattro in punto. *It was exactly four o'clock when he arrived.*

Alla festa ci **saranno** tutti i miei amici. *All my friends will be at the party.*

Italic letters in Italian words show where stress does not follow the usual rules.

fare (to do; make)

PRESENT

(io)	**faccio**
(tu)	**fai**
(lui/lei) (lei/Lei)	**fa**
(noi)	**facciamo**
(voi)	**fate**
(loro)	**fanno**

FUTURE

(io)	**farò**
(tu)	**farai**
(lui/lei) (lei/Lei)	**farà**
(noi)	**faremo**
(voi)	**farete**
(loro)	**faranno**

PERFECT

(io)	**ho fatto**
(tu)	**hai fatto**
(lui/lei) (lei/Lei)	**ha fatto**
(noi)	**abbiamo fatto**
(voi)	**avete fatto**
(loro)	**hanno fatto**

CONDITIONAL

(io)	**farei**
(tu)	**faresti**
(lui/lei) (lei/Lei)	**farebbe**
(noi)	**faremmo**
(voi)	**fareste**
(loro)	**farebbero**

IMPERFECT

(io)	**facevo**
(tu)	**facevi**
(lui/lei) (lei/Lei)	**faceva**
(noi)	**facevamo**
(voi)	**facevate**
(loro)	**facevano**

PRESENT SUBJUNCTIVE

(io)	**faccia**
(tu)	**faccia**
(lui/lei) (lei/Lei)	**faccia**
(noi)	**facciamo**
(voi)	**facciate**
(loro)	**facciano**

IMPERATIVE
fai
facciamo
fate

PAST PARTICIPLE
fatto

GERUND
facendo

EXAMPLE PHRASES

Ho fatto un errore. *I made a mistake.*
Due più due **fa** quattro. *Two and two makes four.*
Cosa **stai facendo**? *What are you doing?*
Fa il medico. *He is a doctor.*
Fa caldo. *It's hot.*

Remember that subject pronouns are not used very often in Italian.

fuggire (to run away)

PRESENT

(io)	**fuggo**
(tu)	**fuggi**
(lui/lei) (lei/Lei)	**fugge**
(noi)	**fuggiamo**
(voi)	**fuggite**
(loro)	**fuggono**

PERFECT

(io)	**sono fuggito/a**
(tu)	**sei fuggito/a**
(lui/lei) (lei/Lei)	**è fuggito/a**
(noi)	**siamo fuggiti/e**
(voi)	**siete fuggiti/e**
(loro)	**sono fuggiti/e**

IMPERFECT

(io)	**fuggivo**
(tu)	**fuggivi**
(lui/lei) (lei/Lei)	**fuggiva**
(noi)	**fuggivamo**
(voi)	**fuggivate**
(loro)	**fuggivano**

IMPERATIVE

fuggi
fuggiamo
fuggite

FUTURE

(io)	**fuggirò**
(tu)	**fuggirai**
(lui/lei) (lei/Lei)	**fuggirà**
(noi)	**fuggiremo**
(voi)	**fuggirete**
(loro)	**fuggiranno**

CONDITIONAL

(io)	**fuggirei**
(tu)	**fuggiresti**
(lui/lei) (lei/Lei)	**fuggirebbe**
(noi)	**fuggiremmo**
(voi)	**fuggireste**
(loro)	**fuggirebbero**

PRESENT SUBJUNCTIVE

(io)	**fugga**
(tu)	**fugga**
(lui/lei) (lei/Lei)	**fugga**
(noi)	**fuggiamo**
(voi)	**fuggiate**
(loro)	**fuggano**

PAST PARTICIPLE

fuggito

GERUND

fuggendo

EXAMPLE PHRASES

È fuggita di casa. *She ran away from home.*
Non c'è bisogno che tu leghi il cane alla sedia: non **fuggirà**. *There is no need for you to tie your dog to the chair, it won't run off.*
La polizia! **Fuggiamo**! *It's the police! Run for it!*

Italic letters in Italian words show where stress does not follow the usual rules.

immergere (to immerse)

PRESENT

(io)	immergo
(tu)	immergi
(lui/lei) (lei/Lei)	immerge
(noi)	immergiamo
(voi)	immergete
(loro)	immergono

FUTURE

(io)	immergerò
(tu)	immergerai
(lui/lei) (lei/Lei)	immergerà
(noi)	immergeremo
(voi)	immergerete
(loro)	immergeranno

PERFECT

(io)	ho immerso
(tu)	hai immerso
(lui/lei) (lei/Lei)	ha immerso
(noi)	abbiamo immerso
(voi)	avete immerso
(loro)	hanno immerso

CONDITIONAL

(io)	immergerei
(tu)	immergeresti
(lui/lei) (lei/Lei)	immergerebbe
(noi)	immergeremmo
(voi)	immergereste
(loro)	immergerebbero

IMPERFECT

(io)	immergevo
(tu)	immergevi
(lui/lei) (lei/Lei)	immergeva
(noi)	immergevamo
(voi)	immergevate
(loro)	immergevano

PRESENT SUBJUNCTIVE

(io)	immerga
(tu)	immerga
(lui/lei) (lei/Lei)	immerga
(noi)	immergiamo
(voi)	immergiate
(loro)	immergano

IMPERATIVE

immergi
immergiamo
immergete

PAST PARTICIPLE

immerso

GERUND

immergendo

EXAMPLE PHRASES

Ha immerso il metallo incandescente nell'acqua. *He plunged the red-hot metal into the water.*

Ci **immergeremo** nelle acque dell'Adriatico. *We'll dive in the waters of the Adriatic.*

Si **immergevano** nello studio ogni sera. *They immersed themselves in their studies every evening.*

Remember that subject pronouns are not used very often in Italian.

invecchiare (to get old)

PRESENT

(io)	invecchio
(tu)	invecchi
(lui/lei) (lei/Lei)	invecchia
(noi)	invecchiamo
(voi)	invecchiate
(loro)	invecchiano

PERFECT

(io)	sono invecchiato/a
(tu)	sei invecchiato/a
(lui/lei) (lei/Lei)	è invecchiato/a
(noi)	siamo invecchiati/e
(voi)	siete invecchiati/e
(loro)	sono invecchiati/e

IMPERFECT

(io)	invecchiavo
(tu)	invecchiavi
(lui/lei) (lei/Lei)	invecchiava
(noi)	invecchiavamo
(voi)	invecchiavate
(loro)	invecchiavano

IMPERATIVE

invecchia
invecchiamo
invecchiate

FUTURE

(io)	invecchierò
(tu)	invecchierai
(lui/lei) (lei/Lei)	invecchierà
(noi)	invecchieremo
(voi)	invecchierete
(loro)	invecchieranno

CONDITIONAL

(io)	invecchierei
(tu)	invecchieresti
(lui/lei) (lei/Lei)	invecchierebbe
(noi)	invecchieremmo
(voi)	invecchiereste
(loro)	invecchierebbero

PRESENT SUBJUNCTIVE

(io)	invecchi
(tu)	invecchi
(lui/lei) (lei/Lei)	invecchi
(noi)	invecchiamo
(voi)	invecchiate
(loro)	invecchino

PAST PARTICIPLE

invecchiato

GERUND

invecchiando

EXAMPLE PHRASES

Tutti **invecchiano** prima o poi. *Everyone gets old sooner or later.*
Questo vino **è invecchiato** in botti di rovere. *This wine is aged in oak casks.*
Molti hanno paura di **invecchiare**. *A lot of people are afraid of getting old.*

Italic letters in Italian words show where stress does not follow the usual rules.

inviare (to send)

PRESENT

(io)	**invio**
(tu)	**invii**
(lui/lei) (lei/Lei)	**invia**
(noi)	**inviamo**
(voi)	**inviate**
(loro)	**inviino**

PERFECT

(io)	**ho inviato**
(tu)	**hai inviato**
(lui/lei) (lei/Lei)	**ha inviato**
(noi)	**abbiamo inviato**
(voi)	**avete inviato**
(loro)	**hanno inviato**

IMPERFECT

(io)	**inviavo**
(tu)	**inviavi**
(lui/lei) (lei/Lei)	**inviava**
(noi)	**inviavamo**
(voi)	**inviavate**
(loro)	**inviavano**

IMPERATIVE

invia
inviamo
inviate

FUTURE

(io)	**invierò**
(tu)	**invierai**
(lui/lei) (lei/Lei)	**invierà**
(noi)	**invieremo**
(voi)	**invierete**
(loro)	**invieranno**

CONDITIONAL

(io)	**invierei**
(tu)	**invieresti**
(lui/lei) (lei/Lei)	**invierebbe**
(noi)	**invieremmo**
(voi)	**inviereste**
(loro)	**invierebbero**

PRESENT SUBJUNCTIVE

(io)	**invii**
(tu)	**invii**
(lui/lei) (lei/Lei)	**invii**
(noi)	**inviamo**
(voi)	**inviate**
(loro)	**inviino**

PAST PARTICIPLE

inviato

GERUND

inviando

EXAMPLE PHRASES

Non **ho** ancora **inviato** la domanda di iscrizione. *I haven't sent the enrolment form off yet.*

Quando arrivi, **inviami** un sms. *Text me when you arrive.*

Vi **invieremo** ulteriori dettagli in seguito. *We will send you further details later.*

Remember that subject pronouns are not used very often in Italian.

lasciare (to leave)

PRESENT

(io)	lascio
(tu)	lasci
(lui/lei) (lei/Lei)	lascia
(noi)	lasciamo
(voi)	lasciate
(loro)	lasciano

PERFECT

(io)	ho lasciato
(tu)	hai lasciato
(lui/lei) (lei/Lei)	ha lasciato
(noi)	abbiamo lasciato
(voi)	avete lasciato
(loro)	hanno lasciato

IMPERFECT

(io)	lasciavo
(tu)	lasciavi
(lui/lei) (lei/Lei)	lasciava
(noi)	lasciavamo
(voi)	lasciavate
(loro)	lasciavano

IMPERATIVE

lascia
lasciamo
lasciate

FUTURE

(io)	lascerò
(tu)	lascerai
(lui/lei) (lei/Lei)	lascerà
(noi)	lasceremo
(voi)	lascerete
(loro)	lasceranno

CONDITIONAL

(io)	lascerei
(tu)	lasceresti
(lui/lei) (lei/Lei)	lascerebbe
(noi)	lasceremmo
(voi)	lascereste
(loro)	lascerebbero

PRESENT SUBJUNCTIVE

(io)	lasci
(tu)	lasci
(lui/lei) (lei/Lei)	lasci
(noi)	lasciamo
(voi)	lasciate
(loro)	lascino

PAST PARTICIPLE

lasciato

GERUND

lasciando

EXAMPLE PHRASES

Mio padre non mi **lascia** uscire fino a tardi. *My father doesn't let me stay out late.*
Lascia stare mia sorella! *Leave my sister alone!*
I miei si **sono lasciati** un anno fa. *My parents split up a year ago.*

Italic letters in Italian words show where stress does not follow the usual rules.

leggere (to read)

PRESENT

(io)	**leggo**
(tu)	**leggi**
(lui/lei) (lei/Lei)	**legge**
(noi)	**leggiamo**
(voi)	**leggete**
(loro)	**leggono**

PERFECT

(io)	**ho letto**
(tu)	**hai letto**
(lui/lei) (lei/Lei)	**ha letto**
(noi)	**abbiamo letto**
(voi)	**avete letto**
(loro)	**hanno letto**

IMPERFECT

(io)	**leggevo**
(tu)	**leggevi**
(lui/lei) (lei/Lei)	**leggeva**
(noi)	**leggevamo**
(voi)	**leggevate**
(loro)	**leggevano**

IMPERATIVE

leggi
leggiamo
leggete

FUTURE

(io)	**leggerò**
(tu)	**leggerai**
(lui/lei) (lei/Lei)	**leggerà**
(noi)	**leggeremo**
(voi)	**leggerete**
(loro)	**leggeranno**

CONDITIONAL

(io)	**leggerei**
(tu)	**leggeresti**
(lui/lei) (lei/Lei)	**leggerebbe**
(noi)	**leggeremmo**
(voi)	**leggereste**
(loro)	**leggerebbero**

PRESENT SUBJUNCTIVE

(io)	**legga**
(tu)	**legga**
(lui/lei) (lei/Lei)	**legga**
(noi)	**leggiamo**
(voi)	**leggiate**
(loro)	**leggano**

PAST PARTICIPLE

letto

GERUND

leggendo

EXAMPLE PHRASES

Non **ho** ancora **letto** quel libro. *I haven't read that book yet.*
Legge il giornale tutti i giorni. *He reads the paper every day.*
Leggevo molto prima di iniziare a lavorare. *I read a lot before I started working.*

Remember that subject pronouns are not used very often in Italian.

mangiare (to eat)

PRESENT

(io)	**mangio**
(tu)	**mangi**
(lui/lei) (lei/Lei)	**mangia**
(noi)	**mangiamo**
(voi)	**mangiate**
(loro)	**mangiano**

PERFECT

(io)	**ho mangiato**
(tu)	**hai mangiato**
(lui/lei) (lei/Lei)	**ha mangiato**
(noi)	**abbiamo mangiato**
(voi)	**avete mangiato**
(loro)	**hanno mangiato**

IMPERFECT

(io)	**mangiavo**
(tu)	**mangiavi**
(lui/lei) (lei/Lei)	**mangiava**
(noi)	**mangiavamo**
(voi)	**mangiavate**
(loro)	**mangiavano**

IMPERATIVE

mangia
mangiamo
mangiate

FUTURE

(io)	**mangerò**
(tu)	**mangerai**
(lui/lei) (lei/Lei)	**mangerà**
(noi)	**mangeremo**
(voi)	**mangerete**
(loro)	**mangeranno**

CONDITIONAL

(io)	**mangerei**
(tu)	**mangeresti**
(lui/lei) (lei/Lei)	**mangerebbe**
(noi)	**mangeremmo**
(voi)	**mangereste**
(loro)	**mangerebbero**

PRESENT SUBJUNCTIVE

(io)	**mangi**
(tu)	**mangi**
(lui/lei) (lei/Lei)	**mangi**
(noi)	**mangiamo**
(voi)	**mangiate**
(loro)	**mangino**

PAST PARTICIPLE

mangiato

GERUND

mangiando

EXAMPLE PHRASES

Non **mangio** carne. *I don't eat meat.*
Si **mangia** bene in quel ristorante. *The food is good in that restaurant.*
Ultimamente **sto mangiando** troppo. *I've been eating too much lately.*

Italic letters in Italian words show where stress does not follow the usual rules.

mettere (to put)

PRESENT

(io)	**metto**
(tu)	**metti**
(lui/lei) (lei/Lei)	**mette**
(noi)	**mettiamo**
(voi)	**mettete**
(loro)	**mettono**

PERFECT

(io)	**ho messo**
(tu)	**hai messo**
(lui/lei) (lei/Lei)	**ha messo**
(noi)	**abbiamo messo**
(voi)	**avete messo**
(loro)	**hanno messo**

IMPERFECT

(io)	**mettevo**
(tu)	**mettevi**
(lui/lei) (lei/Lei)	**metteva**
(noi)	**mettevamo**
(voi)	**mettevate**
(loro)	**mettevano**

IMPERATIVE

metti
mettiamo
mettete

FUTURE

(io)	**metterò**
(tu)	**metterai**
(lui/lei) (lei/Lei)	**metterà**
(noi)	**metteremo**
(voi)	**metterete**
(loro)	**metteranno**

CONDITIONAL

(io)	**metterei**
(tu)	**metteresti**
(lui/lei) (lei/Lei)	**metterebbe**
(noi)	**metteremmo**
(voi)	**mettereste**
(loro)	**metterebbero**

PRESENT SUBJUNCTIVE

(io)	**metta**
(tu)	**metta**
(lui/lei) (lei/Lei)	**metta**
(noi)	**mettiamo**
(voi)	**mettiate**
(loro)	**mettano**

PAST PARTICIPLE

messo

GERUND

mettendo

EXAMPLE PHRASES

Hai messo i bambini a letto? *Have you put the children to bed?*
Metterò un annuncio sul Internet. *I'll put an advert online.*
Mettiti là e aspetta. *Wait there.*
Quanto tempo ci **hai messo**? *How long did it take you?*
Non **metto** più quelle scarpe. *I don't wear those shoes any more.*

Remember that subject pronouns are not used very often in Italian.

morire (to die)

PRESENT

(io)	mu*o*io
(tu)	mu*o*ri
(lui/lei) (lei/Lei)	mu*o*re
(noi)	moriamo
(voi)	morite
(loro)	mu*o*iono

PERFECT

(io)	sono morto/a
(tu)	sei morto/a
(lui/lei) (lei/Lei)	è morto/a
(noi)	siamo morti/e
(voi)	siete morti/e
(loro)	sono morti/e

IMPERFECT

(io)	morivo
(tu)	morivi
(lui/lei) (lei/Lei)	moriva
(noi)	morivamo
(voi)	morivate
(loro)	morivano

IMPERATIVE

muori
moriamo
morite

FUTURE

(io)	morirò
(tu)	morirai
(lui/lei) (lei/Lei)	morir*à*
(noi)	moriremo
(voi)	morirete
(loro)	moriranno

CONDITIONAL

(io)	morirei
(tu)	moriresti
(lui/lei) (lei/Lei)	morirebbe
(noi)	moriremmo
(voi)	morireste
(loro)	morir*e*bbero

PRESENT SUBJUNCTIVE

(io)	mu*o*ia
(tu)	mu*o*ia
(lui/lei) (lei/Lei)	mu*o*ia
(noi)	moriamo
(voi)	moriate
(loro)	mu*o*iano

PAST PARTICIPLE

morto

GERUND

morendo

EXAMPLE PHRASES

Mu*o*io di sete. *I'm dying of thirst.*
Sta morendo di fame. *She's starving.*
Moriva dalla voglia di raccontarle tutto. *He was dying to tell her everything.*

Italic letters in Italian words show where stress does not follow the usual rules.

muovere (to move)

PRESENT

(io)	muovo
(tu)	muovi
(lui/lei) (lei/Lei)	muove
(noi)	muoviamo
(voi)	muovete
(loro)	muovono

PERFECT

(io)	ho mosso
(tu)	hai mosso
(lui/lei) (lei/Lei)	ha mosso
(noi)	abbiamo mosso
(voi)	avete mosso
(loro)	hanno mosso

IMPERFECT

(io)	muovevo
(tu)	muovevi
(lui/lei) (lei/Lei)	muoveva
(noi)	muovevamo
(voi)	muovevate
(loro)	muovevano

IMPERATIVE

muovi
muoviamo
muovete

FUTURE

(io)	muoverò
(tu)	muoverai
(lui/lei) (lei/Lei)	muoverà
(noi)	muoveremo
(voi)	muoverete
(loro)	muoveranno

CONDITIONAL

(io)	muoverei
(tu)	muoveresti
(lui/lei) (lei/Lei)	muoverebbe
(noi)	muoveremmo
(voi)	muovereste
(loro)	muoverebbero

PRESENT SUBJUNCTIVE

(io)	muova
(tu)	muova
(lui/lei) (lei/Lei)	muova
(noi)	muoviamo
(voi)	muoviate
(loro)	muovano

PAST PARTICIPLE

mosso

GERUND

muovendo

EXAMPLE PHRASES

Non **muovevo** più la gamba per il dolore. *I couldn't move my leg because of the pain.*
Non si **muove**. *It won't move.*
Muoviti, o perdiamo il treno! *Hurry up, or we'll miss the train!*

nascere (to be born)

PRESENT

(io)	nasco
(tu)	nasci
(lui/lei)(lei/Lei)	nasce
(noi)	nasciamo
(voi)	nascete
(loro)	nascono

FUTURE

(io)	nascerò
(tu)	nascerai
(lui/lei)(lei/Lei)	nascerà
(noi)	nasceremo
(voi)	nascerete
(loro)	nasceranno

PERFECT

(io)	sono nato/a
(tu)	sei nato/a
(lui/lei)(lei/Lei)	è nato/a
(noi)	siamo nati/e
(voi)	siete nati/e
(loro)	sono nati/e

CONDITIONAL

(io)	nascerei
(tu)	nasceresti
(lui/lei)(lei/Lei)	nascerebbe
(noi)	nasceremmo
(voi)	nascereste
(loro)	nascerebbero

IMPERFECT

(io)	nascevo
(tu)	nascevi
(lui/lei)(lei/Lei)	nasceva
(noi)	nascevamo
(voi)	nascevate
(loro)	nascevano

PRESENT SUBJUNCTIVE

(io)	nasca
(tu)	nasca
(lui/lei)(lei/Lei)	nasca
(noi)	nasciamo
(voi)	nasciate
(loro)	nascano

IMPERATIVE

nasci
nasciamo
nascete

PAST PARTICIPLE

nato

GERUND

nascendo

EXAMPLE PHRASES

È nato nel 1998. *He was born in 1998.*
Il bambino **nascerà** tra due settimane. *The baby is due in two weeks.*
Sono nata il 28 aprile. *I was born on the 28th of April.*

Italic letters in Italian words show where stress does not follow the usual rules.

pagare (to pay)

PRESENT

(io)	pago
(tu)	paghi
(lui/lei)(lei/Lei)	paga
(noi)	paghiamo
(voi)	pagate
(loro)	pagano

FUTURE

(io)	pagherò
(tu)	pagherai
(lui/lei)(lei/Lei)	pagherà
(noi)	pagheremo
(voi)	pagherete
(loro)	pagheranno

PERFECT

(io)	ho pagato
(tu)	hai pagato
(lui/lei)(lei/Lei)	ha pagato
(noi)	abbiamo pagato
(voi)	avete pagato
(loro)	hanno pagato

CONDITIONAL

(io)	pagherei
(tu)	pagheresti
(lui/lei)(lei/Lei)	pagherebbe
(noi)	pagheremmo
(voi)	paghereste
(loro)	pagherebbero

IMPERFECT

(io)	pagavo
(tu)	pagavi
(lui/lei)(lei/Lei)	pagava
(noi)	pagavamo
(voi)	pagavate
(loro)	pagavano

PRESENT SUBJUNCTIVE

(io)	paghi
(tu)	paghi
(lui/lei)(lei/Lei)	paghi
(noi)	paghiamo
(voi)	paghiate
(loro)	paghino

IMPERATIVE

paga
paghiamo
pagate

PAST PARTICIPLE

pagato

GERUND

pagando

EXAMPLE PHRASES

Hai pagato il conto? *Have you paid the bill?*
Pagherei io, ma non accettano la carta di credito. *I'd pay, but they don't take credit cards.*
La **pagherai**! *You'll pay for this!*

Remember that subject pronouns are not used very often in Italian.

parere (to appear)

PRESENT

(io)	paio
(tu)	pari
(lui/lei) (lei/Lei)	pare
(noi)	pariamo
(voi)	parete
(loro)	paiono

PERFECT

(io)	sono parso/a
(tu)	sei parso/a
(lui/lei) (lei/Lei)	è parso/a
(noi)	siamo parsi/e
(voi)	siete parsi/e
(loro)	sono parsi/e

IMPERFECT

(io)	parevo
(tu)	parevi
(lui/lei) (lei/Lei)	pareva
(noi)	parevamo
(voi)	parevate
(loro)	parevano

IMPERATIVE

pari
pariamo
parete

FUTURE

(io)	parrò
(tu)	parrai
(lui/lei) (lei/Lei)	parrà
(noi)	parremo
(voi)	parrete
(loro)	parranno

CONDITIONAL

(io)	parrei
(tu)	parresti
(lui/lei) (lei/Lei)	parrebbe
(noi)	parremmo
(voi)	parreste
(loro)	parrebbero

PRESENT SUBJUNCTIVE

(io)	paia
(tu)	paia
(lui/lei) (lei/Lei)	paia
(noi)	paiamo
(voi)	paiate
(loro)	paiano

PAST PARTICIPLE

parso

GERUND

parendo

EXAMPLE PHRASES

Mi **pare** che sia già arrivato. *I think he's already here.*
Ci **è parso** che foste stanchi. *We thought you were tired.*
Faceva solo ciò che gli **pareva**. *He did just what he wanted.*

Italic letters in Italian words show where stress does not follow the usual rules.

parlare (to speak)

PRESENT

(io)	**parlo**
(tu)	**parli**
(lui/lei) (lei/Lei)	**parla**
(noi)	**parliamo**
(voi)	**parlate**
(loro)	**parlano**

PERFECT

(io)	**ho parlato**
(tu)	**hai parlato**
(lui/lei) (lei/Lei)	**ha parlato**
(noi)	**abbiamo parlato**
(voi)	**avete parlato**
(loro)	**hanno parlato**

IMPERFECT

(io)	**parlavo**
(tu)	**parlavi**
(lui/lei) (lei/Lei)	**parlava**
(noi)	**parlavamo**
(voi)	**parlavate**
(loro)	**parlavano**

IMPERATIVE

parla
parliamo
parlate

FUTURE

(io)	**parlerò**
(tu)	**parlerai**
(lui/lei) (lei/Lei)	**parlerà**
(noi)	**parleremo**
(voi)	**parlerete**
(loro)	**parleranno**

CONDITIONAL

(io)	**parlerei**
(tu)	**parleresti**
(lui/lei) (lei/Lei)	**parlerebbe**
(noi)	**parleremmo**
(voi)	**parlereste**
(loro)	**parlerebbero**

PRESENT SUBJUNCTIVE

(io)	**parli**
(tu)	**parli**
(lui/lei) (lei/Lei)	**parli**
(noi)	**parliamo**
(voi)	**parliate**
(loro)	**parlino**

PAST PARTICIPLE

parlato

GERUND

parlando

EXAMPLE PHRASES

Pronto, chi **parla**? *Hello, who's speaking?*
Non **parliamone** più. *Let's just forget about it.*
Abbiamo parlato per ore. *We talked for hours.*
Gli **parlerò** di te. *I'll talk to him about you.*
Di cosa **parla** quel libro? *What is that book about?*

Remember that subject pronouns are not used very often in Italian.

pescare (to fish)

PRESENT

(io)	**pesco**
(tu)	**peschi**
(lui/lei) (lei/Lei)	**pesca**
(noi)	**peschiamo**
(voi)	**pescate**
(loro)	**pescano**

PERFECT

(io)	**ho pescato**
(tu)	**hai pescato**
(lui/lei) (lei/Lei)	**ha pescato**
(noi)	**abbiamo pescato**
(voi)	**avete pescato**
(loro)	**hanno pescato**

IMPERFECT

(io)	**pescavo**
(tu)	**pescavi**
(lui/lei) (lei/Lei)	**pescava**
(noi)	**pescavamo**
(voi)	**pescavate**
(loro)	**pescavano**

IMPERATIVE

pesca
peschiamo
pescate

FUTURE

(io)	**pescherò**
(tu)	**pescherai**
(lui/lei) (lei/Lei)	**pescherà**
(noi)	**pescheremo**
(voi)	**pescherete**
(loro)	**pescheranno**

CONDITIONAL

(io)	**pescherei**
(tu)	**pescheresti**
(lui/lei) (lei/Lei)	**pescherebbe**
(noi)	**pescheremmo**
(voi)	**peschereste**
(loro)	**pescherebbero**

PRESENT SUBJUNCTIVE

(io)	**peschi**
(tu)	**peschi**
(lui/lei) (lei/Lei)	**peschi**
(noi)	**peschiamo**
(voi)	**peschiate**
(loro)	**peschino**

PAST PARTICIPLE

pescato

GERUND

pescando

EXAMPLE PHRASES

Ti insegnerò a **pescare**. *I'll teach you how to fish.*
Ho pescato un pesce enorme. *I caught an enormous fish.*
Dove diavolo **hai pescato** quella giacca? *Where on earth did you get that jacket?*

Italic letters in Italian words show where stress does not follow the usual rules.

piacere (to be pleasing)

PRESENT

(io)	**piaccio**
(tu)	**piaci**
(lui/lei) (lei/Lei)	**piace**
(noi)	**piacciamo**
(voi)	**piacete**
(loro)	**piacciono**

PERFECT

(io)	**sono piaciuto/a**
(tu)	**sei piaciuto/a**
(lui/lei) (lei/Lei)	**è piaciuto/a**
(noi)	**siamo piaciuti/e**
(voi)	**siete piaciuti/e**
(loro)	**sono piaciuti/e**

IMPERFECT

(io)	**piacevo**
(tu)	**piacevi**
(lui/lei) (lei/Lei)	**piaceva**
(noi)	**piacevamo**
(voi)	**piacevate**
(loro)	**piacevano**

IMPERATIVE

piaci
piacciamo
piacete

FUTURE

(io)	**piacerò**
(tu)	**piacerai**
(lui/lei) (lei/Lei)	**piacerà**
(noi)	**piaceremo**
(voi)	**piacerete**
(loro)	**piaceranno**

CONDITIONAL

(io)	**piacerei**
(tu)	**piaceresti**
(lui/lei) (lei/Lei)	**piacerebbe**
(noi)	**piaceremmo**
(voi)	**piacereste**
(loro)	**piacerebbero**

PRESENT SUBJUNCTIVE

(io)	**piaccia**
(tu)	**piaccia**
(lui/lei) (lei/Lei)	**piaccia**
(noi)	**piacciamo**
(voi)	**piacciate**
(loro)	**piacciano**

PAST PARTICIPLE

piaciuto

GERUND

piacendo

EXAMPLE PHRASES

Questa musica non **mi piace**. *I don't like this music.*
Cosa **ti piacerebbe** fare? *What would you like to do?*
Da piccola non **mi piacevano** i ragni. *When I was little I didn't like spiders.*

Remember that subject pronouns are not used very often in Italian.

piovere (to rain)

PRESENT
piove

FUTURE
piover*à*

PERFECT
ha piovuto

CONDITIONAL
pioverebbe

IMPERFECT
pioveva

PRESENT SUBJUNCTIVE
piova

IMPERATIVE
–

PAST PARTICIPLE
piovuto

GERUND
piovendo

EXAMPLE PHRASES

Piove. *It's raining.*
Ha piovuto tutto il giorno. *It rained all day.*
Quando sono uscito **pioveva**. *When I went out it was raining.*

Italic letters in Italian words show where stress does not follow the usual rules.

potere (to be able)

PRESENT

(io)	posso
(tu)	puoi
(lui/lei) (lei/Lei)	può
(noi)	possiamo
(voi)	potete
(loro)	possono

FUTURE

(io)	potrò
(tu)	potrai
(lui/lei) (lei/Lei)	potrà
(noi)	potremo
(voi)	potrete
(loro)	potranno

PERFECT

(io)	ho potuto
(tu)	hai potuto
(lui/lei) (lei/Lei)	ha potuto
(noi)	abbiamo potuto
(voi)	avete potuto
(loro)	hanno potuto

CONDITIONAL

(io)	potrei
(tu)	potresti
(lui/lei) (lei/Lei)	potrebbe
(noi)	potremmo
(voi)	potreste
(loro)	potrebbero

IMPERFECT

(io)	potevo
(tu)	potevi
(lui/lei) (lei/Lei)	poteva
(noi)	potevamo
(voi)	potevate
(loro)	potevano

PRESENT SUBJUNCTIVE

(io)	possa
(tu)	possa
(lui/lei) (lei/Lei)	possa
(noi)	possiamo
(voi)	possiate
(loro)	possano

IMPERATIVE

–

PAST PARTICIPLE

potuto

GERUND

potendo

EXAMPLE PHRASES

Si **può** visitare il castello tutti i giorni dell'anno. *You can visit the castle any day of the year.*

Non **è potuto** venire. *He couldn't come.*

Non **potrò** venire domani. *I won't be able to come tomorrow.*

Può aver avuto un incidente. *He may have had an accident.*

Potrebbe essere vero. *It could be true.*

Remember that subject pronouns are not used very often in Italian.

prendere (to take)

PRESENT

(io)	prendo
(tu)	prendi
(lui/lei) (lei/Lei)	prende
(noi)	prendiamo
(voi)	prendete
(loro)	prendono

PERFECT

(io)	ho preso
(tu)	hai preso
(lui/lei) (lei/Lei)	ha preso
(noi)	abbiamo preso
(voi)	avete preso
(loro)	hanno preso

IMPERFECT

(io)	prendevo
(tu)	prendevi
(lui/lei) (lei/Lei)	prendeva
(noi)	prendevamo
(voi)	prendevate
(loro)	prendevano

IMPERATIVE

prendi
prendiamo
prendete

FUTURE

(io)	prenderò
(tu)	prenderai
(lui/lei) (lei/Lei)	prenderà
(noi)	prenderemo
(voi)	prenderete
(loro)	prenderanno

CONDITIONAL

(io)	prenderei
(tu)	prenderesti
(lui/lei) (lei/Lei)	prenderebbe
(noi)	prenderemmo
(voi)	prendereste
(loro)	prenderebbero

PRESENT SUBJUNCTIVE

(io)	prenda
(tu)	prenda
(lui/lei) (lei/Lei)	prenda
(noi)	prendiamo
(voi)	prendiate
(loro)	prendano

PAST PARTICIPLE

preso

GERUND

prendendo

EXAMPLE PHRASES

Prendi quella borsa. *Take that bag.*
Ho preso un bel voto. *I got a good mark.*
Prende qualcosa da bere? *Would you like something to drink?*
Per chi mi **prendi**? *Who do you think I am?*

Italic letters in Italian words show where stress does not follow the usual rules.

procedere (to move along)

PRESENT

(io)	procedo
(tu)	procedi
(lui/lei) (lei/Lei)	procede
(noi)	procediamo
(voi)	procedete
(loro)	procedono

PERFECT

(io)	**sono proceduto/a**
(tu)	**sei proceduto/a**
(lui/lei) (lei/Lei)	**è proceduto/a**
(noi)	**siamo proceduti/e**
(voi)	**siete proceduti/e**
(loro)	**sono proceduti/e**

IMPERFECT

(io)	procedevo
(tu)	procedevi
(lui/lei) (lei/Lei)	procedeva
(noi)	procedevamo
(voi)	procedevate
(loro)	procedevano

IMPERATIVE

procedi
procediamo
procedete

FUTURE

(io)	procederò
(tu)	procederai
(lui/lei) (lei/Lei)	procederà
(noi)	procederemo
(voi)	procederete
(loro)	procederanno

CONDITIONAL

(io)	procederei
(tu)	procederesti
(lui/lei) (lei/Lei)	procederebbe
(noi)	procederemmo
(voi)	procedereste
(loro)	procederebbero

PRESENT SUBJUNCTIVE

(io)	proceda
(tu)	proceda
(lui/lei) (lei/Lei)	proceda
(noi)	procediamo
(voi)	procediate
(loro)	procedano

PAST PARTICIPLE

proceduto

GERUND

procedendo

EXAMPLE PHRASES

Come **procede** il lavoro? *How's the work going?*
Gli affari **procedono** bene. *Business is going well.*
Il traffico **sta procedendo** lentamente. *The traffic is moving slowly.*

Remember that subject pronouns are not used very often in Italian.

produrre (to produce)

PRESENT

(io)	produco
(tu)	produci
(lui/lei) (lei/Lei)	produce
(noi)	produciamo
(voi)	producete
(loro)	producono

PERFECT

(io)	ho prodotto
(tu)	hai prodotto
(lui/lei) (lei/Lei)	ha prodotto
(noi)	abbiamo prodotto
(voi)	avete prodotto
(loro)	hanno prodotto

IMPERFECT

(io)	producevo
(tu)	producevi
(lui/lei) (lei/Lei)	produceva
(noi)	producevamo
(voi)	producevate
(loro)	producevano

IMPERATIVE

produci
produciamo
producete

FUTURE

(io)	produrrò
(tu)	produrrai
(lui/lei) (lei/Lei)	produrrà
(noi)	produrremo
(voi)	produrrete
(loro)	produrranno

CONDITIONAL

(io)	produrrei
(tu)	produrresti
(lui/lei) (lei/Lei)	produrrebbe
(noi)	produrremmo
(voi)	produrreste
(loro)	produrrebbero

PRESENT SUBJUNCTIVE

(io)	produca
(tu)	produca
(lui/lei) (lei/Lei)	produca
(noi)	produciamo
(voi)	produciate
(loro)	producano

PAST PARTICIPLE

prodotto

GERUND

producendo

EXAMPLE PHRASES

La ditta **produce** scarpe. *The company makes shoes.*
Questa soluzione non **ha prodotto** buoni risultati. *This solution did not produce good results.*
L'Italia **produceva** molto grano. *Italy used to produce a lot of wheat.*

Italic letters in Italian words show where stress does not follow the usual rules.

proporre (to suggest)

PRESENT

(io)	propongo
(tu)	proponi
(lui/lei) (lei/Lei)	propone
(noi)	proponiamo
(voi)	proponete
(loro)	propongono

FUTURE

(io)	proporrò
(tu)	proporrai
(lui/lei) (lei/Lei)	proporrà
(noi)	proporremo
(voi)	proporrete
(loro)	proporranno

PERFECT

(io)	ho proposto
(tu)	hai proposto
(lui/lei) (lei/Lei)	ha proposto
(noi)	abbiamo proposto
(voi)	avete proposto
(loro)	hanno proposto

CONDITIONAL

(io)	proporrei
(tu)	proporresti
(lui/lei) (lei/Lei)	proporrebbe
(noi)	proporremmo
(voi)	proporreste
(loro)	proporrebbero

IMPERFECT

(io)	proponevo
(tu)	proponevi
(lui/lei) (lei/Lei)	proponeva
(noi)	proponevamo
(voi)	proponevate
(loro)	proponevano

PRESENT SUBJUNCTIVE

(io)	proponga
(tu)	proponga
(lui/lei) (lei/Lei)	proponga
(noi)	proponiamo
(voi)	proponiate
(loro)	propongano

IMPERATIVE

proponi
proponiamo
proponete

PAST PARTICIPLE

proposto

GERUND

proponendo

EXAMPLE PHRASES

Ho proposto di andare al cinema. *I suggested going to the cinema.*
Che cosa **propone** lo chef? *What does the chef recommend?*
Marco **proponeva** una pizza, ma non ne ho voglia. *Marco suggested a pizza but I don't feel like one.*

raggiungere (to reach)

PRESENT

(io)	**raggiungo**
(tu)	**raggiungi**
(lui/lei) (lei/Lei)	**raggiunge**
(noi)	**raggiungiamo**
(voi)	**raggiungete**
(loro)	**raggiungono**

FUTURE

(io)	**raggiungerò**
(tu)	**raggiungerai**
(lui/lei) (lei/Lei)	**raggiungerà**
(noi)	**raggiungeremo**
(voi)	**raggiungerete**
(loro)	**raggiungeranno**

PERFECT

(io)	**ho raggiunto**
(tu)	**hai raggiunto**
(lui/lei) (lei/Lei)	**ha raggiunto**
(noi)	**abbiamo raggiunto**
(voi)	**avete raggiunto**
(loro)	**hanno raggiunto**

CONDITIONAL

(io)	**raggiungerei**
(tu)	**raggiungeresti**
(lui/lei) (lei/Lei)	**raggiungerebbe**
(noi)	**raggiungeremmo**
(voi)	**raggiungereste**
(loro)	**raggiungerebbero**

IMPERFECT

(io)	**raggiungevo**
(tu)	**raggiungevi**
(lui/lei) (lei/Lei)	**raggiungeva**
(noi)	**raggiungevamo**
(voi)	**raggiungevate**
(loro)	**raggiungevano**

PRESENT SUBJUNCTIVE

(io)	**raggiunga**
(tu)	**raggiunga**
(lui/lei) (lei/Lei)	**raggiunga**
(noi)	**raggiungiamo**
(voi)	**raggiungiate**
(loro)	**raggiungano**

IMPERATIVE

raggiungi
raggiungiamo
raggiungete

PAST PARTICIPLE

raggiunto

GERUND

raggiungendo

EXAMPLE PHRASES

La temperatura può **raggiungere** i quaranta gradi. *The temperature can reach forty degrees.*

Vi **raggiungo** più tardi. *I'll join you later.*

Non **ho** ancora **raggiunto** il mio scopo. *I haven't yet achieved my aim.*

Italic letters in Italian words show where stress does not follow the usual rules.

restare (to stay)

PRESENT

(io)	**resto**
(tu)	**resti**
(lui/lei) (lei/Lei)	**resta**
(noi)	**restiamo**
(voi)	**restate**
(loro)	**restano**

FUTURE

(io)	**resterò**
(tu)	**resterai**
(lui/lei) (lei/Lei)	**resterà**
(noi)	**resteremo**
(voi)	**resterete**
(loro)	**resteranno**

PERFECT

(io)	**sono restato/a**
(tu)	**sei restato/a**
(lui/lei) (lei/Lei)	**è restato/a**
(noi)	**siamo restati/e**
(voi)	**siete restati/e**
(loro)	**sono restati/e**

CONDITIONAL

(io)	**resterei**
(tu)	**resteresti**
(lui/lei) (lei/Lei)	**resterebbe**
(noi)	**resteremmo**
(voi)	**restereste**
(loro)	**resterebbero**

IMPERFECT

(io)	**restavo**
(tu)	**restavi**
(lui/lei) (lei/Lei)	**restava**
(noi)	**restavamo**
(voi)	**restavate**
(loro)	**restavano**

PRESENT SUBJUNCTIVE

(io)	**resti**
(tu)	**resti**
(lui/lei) (lei/Lei)	**resti**
(noi)	**restiamo**
(voi)	**restiate**
(loro)	**restino**

IMPERATIVE

resta
restiamo
restate

PAST PARTICIPLE

restato

GERUND

restando

EXAMPLE PHRASES

Dai, **resta** ancora un po'. *Go on, stay a bit longer.*
Sono restato a casa tutto il giorno. *I stayed at home all day.*
Ne **restano** solo due. *There are only two left.*

Remember that subject pronouns are not used very often in Italian.

riempire (to fill)

PRESENT

(io)	riempio
(tu)	riempi
(lui/lei) (lei/Lei)	riempie
(noi)	riempiamo
(voi)	riempite
(loro)	riempiono

PERFECT

(io)	ho riempito
(tu)	hai riempito
(lui/lei) (lei/Lei)	ha riempito
(noi)	abbiamo riempito
(voi)	avete riempito
(loro)	hanno riempito

IMPERFECT

(io)	riempivo
(tu)	riempivi
(lui/lei) (lei/Lei)	riempiva
(noi)	riempivamo
(voi)	riempivate
(loro)	riempivano

IMPERATIVE

riempi
riempiamo
riempite

FUTURE

(io)	riempirò
(tu)	riempirai
(lui/lei) (lei/Lei)	riempirà
(noi)	riempiremo
(voi)	riempirete
(loro)	riempiranno

CONDITIONAL

(io)	riempirei
(tu)	riempiresti
(lui/lei) (lei/Lei)	riempirebbe
(noi)	riempiremmo
(voi)	riempireste
(loro)	riempirebbero

PRESENT SUBJUNCTIVE

(io)	riempia
(tu)	riempia
(lui/lei) (lei/Lei)	riempia
(noi)	riempiamo
(voi)	riempiate
(loro)	riempiano

PAST PARTICIPLE

riempito

GERUND

riempiendo

EXAMPLE PHRASES

Tieni, **ho riempito** il termos di caffè, va bene? *Here, I've filled the flask with coffee, okay?*
Riempi il modulo, per favore. *Fill in the form, please.*
Vedervi ci **riempie** di gioia. *It's a joy to see you.*

Italic letters in Italian words show where stress does not follow the usual rules.

riflettere (to think)

PRESENT

(io)	**rifletto**
(tu)	**rifletti**
(lui/lei) (lei/Lei)	**riflette**
(noi)	**riflettiamo**
(voi)	**riflettete**
(loro)	**riflettono**

PERFECT

(io)	**ho riflettuto**
(tu)	**hai riflettuto**
(lui/lei) (lei/Lei)	**ha riflettuto**
(noi)	**abbiamo riflettuto**
(voi)	**avete riflettuto**
(loro)	**hanno riflettuto**

IMPERFECT

(io)	**riflettevo**
(tu)	**riflettevi**
(lui/lei) (lei/Lei)	**rifletteva**
(noi)	**riflettevamo**
(voi)	**riflettevate**
(loro)	**riflettevano**

IMPERATIVE

rifletti
riflettiamo
riflettete

FUTURE

(io)	**rifletterò**
(tu)	**rifletterai**
(lui/lei) (lei/Lei)	**rifletterà**
(noi)	**rifletteremo**
(voi)	**rifletterete**
(loro)	**rifletteranno**

CONDITIONAL

(io)	**rifletterei**
(tu)	**rifletteresti**
(lui/lei) (lei/Lei)	**rifletterebbe**
(noi)	**rifletteremmo**
(voi)	**riflettereste**
(loro)	**rifletterebbero**

PRESENT SUBJUNCTIVE

(io)	**rifletta**
(tu)	**rifletta**
(lui/lei) (lei/Lei)	**rifletta**
(noi)	**riflettiamo**
(voi)	**riflettiate**
(loro)	**riflettano**

PAST PARTICIPLE

riflettuto

GERUND

riflettendo

EXAMPLE PHRASES

Agisce senza **riflettere**. *He does things without thinking.*
Ci **ho riflettuto** su e ho deciso di accettare. *I've thought about it and have decided to accept.*
Rifletti prima di parlare! *Think before you speak!*

Remember that subject pronouns are not used very often in Italian.

rimanere (to stay)

PRESENT

(io)	rimango
(tu)	rimani
(lui/lei) (lei/Lei)	rimane
(noi)	rimaniamo
(voi)	rimanete
(loro)	rimangono

PERFECT

(io)	sono rimasto/a
(tu)	sei rimasto/a
(lui/lei) (lei/Lei)	è rimasto/a
(noi)	siamo rimasti/e
(voi)	siete rimasti/e
(loro)	sono rimasti/e

IMPERFECT

(io)	rimanevo
(tu)	rimanevi
(lui/lei) (lei/Lei)	rimaneva
(noi)	rimanevamo
(voi)	rimanevate
(loro)	rimanevano

IMPERATIVE

rimani
rimaniamo
rimanete

FUTURE

(io)	rimarrò
(tu)	rimarrai
(lui/lei) (lei/Lei)	rimarrà
(noi)	rimarremo
(voi)	rimarrete
(loro)	rimarranno

CONDITIONAL

(io)	rimarrei
(tu)	rimarresti
(lui/lei) (lei/Lei)	rimarrebbe
(noi)	rimarremmo
(voi)	rimarreste
(loro)	rimarrebbero

PRESENT SUBJUNCTIVE

(io)	rimanga
(tu)	rimanga
(lui/lei) (lei/Lei)	rimanga
(noi)	rimaniamo
(voi)	rimaniate
(loro)	rimangano

PAST PARTICIPLE

rimasto

GERUND

rimanendo

EXAMPLE PHRASES

Sono rimasto a casa tutto il giorno. *I stayed at home all day.*
Mi piacerebbe **rimanere** qualche altro giorno. *I'd like to stay a few more days.*
Ci **rimarrebbero** molto male. *They'd be very upset.*

Italic letters in Italian words show where stress does not follow the usual rules.

risolvere (to solve)

PRESENT

(io)	**risolvo**
(tu)	**risolvi**
(lui/lei) (lei/Lei)	**risolve**
(noi)	**risolviamo**
(voi)	**risolvete**
(loro)	**risolvono**

FUTURE

(io)	**risolverò**
(tu)	**risolverai**
(lui/lei) (lei/Lei)	**risolverà**
(noi)	**risolveremo**
(voi)	**risolverete**
(loro)	**risolveranno**

PERFECT

(io)	**ho risolto**
(tu)	**hai risolto**
(lui/lei) (lei/Lei)	**ha risolto**
(noi)	**abbiamo risolto**
(voi)	**avete risolto**
(loro)	**hanno risolto**

CONDITIONAL

(io)	**risolverei**
(tu)	**risolveresti**
(lui/lei) (lei/Lei)	**risolverebbe**
(noi)	**risolveremmo**
(voi)	**risolvereste**
(loro)	**risolverebbero**

IMPERFECT

(io)	**risolvevo**
(tu)	**risolvevi**
(lui/lei) (lei/Lei)	**risolveva**
(noi)	**risolvevamo**
(voi)	**risolvevate**
(loro)	**risolvevano**

PRESENT SUBJUNCTIVE

(io)	**risolva**
(tu)	**risolva**
(lui/lei) (lei/Lei)	**risolva**
(noi)	**risolviamo**
(voi)	**risolviate**
(loro)	**risolvano**

IMPERATIVE

risolvi
risolviamo
risolvete

PAST PARTICIPLE

risolto

GERUND

risolvendo

EXAMPLE PHRASES

Ho risolto l'indovinello! *I've worked out the riddle!*

Ti calmerai solo se **risolverai** i tuoi problemi. *You'll only calm down if you solve your problems.*

Così non **risolvi** nulla. *You won't solve the problems that way.*

Remember that subject pronouns are not used very often in Italian.

rispondere (to answer)

PRESENT

(io)	rispondo
(tu)	rispondi
(lui/lei) (lei/Lei)	risponde
(noi)	rispondiamo
(voi)	rispondete
(loro)	rispondono

PERFECT

(io)	ho risposto
(tu)	hai risposto
(lui/lei) (lei/Lei)	ha risposto
(noi)	abbiamo risposto
(voi)	avete risposto
(loro)	hanno risposto

IMPERFECT

(io)	rispondevo
(tu)	rispondevi
(lui/lei) (lei/Lei)	rispondeva
(noi)	rispondevamo
(voi)	rispondevate
(loro)	rispondevano

IMPERATIVE

rispondi
rispondiamo
rispondete

FUTURE

(io)	risponderò
(tu)	risponderai
(lui/lei) (lei/Lei)	risponderà
(noi)	risponderemo
(voi)	risponderete
(loro)	risponderanno

CONDITIONAL

(io)	risponderei
(tu)	risponderesti
(lui/lei) (lei/Lei)	risponderebbe
(noi)	risponderemmo
(voi)	rispondereste
(loro)	risponderebbero

PRESENT SUBJUNCTIVE

(io)	risponda
(tu)	risponda
(lui/lei) (lei/Lei)	risponda
(noi)	rispondiamo
(voi)	rispondiate
(loro)	rispondano

PAST PARTICIPLE

risposto

GERUND

rispondendo

EXAMPLE PHRASES

Ho telefonato ma non **ha risposto** nessuno. *I phoned, but nobody answered.*
Rispondi alla mia domanda. *Answer my question.*
Rispondeva sempre di sì a tutti. *He always said yes to everyone.*

Italic letters in Italian words show where stress does not follow the usual rules.

rompere (to break)

PRESENT

(io)	rompo
(tu)	rompi
(lui/lei) (lei/Lei)	rompe
(noi)	rompiamo
(voi)	rompete
(loro)	rompono

PERFECT

(io)	ho rotto
(tu)	hai rotto
(lui/lei) (lei/Lei)	ha rotto
(noi)	abbiamo rotto
(voi)	avete rotto
(loro)	hanno rotto

IMPERFECT

(io)	rompevo
(tu)	rompevi
(lui/lei) (lei/Lei)	rompeva
(noi)	rompevamo
(voi)	rompevate
(loro)	rompevano

IMPERATIVE

rompi
rompiamo
rompete

FUTURE

(io)	romperò
(tu)	romperai
(lui/lei) (lei/Lei)	romperà
(noi)	romperemo
(voi)	romperete
(loro)	romperanno

CONDITIONAL

(io)	romperei
(tu)	romperesti
(lui/lei) (lei/Lei)	romperebbe
(noi)	romperemmo
(voi)	rompereste
(loro)	romperebbero

PRESENT SUBJUNCTIVE

(io)	rompa
(tu)	rompa
(lui/lei) (lei/Lei)	rompa
(noi)	rompiamo
(voi)	rompiate
(loro)	rompano

PAST PARTICIPLE

rotto

GERUND

rompendo

EXAMPLE PHRASES

Ho rotto un bicchiere! *I've broken a glass!*
Uffa quanto **rompi**! *What a pain you are!*
Il piatto si **è rotto**. *The plate broke.*

Remember that subject pronouns are not used very often in Italian.

salire (to go up)

PRESENT

(io)	**salgo**
(tu)	**sali**
(lui/lei) (lei/Lei)	**sale**
(noi)	**saliamo**
(voi)	**salite**
(loro)	**salgono**

PERFECT

(io)	**sono salito/a**
(tu)	**sei salito/a**
(lui/lei) (lei/Lei)	**è salito/a**
(noi)	**siamo saliti/e**
(voi)	**siete saliti/e**
(loro)	**sono saliti/e**

IMPERFECT

(io)	**salivo**
(tu)	**salivi**
(lui/lei) (lei/Lei)	**saliva**
(noi)	**salivamo**
(voi)	**salivate**
(loro)	**salivano**

IMPERATIVE

sali
saliamo
salite

FUTURE

(io)	**salirò**
(tu)	**salirai**
(lui/lei) (lei/Lei)	**salirà**
(noi)	**saliremo**
(voi)	**salirete**
(loro)	**saliranno**

CONDITIONAL

(io)	**salirei**
(tu)	**saliresti**
(lui/lei) (lei/Lei)	**salirebbe**
(noi)	**saliremmo**
(voi)	**salireste**
(loro)	**salirebbero**

PRESENT SUBJUNCTIVE

(io)	**salga**
(tu)	**salga**
(lui/lei) (lei/Lei)	**salga**
(noi)	**saliamo**
(voi)	**saliate**
(loro)	**salgano**

PAST PARTICIPLE

salito

GERUND

salendo

EXAMPLE PHRASES

I prezzi **sono saliti**. *Prices have gone up.*
Dopo cena **salirai** in camera tua. *After dinner you'll go up to your room.*
Sali tu o scendo io? *Are you coming up or shall I come down?*

Italic letters in Italian words show where stress does not follow the usual rules.

sapere (to know)

PRESENT

(io)	so
(tu)	sai
(lui/lei)(lei/Lei)	sa
(noi)	sappiamo
(voi)	sapete
(loro)	sanno

FUTURE

(io)	saprò
(tu)	saprai
(lui/lei)(lei/Lei)	saprà
(noi)	sapremo
(voi)	saprete
(loro)	sapranno

PERFECT

(io)	ho saputo
(tu)	hai saputo
(lui/lei)(lei/Lei)	ha saputo
(noi)	abbiamo saputo
(voi)	avete saputo
(loro)	hanno saputo

CONDITIONAL

(io)	saprei
(tu)	sapresti
(lui/lei)(lei/Lei)	saprebbe
(noi)	sapremmo
(voi)	sapreste
(loro)	saprebbero

IMPERFECT

(io)	sapevo
(tu)	sapevi
(lui/lei)(lei/Lei)	sapeva
(noi)	sapevamo
(voi)	sapevate
(loro)	sapevano

PRESENT SUBJUNCTIVE

(io)	sappia
(tu)	sappia
(lui/lei)(lei/Lei)	sappia
(noi)	sappiamo
(voi)	sappiate
(loro)	sappiano

IMPERATIVE

sappi
sappiamo
sappiate

PAST PARTICIPLE

saputo

GERUND

sapendo

EXAMPLE PHRASES

Sai dove abita? *Do you know where he lives?*
Non **sapeva** andare in bicicletta. *He couldn't ride a bike.*
Sa di fragola. *It tastes of strawberries.*

Remember that subject pronouns are not used very often in Italian.

sbagliare (to make a mistake)

PRESENT

(io)	sbaglio
(tu)	sbagli
(lui/lei) (lei/Lei)	sbaglia
(noi)	sbagliamo
(voi)	sbagliate
(loro)	sbagliano

FUTURE

(io)	sbaglierò
(tu)	sbaglierai
(lui/lei) (lei/Lei)	sbaglierà
(noi)	sbaglieremo
(voi)	sbaglierete
(loro)	sbaglieranno

PERFECT

(io)	ho sbagliato
(tu)	hai sbagliato
(lui/lei) (lei/Lei)	ha sbagliato
(noi)	abbiamo sbagliato
(voi)	avete sbagliato
(loro)	hanno sbagliato

CONDITIONAL

(io)	sbaglierei
(tu)	sbaglieresti
(lui/lei) (lei/Lei)	sbaglierebbe
(noi)	sbaglieremmo
(voi)	sbagliereste
(loro)	sbaglierebbero

IMPERFECT

(io)	sbagliavo
(tu)	sbagliavi
(lui/lei) (lei/Lei)	sbagliava
(noi)	sbagliavamo
(voi)	sbagliavate
(loro)	sbagliavano

PRESENT SUBJUNCTIVE

(io)	sbagli
(tu)	sbagli
(lui/lei) (lei/Lei)	sbagli
(noi)	sbagliamo
(voi)	sbagliate
(loro)	sbaglino

IMPERATIVE

sbaglia
sbagliamo
sbagliate

PAST PARTICIPLE

sbagliato

GERUND

sbagliando

EXAMPLE PHRASES

Mi dispiace, **avete sbagliato**. *I'm sorry, you've made a mistake.*
Scusi, **ho sbagliato** numero. *Sorry, I've got the wrong number.*
Pensavo fosse lei, ma mi **sono sbagliato**. *I thought it was her, but I was wrong.*
Sbagliando s'impara. *You learn by your mistakes.*

Italic letters in Italian words show where stress does not follow the usual rules.

sciare (to ski)

PRESENT

(io)	scio
(tu)	scii
(lui/lei) (lei/Lei)	scia
(noi)	sciamo
(voi)	sciate
(loro)	sciano

PERFECT

(io)	ho sciato
(tu)	hai sciato
(lui/lei) (lei/Lei)	ha sciato
(noi)	abbiamo sciato
(voi)	avete sciato
(loro)	hanno sciato

IMPERFECT

(io)	sciavo
(tu)	sciavi
(lui/lei) (lei/Lei)	sciava
(noi)	sciavamo
(voi)	sciavate
(loro)	sciavano

IMPERATIVE

scia
sciamo
sciate

FUTURE

(io)	scierò
(tu)	scierai
(lui/lei) (lei/Lei)	scierà
(noi)	scieremo
(voi)	scierete
(loro)	scieranno

CONDITIONAL

(io)	scierei
(tu)	scieresti
(lui/lei) (lei/Lei)	scierebbe
(noi)	scieremmo
(voi)	sciereste
(loro)	scierebbero

PRESENT SUBJUNCTIVE

(io)	scii
(tu)	scii
(lui/lei) (lei/Lei)	scii
(noi)	sciamo
(voi)	sciate
(loro)	sciino

PAST PARTICIPLE

sciato

GERUND

sciando

EXAMPLE PHRASES

Sai **sciare**? *Can you ski?*
Si è rotto la gamba **sciando**. *He broke his leg skiing.*
Abbiamo sciato tutto il giorno. *We skied all day.*

Remember that subject pronouns are not used very often in Italian.

scrivere (to write)

PRESENT

(io)	**scrivo**
(tu)	**scrivi**
(lui/lei) (lei/Lei)	**scrive**
(noi)	**scriviamo**
(voi)	**scrivete**
(loro)	**scrivono**

PERFECT

(io)	**ho scritto**
(tu)	**hai scritto**
(lui/lei) (lei/Lei)	**ha scritto**
(noi)	**abbiamo scritto**
(voi)	**avete scritto**
(loro)	**hanno scritto**

IMPERFECT

(io)	**scrivevo**
(tu)	**scrivevi**
(lui/lei) (lei/Lei)	**scriveva**
(noi)	**scrivevamo**
(voi)	**scrivevate**
(loro)	**scrivevano**

IMPERATIVE

scrivi
scriviamo
scrivete

FUTURE

(io)	**scriverò**
(tu)	**scriverai**
(lui/lei) (lei/Lei)	**scriverà**
(noi)	**scriveremo**
(voi)	**scriverete**
(loro)	**scriveranno**

CONDITIONAL

(io)	**scriverei**
(tu)	**scriveresti**
(lui/lei) (lei/Lei)	**scriverebbe**
(noi)	**scriveremmo**
(voi)	**scrivereste**
(loro)	**scriverebbero**

PRESENT SUBJUNCTIVE

(io)	**scriva**
(tu)	**scriva**
(lui/lei) (lei/Lei)	**scriva**
(noi)	**scriviamo**
(voi)	**scriviate**
(loro)	**scrivano**

PAST PARTICIPLE

scritto

GERUND

scrivendo

EXAMPLE PHRASES

Scrivimi presto. *Write to me soon.*
Ho scritto una lettera a Luca. *I wrote Luca a letter.*
Ho scritto una mail a Luca. *I wrote an email to Luca.*
Come **si scrive**? *How do you spell it?*

Italic letters in Italian words show where stress does not follow the usual rules.

scuotere (to shake)

PRESENT

(io)	**scuoto**
(tu)	**scuoti**
(lui/lei) (lei/Lei)	**scuote**
(noi)	**scuotiamo**
(voi)	**scuotete**
(loro)	**scuotono**

FUTURE

(io)	**scuoterò**
(tu)	**scuoterai**
(lui/lei) (lei/Lei)	**scuoterà**
(noi)	**scuoteremo**
(voi)	**scuoterete**
(loro)	**scuoteranno**

PERFECT

(io)	**ho scosso**
(tu)	**hai scosso**
(lui/lei) (lei/Lei)	**ha scosso**
(noi)	**abbiamo scosso**
(voi)	**avete scosso**
(loro)	**hanno scosso**

CONDITIONAL

(io)	**scuoterei**
(tu)	**scuoteresti**
(lui/lei) (lei/Lei)	**scuoterebbe**
(noi)	**scuoteremmo**
(voi)	**scuotereste**
(loro)	**scuoterebbero**

IMPERFECT

(io)	**scuotevo**
(tu)	**scuotevi**
(lui/lei) (lei/Lei)	**scuoteva**
(noi)	**scuotevamo**
(voi)	**scuotevate**
(loro)	**scuotevano**

PRESENT SUBJUNCTIVE

(io)	**scuota**
(tu)	**scuota**
(lui/lei) (lei/Lei)	**scuota**
(noi)	**scuotiamo**
(voi)	**scuotiate**
(loro)	**scuotano**

IMPERATIVE

scuoti
scuotiamo
scuotete

PAST PARTICIPLE

scosso

GERUND

scuotendo

EXAMPLE PHRASES

Ha scosso la testa. *He shook his head.*

È sul terrazzo che **scuote** i tappeti. *She's on the balcony shaking the rugs.*

Scuoteva la scatola per capire cosa conteneva. *He shook the box to see what it had in it.*

Remember that subject pronouns are not used very often in Italian.

sedere (to sit)

PRESENT

(io)	siedo
(tu)	siedi
(lui/lei) (lei/Lei)	siede
(noi)	sediamo
(voi)	sedete
(loro)	siedono

PERFECT

(io)	sono seduto/a
(tu)	sei seduto/a
(lui/lei) (lei/Lei)	è seduto/a
(noi)	siamo seduti/e
(voi)	siete seduti/e
(loro)	sono seduti/e

IMPERFECT

(io)	sedevo
(tu)	sedevi
(lui/lei) (lei/Lei)	sedeva
(noi)	sedevamo
(voi)	sedevate
(loro)	sedevano

IMPERATIVE

siedi
sediamo
sedete

FUTURE

(io)	sederò
(tu)	sederai
(lui/lei) (lei/Lei)	sederà
(noi)	sederemo
(voi)	sederete
(loro)	sederanno

CONDITIONAL

(io)	sederei
(tu)	sederesti
(lui/lei) (lei/Lei)	sederebbe
(noi)	sederemmo
(voi)	sedereste
(loro)	sederebbero

PRESENT SUBJUNCTIVE

(io)	sieda
(tu)	sieda
(lui/lei) (lei/Lei)	sieda
(noi)	sediamo
(voi)	sediate
(loro)	siedano

PAST PARTICIPLE

seduto

GERUND

sedendo

EXAMPLE PHRASES

Era seduta accanto a me. *She was sitting beside me.*
Si **è seduto** per terra. *He sat on the floor.*
Siediti qui! *Sit here!*

Italic letters in Italian words show where stress does not follow the usual rules.

soddisfare (to satisfy)

PRESENT

(io)	**soddisfo**
(tu)	**soddisfi**
(lui/lei) (lei/Lei)	**soddisfa**
(noi)	**soddisfiamo**
(voi)	**soddisfate**
(loro)	**soddisfano**

FUTURE

(io)	**soddisferò**
(tu)	**soddisferai**
(lui/lei) (lei/Lei)	**soddisferà**
(noi)	**soddisferemo**
(voi)	**soddisferete**
(loro)	**soddisferanno**

PERFECT

(io)	**ho soddisfatto**
(tu)	**hai soddisfatto**
(lui/lei) (lei/Lei)	**ha soddisfatto**
(noi)	**abbiamo soddisfatto**
(voi)	**avete soddisfatto**
(loro)	**hanno soddisfatto**

CONDITIONAL

(io)	**soddisferei**
(tu)	**soddisferesti**
(lui/lei) (lei/Lei)	**soddisferebbe**
(noi)	**soddisferemmo**
(voi)	**soddisfereste**
(loro)	**soddisferebbero**

IMPERFECT

(io)	**soddisfacevo**
(tu)	**soddisfacevi**
(lui/lei) (lei/Lei)	**soddisfaceva**
(noi)	**soddisfacevamo**
(voi)	**soddisfacevate**
(loro)	**soddisfacevano**

PRESENT SUBJUNCTIVE

(io)	**soddisfi**
(tu)	**soddisfi**
(lui/lei) (lei/Lei)	**soddisfi**
(noi)	**soddisfiamo**
(voi)	**soddisfiate**
(loro)	**soddisfino**

IMPERATIVE

soddisfa
soddisfiamo
soddisfate

PAST PARTICIPLE

soddisfatto

GERUND

soddisfacendo

EXAMPLE PHRASES

Il mio lavoro non mi **soddisfa**. *My job doesn't satisfy me.*
Questo libro **soddisferà** i lettori più esigenti. *This book will please the most demanding readers.*
Soddisfaceva ogni desiderio della moglie. *He satisfied his wife's every wish.*

Remember that subject pronouns are not used very often in Italian.

sognare (to dream)

PRESENT

(io)	sogno
(tu)	sogni
(lui/lei) (lei/Lei)	sogna
(noi)	sogniamo
(voi)	sognate
(loro)	sognano

PERFECT

(io)	ho sognato
(tu)	hai sognato
(lui/lei) (lei/Lei)	ha sognato
(noi)	abbiamo sognato
(voi)	avete sognato
(loro)	hanno sognato

IMPERFECT

(io)	sognavo
(tu)	sognavi
(lui/lei) (lei/Lei)	sognava
(noi)	sognavamo
(voi)	sognavate
(loro)	sognavano

IMPERATIVE

sogna
sogniamo
sognate

FUTURE

(io)	sognerò
(tu)	sognerai
(lui/lei) (lei/Lei)	sognerà
(noi)	sogneremo
(voi)	sognerete
(loro)	sogneranno

CONDITIONAL

(io)	sognerei
(tu)	sogneresti
(lui/lei) (lei/Lei)	sognerebbe
(noi)	sogneremmo
(voi)	sognereste
(loro)	sognerebbero

PRESENT SUBJUNCTIVE

(io)	sogni
(tu)	sogni
(lui/lei) (lei/Lei)	sogni
(noi)	sogniamo
(voi)	sogniate
(loro)	sognino

PAST PARTICIPLE

sognato

GERUND

sognando

EXAMPLE PHRASES

Stanotte ti **ho sognato**. *I dreamt about you last night.*
Ve lo **sognate**! *You can forget it!*
Stavo sognando ad occhi aperti. *I was daydreaming.*

Italic letters in Italian words show where stress does not follow the usual rules.

sparire (to disappear)

PRESENT

(io)	**sparisco**
(tu)	**sparisci**
(lui/lei) (lei/Lei)	**sparisce**
(noi)	**spariamo**
(voi)	**sparite**
(loro)	**spariscono**

PERFECT

(io)	**sono sparito/a**
(tu)	**sei sparito/a**
(lui/lei) (lei/Lei)	**è sparito/a**
(noi)	**siamo spariti/e**
(voi)	**siete spariti/e**
(loro)	**sono spariti/e**

IMPERFECT

(io)	**sparivo**
(tu)	**sparivi**
(lui/lei) (lei/Lei)	**spariva**
(noi)	**sparivamo**
(voi)	**sparivate**
(loro)	**sparivano**

IMPERATIVE

sparisci
spariamo
sparite

FUTURE

(io)	**sparirò**
(tu)	**sparirai**
(lui/lei) (lei/Lei)	**sparirà**
(noi)	**spariremo**
(voi)	**sparirete**
(loro)	**spariranno**

CONDITIONAL

(io)	**sparirei**
(tu)	**spariresti**
(lui/lei) (lei/Lei)	**sparirebbe**
(noi)	**spariremmo**
(voi)	**sparireste**
(loro)	**sparirebbero**

PRESENT SUBJUNCTIVE

(io)	**sparisca**
(tu)	**sparisca**
(lui/lei) (lei/Lei)	**sparisca**
(noi)	**spariamo**
(voi)	**spariate**
(loro)	**spariscano**

PAST PARTICIPLE

sparito

GERUND

sparendo

EXAMPLE PHRASES

La nave **è sparita** all'orizzonte. *The ship disappeared over the horizon.*
Dov'è **sparita** la mia penna? *Where has my pen gone?*
Sparisce ogni volta che c'è bisogno di lui. *He disappears whenever he's needed.*

Remember that subject pronouns are not used very often in Italian.

spegnere (to put out)

PRESENT

(io)	spengo
(tu)	spegni
(lui/lei) (lei/Lei)	spegne
(noi)	spegniamo
(voi)	spegnete
(loro)	spengono

FUTURE

(io)	spegnerò
(tu)	spegnerai
(lui/lei) (lei/Lei)	spegnerà
(noi)	spegneremo
(voi)	spegnerete
(loro)	spegneranno

PERFECT

(io)	ho spento
(tu)	hai spento
(lui/lei) (lei/Lei)	ha spento
(noi)	abbiamo spento
(voi)	avete spento
(loro)	hanno spento

CONDITIONAL

(io)	spegnerei
(tu)	spegneresti
(lui/lei) (lei/Lei)	spegnerebbe
(noi)	spegneremmo
(voi)	spegnereste
(loro)	spegnerebbero

IMPERFECT

(io)	spegnevo
(tu)	spegnevi
(lui/lei) (lei/Lei)	spegneva
(noi)	spegnevamo
(voi)	spegnevate
(loro)	spegnevano

PRESENT SUBJUNCTIVE

(io)	spenga
(tu)	spenga
(lui/lei) (lei/Lei)	spenga
(noi)	spegniamo
(voi)	spegniate
(loro)	spengano

IMPERATIVE

spegni
spegniamo
spegnete

PAST PARTICIPLE

spento

GERUND

spegnendo

EXAMPLE PHRASES

Hai spento la sigaretta? *Have you put your cigarette out?*
Spegnete le luci che guardiamo il film. *Turn off the lights and we'll watch the film.*
La luce si **è spenta** all'improvviso. *The light went off suddenly.*

Italic letters in Italian words show where stress does not follow the usual rules.

sporgersi (to lean out)

PRESENT

(io)	mi sporgo
(tu)	ti sporgi
(lui/lei) (lei/Lei)	si sporge
(noi)	ci sporgiamo
(voi)	vi sporgete
(loro)	si sporgono

PERFECT

(io)	mi sono sporto/a
(tu)	ti sei sporto/a
(lui/lei) (lei/Lei)	si è sporto/a
(noi)	ci siamo sporti/e
(voi)	vi siete sporti/e
(loro)	si sono sporti/e

IMPERFECT

(io)	mi sporgevo
(tu)	ti sporgevi
(lui/lei) (lei/Lei)	si sporgeva
(noi)	ci sporgevamo
(voi)	vi sporgevate
(loro)	si sporgevano

IMPERATIVE

sporgiti
sporgiamoci
sporgetevi

FUTURE

(io)	mi sporgerò
(tu)	ti sporgerai
(lui/lei) (lei/Lei)	si sporgerà
(noi)	ci sporgeremo
(voi)	vi sporgerete
(loro)	si sporgeranno

CONDITIONAL

(io)	mi sporgerei
(tu)	ti sporgeresti
(lui/lei) (lei/Lei)	si sporgerebbe
(noi)	ci sporgeremmo
(voi)	vi sporgereste
(loro)	si sporgerebbero

PRESENT SUBJUNCTIVE

(io)	mi sporga
(tu)	ti sporga
(lui/lei) (lei/Lei)	si sporga
(noi)	ci sporgiamo
(voi)	vi sporgiate
(loro)	si sporgano

PAST PARTICIPLE

sporto

GERUND

sporgendosi

EXAMPLE PHRASES

Non **sporgerti** dal finestrino. *Don't lean out of the window.*
Sporgendoti, vedrai meglio. *If you lean out you'll see better.*

stare (to be)

PRESENT

(io)	**sto**
(tu)	**stai**
(lui/lei) (lei/Lei)	**sta**
(noi)	**stiamo**
(voi)	**state**
(loro)	**stanno**

PERFECT

(io)	**sono stato/a**
(tu)	**sei stato/a**
(lui/lei) (lei/Lei)	**è stato/a**
(noi)	**siamo stati/e**
(voi)	**siete stati/e**
(loro)	**sono stati/e**

IMPERFECT

(io)	**stavo**
(tu)	**stavi**
(lui/lei) (lei/Lei)	**stava**
(noi)	**stavamo**
(voi)	**stavate**
(loro)	**stavano**

IMPERATIVE

stai
stiamo
state

FUTURE

(io)	**starò**
(tu)	**starai**
(lui/lei) (lei/Lei)	**starà**
(noi)	**staremo**
(voi)	**starete**
(loro)	**staranno**

CONDITIONAL

(io)	**starei**
(tu)	**staresti**
(lui/lei) (lei/Lei)	**starebbe**
(noi)	**staremmo**
(voi)	**stareste**
(loro)	**starebbero**

PRESENT SUBJUNCTIVE

(io)	**stia**
(tu)	**stia**
(lui/lei) (lei/Lei)	**stia**
(noi)	**stiamo**
(voi)	**stiate**
(loro)	**stiano**

PAST PARTICIPLE

stato

GERUND

stando

EXAMPLE PHRASES

Sei mai **stato** in Francia? *Have you ever been to France?*
Come **stai**? *How are you?*
Stavo andando a casa. *I was going home.*
A Londra **starò** da amici. *I'll be staying with friends in London.*
Stavo per uscire quando ha squillato il telefono. *I was about to go out when the phone rang.*

Italic letters in Italian words show where stress does not follow the usual rules.

stringere (to tighten)

PRESENT

(io)	stringo
(tu)	stringi
(lui/lei) (lei/Lei)	stringe
(noi)	stringiamo
(voi)	stringete
(loro)	stringono

PERFECT

(io)	ho stretto
(tu)	hai stretto
(lui/lei) (lei/Lei)	ha stretto
(noi)	abbiamo stretto
(voi)	avete stretto
(loro)	hanno stretto

IMPERFECT

(io)	stringevo
(tu)	stringevi
(lui/lei) (lei/Lei)	stringeva
(noi)	stringevamo
(voi)	stringevate
(loro)	stringevano

IMPERATIVE

stringi
stringiamo
stringete

FUTURE

(io)	stringerò
(tu)	stringerai
(lui/lei) (lei/Lei)	stringerà
(noi)	stringeremo
(voi)	stringerete
(loro)	stringeranno

CONDITIONAL

(io)	stringerei
(tu)	stringeresti
(lui/lei) (lei/Lei)	stringerebbe
(noi)	stringeremmo
(voi)	stringereste
(loro)	stringerebbero

PRESENT SUBJUNCTIVE

(io)	stringa
(tu)	stringa
(lui/lei) (lei/Lei)	stringa
(noi)	stringiamo
(voi)	stringiate
(loro)	stringano

PAST PARTICIPLE

stretto

GERUND

stringendo

EXAMPLE PHRASES

Ho stretto la cintura perché sono dimagrita. *I've tightened my belt because I've lost weight.*

Se ci **stringiamo** ci staremo tutti. *If we squeeze up we'll all get in.*

Ci **siamo stretti** la mano. *We shook hands.*

Remember that subject pronouns are not used very often in Italian.

succedere (to happen)

PRESENT
succede
succedono

FUTURE
succederà
succederanno

PERFECT
è successo/a
sono successi/e

CONDITIONAL
succederebbe
succederebbero

IMPERFECT
succedeva
succedevano

PRESENT SUBJUNCTIVE
succede
succedano

IMPERATIVE
–

PAST PARTICIPLE
successo

GERUND
succedendo

EXAMPLE PHRASES

Cos'**è successo**? *What happened?*
Dev'**essergli successo** qualcosa. *Something must have happened to him.*
Sono cose che **succedono**. *These things happen.*

Italic letters in Italian words show where stress does not follow the usual rules.

tenere (to hold)

PRESENT

(io)	tengo
(tu)	tieni
(lui/lei)(lei/Lei)	tiene
(noi)	teniamo
(voi)	tenete
(loro)	tengono

PERFECT

(io)	ho tenuto
(tu)	hai tenuto
(lui/lei)(lei/Lei)	ha tenuto
(noi)	abbiamo tenuto
(voi)	avete tenuto
(loro)	hanno tenuto

IMPERFECT

(io)	tenevo
(tu)	tenevi
(lui/lei)(lei/Lei)	teneva
(noi)	tenevamo
(voi)	tenevate
(loro)	tenevano

IMPERATIVE

tieni
teniamo
tenete

FUTURE

(io)	terrò
(tu)	terrai
(lui/lei)(lei/Lei)	terrà
(noi)	terremo
(voi)	terrete
(loro)	terranno

CONDITIONAL

(io)	terrei
(tu)	terresti
(lui/lei)(lei/Lei)	terrebbe
(noi)	terremmo
(voi)	terreste
(loro)	terrebbero

PRESENT SUBJUNCTIVE

(io)	tenga
(tu)	tenga
(lui/lei)(lei/Lei)	tenga
(noi)	teniamo
(voi)	teniate
(loro)	tengano

PAST PARTICIPLE

tenuto

GERUND

tenendo

EXAMPLE PHRASES

Tiene la racchetta con la sinistra. *He holds the racket with his left hand.*
Tieniti forte! *Hold on tight!*
Si **tenevano** per mano. *They were holding hands.*
Tieniti pronta per le cinque. *Be ready by five.*
Tieni, questo è per te. *Here, this is for you*

Remember that subject pronouns are not used very often in Italian.

togliere (to take off)

PRESENT

(io)	**tolgo**
(tu)	**togli**
(lui/lei) (lei/Lei)	**toglie**
(noi)	**togliamo**
(voi)	**togliete**
(loro)	**tolgono**

PERFECT

(io)	**ho tolto**
(tu)	**hai tolto**
(lui/lei) (lei/Lei)	**ha tolto**
(noi)	**abbiamo tolto**
(voi)	**avete tolto**
(loro)	**hanno tolto**

IMPERFECT

(io)	**toglievo**
(tu)	**toglievi**
(lui/lei) (lei/Lei)	**toglieva**
(noi)	**toglievamo**
(voi)	**toglievate**
(loro)	**toglievano**

IMPERATIVE

togli
togliamo
togliete

FUTURE

(io)	**toglierò**
(tu)	**toglierai**
(lui/lei) (lei/Lei)	**toglierà**
(noi)	**toglieremo**
(voi)	**toglierete**
(loro)	**toglieranno**

CONDITIONAL

(io)	**toglierei**
(tu)	**toglieresti**
(lui/lei) (lei/Lei)	**toglierebbe**
(noi)	**toglieremmo**
(voi)	**togliereste**
(loro)	**toglierebbero**

PRESENT SUBJUNCTIVE

(io)	**tolga**
(tu)	**tolga**
(lui/lei) (lei/Lei)	**tolga**
(noi)	**togliamo**
(voi)	**togliate**
(loro)	**tolgano**

PAST PARTICIPLE

tolto

GERUND

togliendo

EXAMPLE PHRASES

Togliti il cappotto. *Take off your coat.*
Ho tolto il poster dalla parete. *I took the poster off the wall.*
Mi **toglieranno** due denti. *I'm going to have two teeth out.*

Italic letters in Italian words show where stress does not follow the usual rules.

trarre (to draw)

PRESENT

(io)	**traggo**
(tu)	**trai**
(lui/lei) (lei/Lei)	**trae**
(noi)	**traiamo**
(voi)	**traete**
(loro)	**traggono**

PERFECT

(io)	**ho tratto**
(tu)	**hai tratto**
(lui/lei) (lei/Lei)	**ha tratto**
(noi)	**abbiamo tratto**
(voi)	**avete tratto**
(loro)	**hanno tratto**

IMPERFECT

(io)	**traevo**
(tu)	**traevi**
(lui/lei) (lei/Lei)	**traeva**
(noi)	**traevamo**
(voi)	**traevate**
(loro)	**traevano**

IMPERATIVE

trai
traiamo
traete

FUTURE

(io)	**trarrò**
(tu)	**trarrai**
(lui/lei) (lei/Lei)	**trarrà**
(noi)	**trarremo**
(voi)	**trarrete**
(loro)	**trarranno**

CONDITIONAL

(io)	**trarrei**
(tu)	**trarresti**
(lui/lei) (lei/Lei)	**trarrebbe**
(noi)	**trarremmo**
(voi)	**trarreste**
(loro)	**trarrebbero**

PRESENT SUBJUNCTIVE

(io)	**tragga**
(tu)	**tragga**
(lui/lei) (lei/Lei)	**tragga**
(noi)	**traiamo**
(voi)	**traiate**
(loro)	**traggano**

PAST PARTICIPLE

tratto

GERUND

traendo

EXAMPLE PHRASES

Il suo modo di fare **trae** in inganno. *His manner is misleading.*
Sono stati tratti in salvo dai vigili del fuoco. *They were rescued by the firemen.*
Un film **tratto** da un romanzo di Agatha Christie. *A film based on a novel by Agatha Christie.*

uscire (to go out)

PRESENT

(io)	**esco**
(tu)	**esci**
(lui/lei)(lei/Lei)	**esce**
(noi)	**usciamo**
(voi)	**uscite**
(loro)	*e*scono

PERFECT

(io)	**sono uscito/a**
(tu)	**sei uscito/a**
(lui/lei)(lei/Lei)	**è uscito/a**
(noi)	**siamo usciti/e**
(voi)	**siete usciti/e**
(loro)	**sono usciti/e**

IMPERFECT

(io)	**uscivo**
(tu)	**uscivi**
(lui/lei)(lei/Lei)	**usciva**
(noi)	**uscivamo**
(voi)	**uscivate**
(loro)	**uscivano**

IMPERATIVE

esci
usciamo
uscite

FUTURE

(io)	**uscirò**
(tu)	**uscirai**
(lui/lei)(lei/Lei)	**uscir*à***
(noi)	**usciremo**
(voi)	**uscirete**
(loro)	**usciranno**

CONDITIONAL

(io)	**uscirei**
(tu)	**usciresti**
(lui/lei)(lei/Lei)	**uscirebbe**
(noi)	**usciremmo**
(voi)	**uscireste**
(loro)	**uscir*e*bbero**

PRESENT SUBJUNCTIVE

(io)	**esca**
(tu)	**esca**
(lui/lei)(lei/Lei)	**esca**
(noi)	**usciamo**
(voi)	**usciate**
(loro)	*e*scano

PAST PARTICIPLE

uscito

GERUND

uscendo

EXAMPLE PHRASES

È uscita a comprare il giornale. *She's gone out to buy a newspaper.*
Uscirà dall'ospedale domani. *He's coming out of hospital tomorrow.*
L'ho incontrata che **usciva** dalla farmacia. *I met her coming out of the chemist's.*
La rivista **esce** di lunedì. *The magazine comes out on Mondays.*

Italic letters in Italian words show where stress does not follow the usual rules.

valere (to be worth)

PRESENT

(io)	**valgo**
(tu)	**vali**
(lui/lei) (lei/Lei)	**vale**
(noi)	**valiamo**
(voi)	**valete**
(loro)	**valgono**

FUTURE

(io)	**varrò**
(tu)	**varrai**
(lui/lei) (lei/Lei)	**varrà**
(noi)	**varremo**
(voi)	**varrete**
(loro)	**varranno**

PERFECT

(io)	**sono valso/a**
(tu)	**sei valso/a**
(lui/lei) (lei/Lei)	**è valso/a**
(noi)	**siamo valsi/e**
(voi)	**siete valsi/e**
(loro)	**sono valsi/e**

CONDITIONAL

(io)	**varrei**
(tu)	**varresti**
(lui/lei) (lei/Lei)	**varrebbe**
(noi)	**varremmo**
(voi)	**varreste**
(loro)	**varrebbero**

IMPERFECT

(io)	**valevo**
(tu)	**valevi**
(lui/lei) (lei/Lei)	**valeva**
(noi)	**valevamo**
(voi)	**valevate**
(loro)	**valevano**

PRESENT SUBJUNCTIVE

(io)	**valga**
(tu)	**valga**
(lui/lei) (lei/Lei)	**valga**
(noi)	**valiamo**
(voi)	**valiate**
(loro)	**valgano**

IMPERATIVE

vali
valiamo
valete

PAST PARTICIPLE

valso

GERUND

valendo

EXAMPLE PHRASES

L'auto **vale** tremila euro. *The car is worth three thousand euros.*
Non ne **vale** la pena. *It's not worth it.*
Senza il giardino, la casa non **varrebbe** niente. *Without the garden the house wouldn't be worth anything.*

Remember that subject pronouns are not used very often in Italian.

vedere (to see)

PRESENT

(io)	**vedo**
(tu)	**vedi**
(lui/lei) (lei/Lei)	**vede**
(noi)	**vediamo**
(voi)	**vedete**
(loro)	**vedono**

PERFECT

(io)	**ho visto**
(tu)	**hai visto**
(lui/lei) (lei/Lei)	**ha visto**
(noi)	**abbiamo visto**
(voi)	**avete visto**
(loro)	**hanno visto**

IMPERFECT

(io)	**vedevo**
(tu)	**vedevi**
(lui/lei) (lei/Lei)	**vedeva**
(noi)	**vedevamo**
(voi)	**vedevate**
(loro)	**vedevano**

IMPERATIVE

vedi
vediamo
vedete

FUTURE

(io)	**vedrò**
(tu)	**vedrai**
(lui/lei) (lei/Lei)	**vedrà**
(noi)	**vedremo**
(voi)	**vedrete**
(loro)	**vedranno**

CONDITIONAL

(io)	**vedrei**
(tu)	**vedresti**
(lui/lei) (lei/Lei)	**vedrebbe**
(noi)	**vedremmo**
(voi)	**vedreste**
(loro)	**vedrebbero**

PRESENT SUBJUNCTIVE

(io)	**veda**
(tu)	**veda**
(lui/lei) (lei/Lei)	**veda**
(noi)	**vediamo**
(voi)	**vediate**
(loro)	**vedano**

PAST PARTICIPLE

visto

GERUND

vedendo

EXAMPLE PHRASES

Non ci **vedo** senza occhiali. *I can't see without my glasses.*
Ci **vediamo** domani! *See you tomorrow!*
Non **vedevo** l'ora di conoscerlo. *I couldn't wait to meet him.*

Italic letters in Italian words show where stress does not follow the usual rules.

venire (to come)

PRESENT

(io)	**vengo**
(tu)	**vieni**
(lui/lei) (lei/Lei)	**viene**
(noi)	**veniamo**
(voi)	**venite**
(loro)	**vengono**

PERFECT

(io)	**sono venuto/a**
(tu)	**sei venuto/a**
(lui/lei) (lei/Lei)	**è venuto/a**
(noi)	**siamo venuti/e**
(voi)	**siete venuti/e**
(loro)	**sono venuti/e**

IMPERFECT

(io)	**venivo**
(tu)	**venivi**
(lui/lei) (lei/Lei)	**veniva**
(noi)	**venivamo**
(voi)	**venivate**
(loro)	**venivano**

IMPERATIVE

vieni
veniamo
venite

FUTURE

(io)	**verrò**
(tu)	**verrai**
(lui/lei) (lei/Lei)	**verrà**
(noi)	**verremo**
(voi)	**verrete**
(loro)	**verranno**

CONDITIONAL

(io)	**verrei**
(tu)	**verresti**
(lui/lei) (lei/Lei)	**verrebbe**
(noi)	**verremmo**
(voi)	**verreste**
(loro)	**verrebbero**

PRESENT SUBJUNCTIVE

(io)	**venga**
(tu)	**venga**
(lui/lei) (lei/Lei)	**venga**
(noi)	**veniamo**
(voi)	**veniate**
(loro)	**vengano**

PAST PARTICIPLE

venuto

GERUND

venendo

EXAMPLE PHRASES

È venuto in macchina. *He came by car.*
Da dove **vieni**? *Where do you come from?*
Vieni a trovarci! *Come and see us!*
Quanto **viene**? *How much is it?*

Remember that subject pronouns are not used very often in Italian.

vincere (to defeat)

PRESENT

(io)	**vinco**
(tu)	**vinci**
(lui/lei) (lei/Lei)	**vince**
(noi)	**vinciamo**
(voi)	**vincete**
(loro)	**vincono**

FUTURE

(io)	**vincerò**
(tu)	**vincerai**
(lui/lei) (lei/Lei)	**vincerà**
(noi)	**vinceremo**
(voi)	**vincerete**
(loro)	**vinceranno**

PERFECT

(io)	**ho vinto**
(tu)	**hai vinto**
(lui/lei) (lei/Lei)	**ha vinto**
(noi)	**abbiamo vinto**
(voi)	**avete vinto**
(loro)	**hanno vinto**

CONDITIONAL

(io)	**vincerei**
(tu)	**vinceresti**
(lui/lei) (lei/Lei)	**vincerebbe**
(noi)	**vinceremmo**
(voi)	**vincereste**
(loro)	**vince*r*ebbero**

IMPERFECT

(io)	**vincevo**
(tu)	**vincevi**
(lui/lei) (lei/Lei)	**vinceva**
(noi)	**vincevamo**
(voi)	**vincevate**
(loro)	**vinc*e*vano**

PRESENT SUBJUNCTIVE

(io)	**vinca**
(tu)	**vinca**
(lui/lei) (lei/Lei)	**vinca**
(noi)	**vinciamo**
(voi)	**vinciate**
(loro)	**vincano**

IMPERATIVE

vinci
vinciamo
vincete

PAST PARTICIPLE

vinto

GERUND

vincendo

EXAMPLE PHRASES

Ieri abbiamo **vinto** la partita. *We won the match yesterday.*
Quando giochiamo **vince** sempre lui. *When we play he always wins.*
Stavolta **vincerò** io. *This time I'm going to win.*

Italic letters in Italian words show where stress does not follow the usual rules.

vivere (to live)

PRESENT

(io)	**vivo**
(tu)	**vivi**
(lui/lei) (lei/Lei)	**vive**
(noi)	**viviamo**
(voi)	**vivete**
(loro)	**vivono**

FUTURE

(io)	**vivrò**
(tu)	**vivrai**
(lui/lei) (lei/Lei)	**vivrà**
(noi)	**vivremo**
(voi)	**vivrete**
(loro)	**vivranno**

PERFECT

(io)	**ho vissuto**
(tu)	**hai vissuto**
(lui/lei) (lei/Lei)	**ha vissuto**
(noi)	**abbiamo vissuto**
(voi)	**avete vissuto**
(loro)	**hanno vissuto**

CONDITIONAL

(io)	**vivrei**
(tu)	**vivresti**
(lui/lei) (lei/Lei)	**vivrebbe**
(noi)	**vivremmo**
(voi)	**vivreste**
(loro)	**vivrebbero**

IMPERFECT

(io)	**vivevo**
(tu)	**vivevi**
(lui/lei) (lei/Lei)	**viveva**
(noi)	**vivevamo**
(voi)	**vivevate**
(loro)	**vivevano**

PRESENT SUBJUNCTIVE

(io)	**viva**
(tu)	**viva**
(lui/lei) (lei/Lei)	**viva**
(noi)	**viviamo**
(voi)	**viviate**
(loro)	**vivano**

IMPERATIVE

vivi
viviamo
vivete

PAST PARTICIPLE

vissuto

GERUND

vivendo

EXAMPLE PHRASES

Non **vivrei** mai in un Paese caldo. *I'd never live in a hot country.*
Vivendo in città si respira molto smog. *If you live in a town you breathe a lot of smog.*
Vivevano in una piccola casa di periferia. *They lived in a small house in the suburbs.*

Remember that subject pronouns are not used very often in Italian.

volere (to want)

PRESENT

(io)	**voglio**
(tu)	**vuoi**
(lui/lei) (lei/Lei)	**vuole**
(noi)	**vogliamo**
(voi)	**volete**
(loro)	**vogliono**

PERFECT

(io)	**ho voluto**
(tu)	**hai voluto**
(lui/lei) (lei/Lei)	**ha voluto**
(noi)	**abbiamo voluto**
(voi)	**avete voluto**
(loro)	**hanno voluto**

IMPERFECT

(io)	**volevo**
(tu)	**volevi**
(lui/lei) (lei/Lei)	**voleva**
(noi)	**volevamo**
(voi)	**volevate**
(loro)	**volevano**

IMPERATIVE

–

FUTURE

(io)	**vorrò**
(tu)	**vorrai**
(lui/lei) (lei/Lei)	**vorrà**
(noi)	**vorremo**
(voi)	**vorrete**
(loro)	**vorranno**

CONDITIONAL

(io)	**vorrei**
(tu)	**vorresti**
(lui/lei) (lei/Lei)	**vorrebbe**
(noi)	**vorremmo**
(voi)	**vorreste**
(loro)	**vorrebbero**

PRESENT SUBJUNCTIVE

(io)	**voglia**
(tu)	**voglia**
(lui/lei) (lei/Lei)	**voglia**
(noi)	**vogliamo**
(voi)	**vogliate**
(loro)	**vogliano**

PAST PARTICIPLE

voluto

GERUND

volendo

EXAMPLE PHRASES

Voglio comprare una macchina nuova. *I want to buy a new car.*

Devo pagare subito o posso pagare domani? – Come **vuole**. *Do I have to pay now or can I pay tomorrow? – As you prefer.*

Quanto ci **vorrà** prima che finiate? *How long will it take you to finish?*

La campanella **voleva** dire che la lezione era finita. *The bell meant that the lesson was over.*

Anche **volendo** non posso invitarti: la festa è sua. *I'd like to, but I can't invite you: it's his party.*

Italic letters in Italian words show where stress does not follow the usual rules.

How to use the Verb Index

The verbs in **bold** are the model verbs which you will find in the Verb Tables. All the other verbs follow one of these patterns, so the number next to each verb indicates which pattern fits this particular verb. For example, **divertire** (*to amuse*) follows the same pattern as **dormire** (*to sleep*), which is number 29 in the Verb Tables.

All the verbs are in alphabetical order.

Superior numbers ([1], [2] etc) refer you to notes on page 96. These notes explain any differences between the verbs and their model.

With the exception of reflexive verbs which *always* take **essere**, all verbs have the same auxiliary (**essere** or **avere**) as their model verbs. There are a few exceptions which are indicated by superior numbers [1] to [4]. An asterisk (*) means that the verb takes avere when it is used with a direct object, and **essere** when it isn't.

➪ *For more information on verbs that take either* **avere** *or* **essere**, *see pages* 109 *and* 112.

abbaiare	12	accusare	50	allenare	50	approfittare	50
abbandonare	50	acquistare	50	allineare	50	approfondire	13
abbassare	50	**addormentarsi**	**3**	alloggiare	43	approvare	50
abbattere	20	adoperare	50	allontanare	50	**aprire**	**6**
abboccare	14	adorare	50	allungare	48	archiviare	12
abbonarsi	50	adottare	50	amare	50	arrabbiarsi	12
abitare	50	affacciarsi	16	ambientare	50	arrangiarsi	43
abituarsi	50	afferrare	50	ammazzare	50	arrendersi	55
abolire	13	affibbiare	12	ammettere	44	arrestare	50
abusare	50	affidare	50	amministrare	50	**arrivare**	**7**
accadere	11	affittare	50	ammirare	50	arrotondare	50
accantonare	50	affogare[2]	48	ammonire	13	arruolarsi	50
accarezzare	50	affondare*	50	ammucchiare[1]	39	asciugare	48
accavallare	50	affrettarsi	50	**andare**	**4**	ascoltare	50
accelerare	50	affrontare	50	annaffiare	12	aspettare	50
accendere	55	agganciare	16	annegare*	48	assaggiare	43
accennare	50	aggiungere	59	annoiare	12	assicurare	50
accertarsi	50	aggiustare	50	annotare	50	assistere[1]	32
accettare	50	aggrapparsi	50	annullare	50	assolvere	64
acchiappare	50	aggravare	50	annunciare	16	assomigliare[2]	69
accludere	15	aggredire	13	annusare	50	**assumere**	**8**
accogliere	83	agire	13	appannarsi	50	attaccare	14
accomodarsi	50	agitare	50	apparecchiare[1]	39	atterrare[3]	50
accompagnare	75	aiutare	50	**apparire**	**5**	attirare	50
accontentare	50	allacciare	16	appartenere[2]	82	attraversare	50
accorciare	16	allagare	48	appendere	55	aumentare*	50
accordare	50	allargare	48	appiccicare	14	autorizzare	50
accorgersi	**2**	allarmare	50	applaudire	29	avanzare	7
accudire	13	allegare	48	appoggiare	43	**avere**	**9**

Notes
[1] Auxiliary = **avere**.
[2] Auxiliary = **essere**.
[3] Auxiliary = either **essere** or **avere**.
[4] Past participle of this verb is rare.

Collins

easy learning Italian

Easy Learning Italian Dictionary
978-0-00-753093-9 £10.99

Easy Learning Italian Conversation
[Second edition] 978-0-00-811199-1 £8.99

Easy Learning Italian Grammar
978-0-00-814202-5 £7.99

Easy Learning Italian Verbs
978-0-00-815844-6 £7.99

Easy Learning Italian Vocabulary
978-0-00-748394-5 £7.99

Easy Learning Complete Italian Grammar, Verbs and Vocabulary
(3 books in 1) 978-0-00-814175-2 £12.99

Easy Learning Italian Grammar & Practice
978-0-00-745600-0 £10.99

Available to buy from all good booksellers and online.
Many titles are also available as ebooks.
www.collins.co.uk/languagesupport

 facebook.com/collinsdictionary

@collinsdict